How to Avoid
English Teachers'
Pet Peeves

Improve your writing
by eliminating the common errors
that English teachers see most often

Cheryl Miller Thurston

Cottonwood Press, Inc.
Fort Collins, Colorado

Requests for permission should be addressed to:

Cottonwood Press, Inc.
107 Cameron Drive
Fort Collins, Colorado 80525
800-864-4297
e-mail: cottonwood@cottonwoodpress.com

www.cottonwoodpress.com

ISBN 1-877673-51-X

Printed in the United States of America

Table of Contents

Introduction

How to Avoid English Teachers' Pet Peeves is a book that helps writers avoid the annoying little errors that English teachers encounter nearly every day as they read student papers. It addresses the mistakes that make English teachers wince or, on really bad days, want to give up teaching and embark on a career selling real estate or life insurance. It is not intended to address major problems, like disorganized writing or writing that doesn't make sense.

English teachers are not unreasonably persnickety. They just love words and like to see them used correctly. In college, they major in English because they love reading and writing. Then they become teachers and see their beloved language mangled countless times a day, day after day. Seeing *a lot* misspelled once isn't so bad. Seeing it misspelled as "alot" 57 times in one week does tend to ruin a teacher's sense of perspective.

The pet peeves included in this book were chosen in a survey of 125 English teachers from across the United States. Pet peeves mentioned by more than one teacher were included in this edition.

The pet peeve mentioned most often was writing *should of* and *would of* instead of *should have* and *would have*. Another one of the most "popular" choices was the misuse of *its* and *it's*.

For students using this book. If you are a student using *How to Avoid English Teachers' Pet Peeves* on your own, proceed at your own pace. Study the explanations and examples, and try the exercises. You can check your own work, using the answer key at the end of the book.

How to Avoid English Teachers' Pet Peeves does not use a lot of technical language, so it is easy to understand. It won't matter at all if you can't recognize a participle when you see one or identify an infinitive phrase used as a predicate nominative. The explanations are purposely kept short and simple.

For teachers using this book. The exercises and explanations in *How to Avoid English Teachers' Pet Peeves* are purposely short. Let's face it — the study of picky little grammar problems is not going to keep most students on the edge of their seats. Quick lessons are much more effective than long ones.

Reproduce the explanations and/or exercises in this book and put them on the overhead a couple of times a week. (You *do* have permission to reproduce pages in the book for your own classroom use.) Have students complete the exercises, which take only a few minutes each.

Even better, study all of the pet peeves, one or two a day, at the start of the school year. Then have students enter the "Aggravate Your English Teacher!" contest. (See page 7 for details.)

The list of pet peeves in this book is by no means comprehensive. The book is intended to be the first volume of a series. If you have pet peeves that you would like to see addressed in future volumes, please send them to the author, in care of Cottonwood Press, Inc., 107 Cameron Drive, Fort Collins, CO 80525. You may also e-mail them to cottonwood@cottonwoodpress.com.

For parents using this book. Use *How to Avoid English Teachers' Pet Peeves* to find ways to help your children improve their writing skills. Even better, encourage your children to complete the book on their own. You will find that it contains explanations that make sense to young people — or anyone. In fact, you might take the opportunity to brush up on some writing skills yourself.

Benefits. *How to Avoid English Teachers' Pet Peeves* won't work miracles. However, it will help students learn to avoid the kinds of errors that can cause others to take them, or their work, less seriously. It will help them learn to pay closer attention to their work and to what they are saying.

Paying attention — close attention — is a big step in learning to communicate more clearly and more effectively.

"Aggravate Your English Teacher!" Contest
For writers of any age, grade five to adult

Aggravate your English teacher, learn and compete for cash prizes — all at the same time! Just this once, see how many of the 50 pet peeves in *How to Avoid English Teachers' Pet Peeves* you can "commit" in a short paper of 750 words or less. The paper may be on any topic and in any form, fiction or non-fiction. Just a few ideas: a letter, an essay, a short story, a book or movie review, a report.

The "Aggravate Your English Teacher!" contest will be held each year, 2001-2003, for writers of any age, grade five to adult. According to author Cheryl Miller Thurston, "People love to do what they are not supposed to do. To break all the rules in this book, you have to pay attention to what the rules *are*. Breaking the rules can help you learn them. It's a technique I have found very successful in teaching."

Contestants must enter in one of three categories:

Grades 5–8

Grades 9–12

Adult

Prizes. When discussing prizes for this contest, the publisher's first suggestion was dinner at a nice restaurant for winning students and their English teachers.

The author, a former teacher, pointed out that a better prize, from a student perspective, might be that winners *don't* have to go to dinner with their English teachers!

The compromise was cash. Prizes will be awarded each year, as follows:

First prize in each age group: $50.00

Second prize in each age group: $30.00

Third prize in each age group: $20.00

Some entries will also be published as review exercises in future editions of *How to Avoid English Teachers' Pet Peeves.*

Contest entries must include the contestant's name, age, address and phone number. They must be typed, preferably double-spaced. Mail to:

Cottonwood Press, Inc.

107 Cameron Drive

Fort Collins, Colorado 80525.

Entries may also be submitted by e-mail to:

cottonwood@cottonwoodpress.com

All entries must be received by the following deadlines:

For the year 2001: December 1, 2001

For the year 2002: December 1, 2002

For the year 2003: December 1, 2003

Judging. In choosing winners, judges will look for papers that "commit" at least 90% of the pet peeves. They will also look for papers that make them laugh, show creativity, or — in some other fashion — amuse them. After all, it's not going to be easy to read what the publisher hopes will be hundreds of error-filled papers. The judges will *need* to be amused!

English Teachers' Pet Peeves

Pet Peeve 1: Using spell check without rereading a paper

Spell check on a computer is a wonderful tool. However, it is not perfect. If a word in a document really is a word, spell check won't tell you that it is the *wrong* word. For example, many people write the word *are* when they mean the word *our*, perhaps because they pronounce the words almost the same. Spell check won't catch the mistake. If you don't reread your paper carefully, you may end up with a lot of spelling mistakes, even though spell check tells you the paper is perfect.

According to spell check, the paragraphs that follow are perfect. (Spell check is wrong.)

> *"Eye don't won't too go to sleep," wined little Alfred too his sister. "Eye want too stay up and wash TV with ewe."*
>
> *"Eye want too sit hear on the couch with my boyfriend," grumbled Lauren. "Wee want to bee alone."*
>
> *"Y?" asked Alfred.*
>
> *Lauren side. "Ewe err to young too under stand."*
>
> *"Know I'm knot!" cried Alfred. "I am for!" He climbed up and wedged himself between Lauren and her boyfriend. "Sea? I'm a big buoy. Thistle be fun!"*

PRACTICE

Correct the following:

Are trip was supposed to be a wonderful vacation four us, but when wee got off the bus at Shady Beach, we couldn't do anything but stair. I started to wonder, "Wear our we?" because the beach looked nothing like the won in the brochure.

"Where's are beautiful beech?" asked my brother Carlos.

"Wear's are palm trees?" asked my mom.

"Wear are the cute guise?" asked my sister Judy.

"Wear is the travel agent?" fumed my father. "Weight until I get my hands on hymn!"

"Calm down, deer," said Mom. "They're is probably a perfectly good explanation for are problem."

"Yes. Are travel agent is a crook!" yelled Dad.

Dad doesn't take disappointment reel well.

Pet Peeve 2:
Beginning with "Hi. My name is . . ."
or "Now I'm going to tell you about . . ."
or "This paper will be about . . ."

People often don't know how to start. Because they don't know what to say, they sometimes begin by writing something like this: "Hi, my name is Lisa." Such an opening is definitely _not_ a good idea.

First of all, your name is on the paper — or should be. You don't need to introduce yourself by name. What you need to introduce is your _subject_. To do that, simply make a statement about your subject. For example, for a report on gorillas, you might start out by writing, "Most people think of gorillas as vicious, meat-eating animals." For a composition on why school lunch periods should be longer, you might start out by writing, "Lunch should be a time for relaxation, not stress."

It's also not a good idea to start out by writing, "I am going to tell you about how the printing press was invented," or "My paper will be about the printing press." If you are in first grade and doing show and tell, it's fine to start by saying,

"I am going to tell you about . . ." If you are older, you need to do something more sophisticated, more grown up.

Instead of announcing your topic, begin by telling something *about* your topic. You might even tell your main idea. For example, for a report on the invention of the printing press, you might write, "The invention of the printing press in 1455 was a development that changed the world forever." For an essay comparing cats and dogs, you might start out like this: "Though cats may be attractive to some people, dogs really make much better family pets."

Just a few more ideas for ways to begin:

- Tell an anecdote about your experience, or someone else's experience, related to your topic.
- Quote an authority who has said something particularly interesting or colorful about your topic.
- Point out a startling statistic, an interesting fact, or a fascinating bit of trivia related to your topic.

PRACTICE

Below is the introduction to a composition about something called "zigglebots." Rewrite the introduction so that it is more effective. Use the tips from the previous page, *plus* your imagination!

> *Hello. My name is Clarice. I am going to write about zigglebots.*

Pet Peeve 3:
Mixing up *it's* and *its*

Nothing drives an English teacher crazier than apostrophes used incorrectly. Learn to get them right — even right *most* of the time — and you will save your English teacher and yourself a lot of anguish.

The key to success is to remember the Magic Apostrophe Rule. Learn this rule, and dozens of annoying little writing problems will disappear. Here is the rule:

✳ The Magic Apostrophe Rule ✳

Except when it is used with a person's name or a noun,
an apostrophe almost always stands for a letter that has been left out.
If nothing is left out, you don't want an apostrophe.

The word *it's* is not a person's name or a noun. Therefore, the apostrophe stands for a letter that has been left out — the "i" in *is*. *It's* is short for *it is*. The word *it's* should be used only in places where you could say *it is*.

Which word should you use in each of the following sentences?

It's/Its *always exciting to get a gift in the mail.*

(Try substituting *it is* in the sentence: *It is always exciting to get a gift in the mail.* That makes sense. Use *it's.*)

The car flipped on **it's/its** *back in the accident.*

(Try substituting *it is* in the sentence: *The car flipped on it is back in the accident.* No, that doesn't sound right. Use *its.*)

Pet Peeves ©2001 Cottonwood Press, Inc. • www.cottonwoodpress.com • 800-864-4297 • Fort Collins, Colorado

PRACTICE

Choose *it's* or *its* in the following sentences:

1. "*It's/Its* always *me* who gets blamed for everything," whined Felicity.

2. "You get blamed because *it's/its* always your fault," said her brother calmly.

3. "For example, the car is missing *it's/its* front bumper because you failed to notice a stop sign yesterday."

4. "I was putting on lipstick," cried Felicity. "*It's/Its* not my fault. I didn't have time to do it before I left the house."

5. "Yes it is," said Jacob. "*It's/Its* your fault because you slept through your alarm." He looked at her carefully. "I do see why you would be desperate, though. You look pretty bad without lipstick. You might also consider using a little

6. more mascara. *It's/Its* amazing what a little makeup can do for a homely person."

7. Felicity smacked him. Then she went to look for her make-up bag, which, unfortunately, wasn't in *it's/its* usual place.

Pet Peeve 4:
Confusing *you're* and *your*

Remember the Magic Apostrophe Rule, and your problems will be over with *you're* and *your*.

Let's review the rule again: *Except when it is used with a person's name or a noun, an apostrophe almost always stands for a letter left out. If nothing is left out, you don't want an apostrophe.*

Look at the word *you're*. It is not a person's name or a noun. Therefore, the apostrophe must stand for something left out.

It does. The word *you're* is a contraction for *you are*. The apostrophe stands for the missing *a* in *are*. Therefore, the *only* time you should use *you're* is when you can substitute the words *you are* for the word *you're*.

Take a look at a few examples:

Be sure to bring **your/you're** *coat with you.*

(Be sure to bring *you are* coat with you? No, that doesn't make sense. You definitely don't want *you're*. Use *your* instead.)

If **your/you're** going to ask a guy to the dance, at least pick a nice one.

(If *you are* going to ask a guy to the dance, at least pick a nice one. Yes, that sounds right. Use *you're*.)

Pet Peeves ©2001 Cottonwood Press, Inc. • www.cottonwoodpress.com • 800-864-4297 • Fort Collins, Colorado

PRACTICE

Choose **you're** or **your** for each of the following sentences:

The members of the Melting Lemons sauntered on stage. "*You're/Your*¹ going to love our first song," said the lead singer, Clovis. "It's not *you're/your*²˙ average heavy metal tune, man. It's way deeper than anything ever before created. 3˙ *You're/your* just going to be blown away by its brilliance."

He paused. "This tune has a lot of meaning for me, and for the members of the band because it's about a subject very dear to our hearts: toenail clippers. 4˙ *You're/your* so lucky to be here and share in the very first performance of this piece. I know *you're/your*⁵˙ going to enjoy *you're/your*⁶˙ listening experience."

Pet Peeve 5:
Using *to* and *too* incorrectly

People are always mixing up *to*, *too*, and *two*. Almost everyone knows that the word *two* is the one that refers to a number. Let's assume you do, too.

The biggest problem people usually have is mixing up *to* and *too*. Luckily, there is a very easy way to tell the difference between the words. The key is to remember how we really pronounce the little "filler" word *to*.

Most of us really pronounce *to* so that it sounds kind of like *tuh*, as in "I'm going tuh watch TV now." When you don't know which word to use, try saying *tuh* in the sentence. If *tuh* makes sense, use the word *to*. If *tuh* sounds silly, use the word *too*. (Warning: This trick works only if you try *tuh* first. Don't do it the other way around and try *too* first. *Everything* sounds all right with *too*.)

Let's look at some examples:

*Joleen said, "I'm going **to/too** buy a new hamster."*
(Try substituting **tuh** in the sentence: *I'm going tuh buy a new hamster.* That sounds okay. Use *to*.)

*Blake likes chocolate cake, chocolate milk, and chocolate pie, **to/too**."*
(Try substituting *tuh* in the sentence: *Blake likes chocolate cake, chocolate milk, and chocolate pie, tuh. Tuh sounds wrong. Use too.*)

PRACTICE !

Choose **to** or **too** in the sentences below:

"We should look **to/too** the future when deciding who should have our vote," announced the candidate for the Senate. "It is **to/too** expensive for our future if you choose my opponent."

"Why?" asked Maria. "I am planning **to/too** vote for the other guy, and most of the rest of us here are, **to/too**."

"My opponent, unfortunately, is veracity-challenged. He also is less than respectful **to/too** his constituents and tends **to/too** alienate those with whom he has contact."

"Tell us in plain English," said Maria. "What's wrong with the guy?"

"**To/too** get right **to/too** the point, he lies," said the candidate. "He's a big jerk, **to/too**."

Pet Peeve 6:
Writing "could of," "should of," "would of," or "shoulda," "coulda," "woulda" instead of *could have, should have,* or *would have*

Teachers really hate seeing the word *of* used as a verb. Unless you want the person grading your paper to get *very* cranky, don't write *could of* when you mean *could have*. Don't write *should of* when you mean *should have*. Don't write *would of* when you mean *would have*.

When we speak, we say something that sounds a lot like *could of*. What we are really saying, though, is *could've*. We are contracting, or shrinking, the words *could* and *have* into one word, *could've*. It's not really surprising that people sometimes confuse the words.

They also confuse the words in another way. When speaking informally, people often say something that sounds like *coulda* or *shoulda* or *woulda*, as in "I coulda earned an A if had studied harder. I guess that's what I shoulda done." The proper way to write the sentence, however is like this: "I could've earned an A if I had studied harder. I guess that's what I should've done." Another solution is to simply spell out the words, like this: "I could have earned an A if I had studied harder. I guess that's what I should have done."

PRACTICE

Complete each statement below, using *could have*, *should have*, or *would have*.

Jacob sighed. "Imagine what I _____ done if only I'd remembered that I need to *apply* to colleges if I want to have a chance at being admitted to one."

Hallie's mother yelled at her, "You _____ told me you were borrowing my white silk dress! You _____ told me you spilled mustard on it. You _____ taken it to the dry cleaner immediately, begged my forgiveness, and offered to clean the kitchen every night for the next year and a half!"

"I _____ given you a passing grade," said Mrs. Turnblossom, "if only you had indicated in any way to me, at any time during the quarter, that you were actually conscious."

Mike thought he _____ won the contest if he had worn his lucky skull earring and his Goofy T-shirt.

Pet Peeve 7:
Writing *a lot* as one word

"Alot" is not a word. It is *two* words: *a* and *lot*.

Most people would never even consider writing, "I think I might buy *adog*," or "Thanks *amillion*," or "Please give me just *alittle*." Why, then, do people think of writing *alot*? It doesn't make sense.

Still, people do it all the time. *A lot* is misspelled so frequently that some day it may even be considered just fine to spell it as one word. Rules often do change over time, even spelling rules.

However, the rule hasn't changed yet. It may never change, or it may not change for another 100 years. We are living now and need to follow the acceptable spelling of the word now, according to today's rules. The correct spelling is *a lot* – two words, not one.

PRACTICE

Imagine that you are a teenager with a little brother or sister who keeps doing things to aggravate you. Tell about your suffering in a paragraph of no more than five sentences. See how many times you can use the words *a lot* — spelled correctly, of course — in the paragraph. Try to use the words at least seven times. (No, this paragraph won't be the best paragraph ever written, but it should help you remember the correct spelling of *a lot!*)

Pet Peeve 8:
Mixing up *they're*, *there*, and *their*

One of the easiest pet peeves to avoid is mixing up *they're, there* and *their*.

- *They're* stands for *they are*. (Remember the Magic Apostrophe Rule?) Use it only when you can substitute *they are* in the sentence and have it make sense.
- *There* has the word *here* in it. Use it when you can substitute *here* in the sentence and have it make sense.
- *Their* is used whenever *they're* and *there* don't work. (Another way to look at it is to remember that *their* shows possession — *their* car, *their* dog, *their* test scores.)

Take a look at the following examples:

They're/There/Their *going to get in trouble if they don't shape up.*
(*They are going to get in trouble?* That makes sense. Use *they're*.)

They're/There/Their *are three reasons why Ashley should be named Miss America.*
(*They are three reasons Ashley should be named Miss America?* That doesn't sound right. We know we don't want *they're*. *Here are three reasons Ashley should be named Miss America?* That sounds fine. Use *there*.)

We decided to walk over to **they're/there/their** house.

(*We decided to walk over to they're house?* That doesn't make sense. *We decided to walk over to here house?* That doesn't sound right either. The correct choice is the one left over: *their*, which shows possession.)

PRACTICE

Choose *they're*, *there*, or *their* in the sentences below:

1. *"They're/There/Their* is no excuse for locking Fluffy and Puff in the closet," cried Mrs. Hagglemeister. *"They're/There/Their* 2. such darling little kitties, and as my pet sitter, you were entrusted with *they're/there/their* safety." 3.

"They kept hissing at me," said Arnold. 4.

"My kitties do not hiss unless *they're/there/their* given a good reason," said Mrs. Hagglemeister sternly. "What happened before they hissed?"

5. *"They're/There/Their* was this ugly stuffed mouse they kept trying to drop on my head," answered Arnold. "Then they wanted to climb on my shoulder and sit draped around my neck while I was watering your plants."

"And that's when they hissed?"

6. "No. They seemed to get *they're/there/their* feelings hurt or something when I squirted them with the plant mister. That's when they hissed."

"So your solution was to lock them in a closet. That's unbelievable!" cried Mrs. Hagglemeister. "What kind of pet sitter are you, anyway?"

"Maybe I should have mentioned that I hate cats," confessed Arnold.

7. *They're/There/Their* awful."

Pet Peeve 9:
Mixing up verb tenses

An easy and quick definition of "tense" is "time." Although that doesn't tell the whole story, it does lead you in the right direction. Also, it is easy to remember because both *tense* and *time* begin with the letter "t."

The three most common tenses are present, past and future. Look at the tenses of the verb *jump*:

Today I *jump*. (present tense)
Yesterday I *jumped*. (past tense)
Tomorrow I *will jump*. (future tense)

Look at the verb *frown*:

Today I *frown*. (present tense)
Yesterday I *frowned*. (past tense)
Tomorrow I *will frown*. (future tense)

Look at a harder one, the verb *am*:

Today I *am*. (present tense)
Yesterday I *was*. (past tense)
Tomorrow I *will be*. (future tense)

When you are writing something, remember to stick to one tense. Don't wander around from past to present to future tense. Doing so is very confusing to the reader. Here's an example of what *not* to do:

I went to the bank for some cash. There I see this guy with a mask on. I wondered what he was doing. I think to myself, "I am about to witness a bank robbery." I hoped he didn't have a gun. It turns out that he doesn't. He did, however, have a big tarantula perched on his arm. That was good enough.

This paragraph is a mishmash of past and present tense. I *went* is past tense. I *see* is present tense. I *wondered* is past tense again. I *think* is present tense again. I *hoped* is past tense. It *turns* and he *doesn't* are present tense. He *did* and that *was* are back to past tense. Here's one way to correct the paragraph:

I went to the bank for some cash. There I saw this guy with a mask on. I wondered what he was doing. I thought to myself, "I am about to witness a bank robbery." I hoped he didn't have a gun. It turned out that he didn't. He did, however, have a big tarantula perched on his arm. That was good enough.

Another solution is to put the whole thing in present tense:

I go to the bank for some cash. There I see this guy with a mask on. I wonder what he is doing. I think to myself, "I am about to witness a bank robbery." I hope he doesn't have a gun. It turns out that he doesn't. He does, however, have a big tarantula perched on his arm. That is good enough.

PRACTICE

Correct each of the following paragraphs so that they remain in the same tense:

I was walking along the beach when something moved in the water. I shield my eyes from the sun and look. It is the Loch Ness monster! I will be freaking out. What is it doing in Teal Lake? Was it hungry?

The waiter at *Le Fancy* restaurant was obnoxious. He pours hot tomato soup down my arm, and all he had to say was "Oops." He brought our salads, but he doesn't bring us forks. Then he disappears for 20 minutes. When he finally showed up again, he is bringing me halibut instead of the T-bone steak I ordered. When I complain, he says, "You'll like the halibut better." Then he dripped chocolate fudge sauce on my date's white silk jacket. Finally, when I get mad and ask for the manager, he says, "Dude! Like, chill out!"

Write a paragraph about a child misbehaving in a public place. Write the paragraph in present tense. Then write the same paragraph in past tense.

Pet Peeve 10:
Using casual spellings and symbols in formal writing

It's fine to use casual spellings in casual situations. Who cares if you write *cuz* instead of *because* in an e-mail note to a friend? Who would spell out *and* while taking notes at a lecture when it is so much faster to use the "&" sign?

In formal writing, however, you should spell words with their traditional spelling. (Formal writing refers to just about any communication intended for others, except for very casual notes to friends or family — or to yourself.) Your grocery list would be considered casual. A letter to the editor would be considered formal.

Write *because*, not *cause* or *becuz* or *cuz*.

Write *through*, not *thru*.

Write *okay*, not *O.K.*

Write *and*, not *&*.

Write *light*, not *lite*.

Write *money*, not *$$$$*.

PRACTICE

Correct the casual spellings in the following letter to the editor:

Dear Editor:

Cuz I think your article on education was so unfair, I am canceling my subscription. It is not O.K. to badmouth kids & teachers and schools thru unfair articles like these. Becuz of articles like yours, people think that all schools are bad, & that, in my opinion is definitely not O.K.! Thru the commitment of many people, including parents & other concerned people, we are trying to change the image of schools & build a positive environment for everyone, cuz we really care about education. We're thru with negative attitudes! Please shine your lite on the *good* things kids are doing cause then you will be helping make the world a better place.

Sincerely,
Constance Spooner

P.S. My son is selling chocolates to raise $$$$$ for his school. Do you want to buy some?

Pet Peeves ©2001 Cottonwood Press, Inc. • www.cottonwoodpress.com • 800-864-4297 • Fort Collins, Colorado

Pet Peeve 11: Writing "I seen"

Writing "I seen" is not a good idea. It is not considered "proper" English. Now *why* it is not considered proper is another question. Why is a suit considered proper for a funeral, while a bathing suit is not? Why is it proper to thank your hosts after a party? Why is it proper to eat with a fork in your right hand in the United States but in your left hand in Europe?

Sometimes it is just custom that determines what is proper. Of course, you don't have to follow custom, but if you don't, you won't always get the respect you might deserve. For example, imagine that you are applying for a high-paying job that requires you to travel around the country and talk to various clients. In the interview, the company president asks, "How did you hear about this position?"

"I *seen* a description of it in the newsletter you publish," you answer. With those words, you will probably lose the job. It's very unlikely that the company president will hire someone who doesn't use what is considered proper English, at least not for a well-paying position that involves representing the company to others. Right or wrong, people often *do* judge others by their words. That doesn't mean they are right to do so. However, it is a fact. If you don't want opportunities closed to you, it's important to know how to speak what is considered standard or proper English. If you know how, you can choose to speak it or not. If you don't know how, you have fewer choices in life.

Now — back to the word *seen*. *Seen* always needs a helping verb with it, like *have, had,* or *was*. Instead of "I seen the Empire State Building," you should say, "I *have* seen the Empire State Building," or "I *had* seen the Empire State Building." You *always* need a helping verb with the word *seen*.

If you don't have a helping verb, the word you should use is *saw*, as in, "I *saw* the Empire State Building."

Correct: I saw.

I have seen.

I had seen.

I was seen.

I saw a boa constrictor.

I saw a mouse.

I was seen with a mouse.

I have seen a mouse die at the hands of a boa constrictor.

I saw this.

I saw that.

PRACTICE

Correct the following:

"I never seen anyone with such a bad cold," said Doctor Gutting. "I seen a lady yesterday who was coughing so much it drove everyone in the waiting room crazy. Still, her cold was nothing compared to yours."

"Great," said Gregory. "I'm thrilled."

"I seen a guy once who couldn't stop sneezing. He sneezed constantly for an hour straight and used up three boxes of Kleenex. Still, his cold is not nearly as bad as yours. I never seen anyone with such red eyes and such a swollen nose. I never seen anyone with such a runny nose and such a puffy face. I never seen . . ."

"This is all very interesting," said Gregory, losing the little bit of patience he had left. He peered at the doctor through his very red eyes. "I don't really want to know how bad my cold is, though. I want you to *fix* it!"

"Oh, there's nothing you can do for a cold," said Doctor Gutting.

Pet Peeve 12:
Writing "kinda," "sorta," and "hafta" instead of *kind of, sort of,* and *have to*

In everyday speech, many people say something that sounds like *kinda*, as in "I'm kinda hungry." "Kinda" is really just a sloppy version of *kind of*. When writing, use *kind of,* not "kinda." Also use *sort of,* not "sorta," and *have to,* not "hafta."

If you are thinking, "My best friend Claire isn't going to care if I write her a note about the 'kinda' funny thing that happened at lunch," you are probably right. She also won't care if you show up at her house for dinner in a torn T-shirt and dirty jeans. That's because she's your friend. People who aren't your friends will just think you don't know how to spell.

Pet Peeves ©2001 Cottonwood Press, Inc. • www.cottonwoodpress.com • 800-864-4297 • Fort Collins, Colorado

Correct the following:

Maya kinda wanted to go, but, on the other hand, she kinda wanted to stay home. She thought that a quiet night watching TV might be better than a night at the mall hoping the guy she kinda liked would say "Hey!" to her like he had last Friday night. She kinda liked him, but she wasn't sure. "He's sorta weird," she confessed to her friend Allison.

"Sorta?" cried Allison. "He's the weirdest guy to set foot in the mall in the last ten years!" She saw the look on Maya's face. "I meant that in a *good* way, of course."

Pet Peeve 13:
Starting sentence
after sentence with *well*

Sometimes writers act as though they are afraid to plunge right into a sentence. They tiptoe in by starting off with a *well*. They write, "Well, I called my girlfriend up. Well, she didn't want to talk to me. Well, I got mad."

Most of the time, you are better off without that introductory *well*. It adds nothing and makes your writing sound wimpy. Just get rid of it.

If, once in a while, you do use a *well* to introduce a sentence, put a comma after it to separate it from the rest of the sentence. The same goes for other introductory words like *yes*, *no*, and *oh*.

PRACTICE

Correct the following:

Well here's what happened when I tried to take back the shirt I bought. There was a crabby lady at the counter and she insisted that I had to have a receipt. Well I didn't have a receipt. I don't keep receipts.

The lady said, "Well I can't give you a full-price refund without the receipt. I can only give you a refund of the sales price."

"Well fine," I said. "What is the sales price?"

"Well let's see. That shirt was on the 90% off rack. Here's your $2.00."

Well I was pretty mad. I decided it would be better to keep the shirt than get only $2.00 for it. By the way, I hope a shirt is just what you wanted for your birthday because that is what you are getting.

Pet Peeve 14 :
Beginning sentence after sentence with *so* or *then*

A string of sentences beginning with *so* or *then* is boring. Take a look at the following:

> Janine and I went to the mall. Then we decided to go hang out at the food court. Then we saw some cute guys there. So then we went to talk to them. Then we got tired of that. So then we went to try on pants and tops. Then we got tired of that. So then we left.

You can correct paragraphs like this one by eliminating the words *then* and *so*, at least some of the time. You can also substitute other words, like *after that, soon, next* and *and.* Here is just one way to correct the paragraph above:

> Janine and I went to the mall. We decided to go hang out at the food court. There we saw some cute guys and went to talk to them. After awhile, we got tired of that. Then we went to try on pants and tops. Soon we got tired of that, too, and left.

PRACTICE

Correct the following:

Why I Didn't Turn in My Report on the Battle of Bunker Hill

Our computer crashed this weekend, so I couldn't look up anything on the Internet for my report on the Battle of Bunker Hill. So I decided to go to the library on Sunday. Then my mom's car got a flat, and she didn't have time to change it. So I called my dad to see if he could take me, but I got his answering machine. So then I begged my mom to fix the flat and take me, and she finally said she would. So she got out the jack, but she couldn't get it to work right. So then she asked the neighbor boy Peter to help. So he tried, but the jack slipped, and somehow he managed to cut a big gash in his hand. So I ran over to get his mom because it looked pretty bad. So his mom came running over and took one look at the blood and started crying. She doesn't like blood. So my mom said she would drive him to the hospital, but she would have to use the neighbor's car because ours still had a flat. So she did, but it took four hours in the emergency room. So when she finally got home it was too late to take me to the library because it closes at 6:00 p.m. on Sundays. So that's why I don't have my report finished.

Pet Peeves ©2001 Cottonwood Press, Inc. • www.cottonwoodpress.com • 800-864-4297 • Fort Collins, Colorado

Pet Peeve 15:
Saying "me and my friends"

No one would think of writing "Me went out to eat." Why, then, do people write, "Me and my friends went out to eat"?

The proper phrase is "My friends and I." Use *I* because that's what you would use if you weren't mentioning the friends. Out of politeness, put yourself second. The same idea, of course, applies to other doubled-up phrases, like "My mother and I" or "Joe and I" or "the dogs and I."

Pet Peeves ©2001 Cottonwood Press, Inc. • www.cottonwoodpress.com • 800-864-4297 • Fort Collins, Colorado

PRACTICE

Correct the following:

Me and Dad and Mom and my brother Sam went to a hockey game. There was an awful lot of fighting going on. Me and Mom didn't like it much. Dad and Sam did. They thought it was "action-packed." Me and Mom thought it was bloody.

Dad said me and Mom could stay home next time.

Pet Peeve 16:
Using "go" instead of *say* or *said*

Two little words in the English language are short, simple and effective. The words are *say* and *said*. Unfortunately, many people instead use the word *go*. It is a language fad. Because of it, people write things like this:

My friend takes one look and goes, "Unbelievable!"

That's fine in very informal situations. However, for most situations, you should use either *say* or *said* instead of *go*.

(Of course, if you really are *going* somewhere, that's a different matter. *Go* is a perfectly fine word, used in the right circumstances. It just shouldn't be used to refer to speaking or saying something.)

PRACTICE

Correct the following:

The pizza delivery guy at the door goes, "That will be $12.99."

Jill and I looked at each other. We hadn't ordered a pizza. Jill goes, "You must have the wrong house."

The pizza guy goes, "Nope. This is the house."

Jill goes, "But we didn't order a pizza."

The pizza guy goes, "I have a delivery here for 630 Break Street. You need to pay for it."

Jill and I laughed. As she shut the door, she goes, "You clearly don't know the state of our finances."

Pet Peeve 17:
Using "and stuff"
instead of specific examples

People sometimes write sentences like this:

We went shopping and came home with some food and stuff.

What does *stuff* mean? Did the people bring home food and a new yo-yo? Food and a new set of living room furniture? Food and a pair of earrings? Food and some gum out of a bubblegum machine? Food and a health insurance policy? Food and a leather coat?

Stuff is pretty vague. People use it in writing because they don't want to take time to be specific or clear. They hope "and stuff" will be good enough.

It isn't.

Good writers try to be as specific as possible. The sentence would be better like this:

We went shopping and came home with some food, a year's supply of dog food, and new underwear for everybody in the family.

Sometimes people throw in "and stuff" just as filler. They don't mean a thing by it. Here's an example:

"My paper is late," said Erin, "because we had to go to a meeting and stuff with my dad last night. He was getting some award and my mom said we had to be there and stuff."

Here Erin doesn't really have any meaning at all for "stuff." What they did was go to a meeting. Her mom said they had to be there. Perhaps she had some vague intention of saying that they ate and listened to speeches at the meeting, but it is more likely that "and stuff" means nothing at all. Erin would be better off just leaving it out.

PRACTICE

Correct the following:

Caroline and Sophie walked home after school. They ate some ice cream and stuff. After that, they watched TV and stuff. They were supposed to put the roast and stuff in the oven at 4:00 p.m., but they forgot. They were too busy doing other stuff.

Pet Peeve 18:
Using "use to" for *used to* and "suppose to" for *supposed to*

As you undoubtedly have noticed, words aren't always spelled the way they sound. One example is *used to*, as in "I used to like strawberries" or "I used to have a horse." When we talk, the phrase often sounds like *yoosta*. Many people write *use to*, which looks about right.

It is not. The phrase is *used to*, with a "d" on the end of *use*.

The same thing is true with *supposed to*. It often sounds like "suppose to," but it is really written *supposed to*, with a "d" on the end of *suppose*.

It may help to say the words aloud 10 or 20 times each, really exaggerating each "d" sound. Such a tactic may seem silly, but it really can work. The next time you write the words, you are likely to remember exaggerating the "d" sound — and then spell the phrase correctly.

useD to	useD to	supposeD to	supposeD to
useD to	useD to	supposeD to	supposeD to
useD to	useD to	supposeD to	supposeD to

PRACTICE

Correct the following:

"I use to like English," said Marvin, "but then I found out that spelling is important. My teacher pointed out that no one but me could read anything I wrote. I use to spell things however I wanted — not the way I was suppose to. I guess that wasn't a good idea. Now I have to pay attention and use a dictionary. I'm trying hard to do what I'm suppose to do.

"Things use to be a lot easier."

Pet Peeves ©2001 Cottonwood Press, Inc. • www.cottonwoodpress.com • 800-864-4297 • Fort Collins, Colorado

56

Pet Peeve 19:
Saying and writing "supposebly"

Many people think the word *supposedly* is pronounced — or even written — *supposeBly.*

It isn't.

The letters "d" and "b" *are* very similar sounding, so it's easy to see why people make the error. Still, one little letter can make a big difference. People named *Bob* don't want to be called *Dob*. People named *Bonnie* don't want to be called *Donnie.*

The word *supposedly* would probably feel the same way, if words could have feelings. The word is *supposeDly*, with a "d," not a "b."

PRACTICE

Correct the following:

The bus driver supposebly warned the kids that they would be kicked off if they didn't settle down. They didn't settle down.

He stopped the bus. Supposebly, he said, "Get off at the corner now, or I'll set you down in the middle of the highway later." He had a very crazed look in his eyes. They believed him.

The driver supposebly let out an insane laugh and threw water balloons at the kids as he drove away.

Then he went to the bus station and retired.

Pet Peeve 20:
Using the word *like* as a meaningless filler

Your teacher will, like, hate it if you, like, write the word *like* after, like, every word or two and, like, repeat it, like, again and again and again.

Overuse of the word *like* is so common today that many people simply can't speak or write a sentence without using it. The word generally doesn't mean much of anything. It's often just a filler, used instead of a pause.

Constant use of *like* in both writing and speaking can make you sound immature or silly. When movies or television show writers want to indicate that a character is not terribly bright or deep, one of the first things they do is have the character say *like* a lot, as in the following:

> *"Dude! Where have you been, like, hanging out? I'm, like, so glad to, like, see you! I was just, like, saying the other day, 'Like, where is Casey?'"*

Imagine a candidate for president speaking with a lot of *likes*:

> *"I'm, like, running for president because I, like, have a vision that this country could, like, be a better place. You know?"*

Using *like* a lot is not the way to be taken seriously.

PRACTICE

Correct the following:

Dear School Board:

    I am writing to, like, ask you to change your policy about the state standard-ized test. It is, like, so useless and, like, wastes all our time. We don't take it seri-ously, and our teachers spend way too much time, like, teaching us to take tests instead of, like, helping us, like, learn something that might like be valuable to us in the future. I'm, like, sick of this.

Sincerely,
Aaron Dimwiddie

Pet Peeve 21:
Overusing exclamation points

Writers sometimes get in the bad habit of sprinkling exclamation points around like salt and pepper. Exclamations points should be used only with exclamations, which are statements that show very strong feeling. "A gorilla just climbed in my window!" is an example of an exclamation. Unless you are Dian Fossey, it is unlikely that you would talk about a gorilla sighting in a calm manner. Therefore, an exclamation point would be appropriate.

An innocent fictional character on his way to prison might say, "I didn't do it!" Again, an exclamation point would be appropriate because the character undoubtedly is expressing *very* strong feelings.

An important thing to remember about exclamation points is that you use them very sparingly. If you don't, they lose their intensity.

For example, imagine that you have a friend who says, twelve times a day, "That's the worst thing that ever happened to me!" After a while, you learn to ignore him. You know that the worst thing in the world can't possibly happen to a person twelve times a day, every day of the week. You learn that his statement is an exaggeration. In the same way, exclamation points lose their strength when they aren't saved for *truly* strong statements.

Some people take a liking to exclamation points and sprinkle them everywhere, like this:

I saw my friend Alicia at the mall today! She had on the cutest skirt! I want one just like it! I just love the way Alicia dresses! I wish I had half the clothes she does! My stuff is so ugly!

Perhaps you are thinking, "Wait a minute! Maybe it really *is* a big deal that the writer saw Alicia at the mall. Maybe she *does* need to use an exclamation point."

You could be right. If Alicia had been missing for three years and suddenly turned up at the mall, yes, "I saw my friend Alicia at the mall today!" *would* deserve an exclamation point. However, that isn't the meaning suggested in the paragraph above. If it were, the writer would probably be talking about a lot more than Alicia's cute skirt.

PRACTICE !

Take out all the unnecessary exclamation points in the following:

"I won the lottery!" cried Delmont. "I won two million dollars!"

"That's nice, dear!" said his mother. "I think I'll run to the grocery store now. Do you want Cocoa Puffs or Wheaties this week? Maybe I'll get some Frosted Flakes!"

"Mom! Did you hear me?" Delmont asked.

"Of course I heard you!" said his mother. "You are so cute when you are excited! Now, let me decide on dinner. Let's have hot dogs! I think I'll also whip up some Jello with bananas! That would be good!"

Delmont shook his head. "You never hear a word I say, Mom."

"Let's invite that nice Olivia from church, too!" said his mother. "She is so cute! Don't you think so, Delmont? She's just your age, too — 32! I think that's a perfect age to get married! I married your father at 32! What do you think, Delmont?""

Delmont shook his head as he went out the door. He was on his way to turn in his lottery ticket and buy a one-way ticket to Acapulco.

Pet Peeve 22:
Using "irregardless" and "ain't"

"Irregardless" is like "ain't." You shouldn't use it, except jokingly or in the most informal situations.

"Then how come it's in the dictionary?" many students say triumphantly, holding the dictionary up and pointing to "irregardless" or "ain't." If they look closely, they will see why. The word "nonstandard" (or something similar, depending on the dictionary) appears after the words. That means they are not considered acceptable words in most situations.

Instead of "irregardless," use "regardless." Instead of *ain't,* use *am not* or *are not.*

PRACTICE

Correct the following:

"I expect you to be home by 10:00," said Troy's dad, "irregardless of when the party is over."

"I ain't going to be getting in any trouble," said Troy.

"I know you aren't. That's because you're going to be home by 10:00."

"It ain't fair," said Troy. "Everybody else gets to stay out later."

"If everybody else jumped off a cliff, would you jump off a cliff?"

"You always say that."

"That's because parents are required to say that at least once a week or so. It's in the *Rule Book for Parents, Volume I.*"

Troy looked at his dad suspiciously. "Is that true?"

"Irregardless of whether it's true or not, I expect you to be home by 10:00."

"But why?"

"Because I said so. That's in *Volume II.*"

Pet Peeve 23:
Using *a* and *an* incorrectly

Nothing sets an English teacher's teeth on edge more than reading a sentence like this: *Eric fried a egg.* It's not that English teachers hate eggs. They just hate the word *a* being used with the word *egg.* The word *a* goes with words that start with a consonant sound. The word *an* goes with words that start with a vowel sound.

Why? Perhaps it's because the pronunciation sounds so "sputtery" otherwise. We pronounce the word *a* as *uh,* not *ay.* Saying "uh apple," "uh egg," "uh ear" or "uh idiot" sounds a little bit like burping. "An apple" or "an egg" sounds smoother, gentler, more attractive.

But what if you can't remember which letters are consonants and which are vowels? Take a moment and learn. It's really easy. There are only five vowels: **a, e, i, o** and **u** (and sometimes **y**). These are the letters that you see most often in words. Every word has to have a vowel. Try to pronounce a word without one, and you can't. Here's an example: clck. How do you pronounce a word like that?

You can't. You need a vowel. You could make it *click* or *clack* or *cluck* or *clock,* for example. The vowel is the letter that makes the word pronounceable.

And what is a consonant? All the letters that aren't vowels are consonants.

Note: If a word starts with a consonant that is silent, treat the word as though it starts with a vowel, and use *an.* Example: "an honest man."

PRACTICE

Correct the following:

"I want a egg for breakfast," said Ed.

"What else?" asked his grandmother.

"A orange. Maybe a apple, too."

"Of course, dear," said Grandma. "Can I iron a shirt for you, too?"

"Sure," said Ed. "I think I want to wear a olive green one today."

"Very well. Can I give you a few dollars for lunch money?"

"Sure. A eight dollar bill would be nice."

"Sweetie, they don't make eight dollar bills."

"Oh. Sure. I knew that."

"Of course you did, dear. Those *Fs* in math were all the teacher's fault. Now — what else can I do for you before you leave? How about if I brush your teeth for you? I have a hour before I have to leave."

"Grandma, that's going too far. You wouldn't want to spoil a excellent grandson like me now, would you?"

Pet Peeves ©2001 Cottonwood Press, Inc. • www.cottonwoodpress.com • 800-864-4297 • Fort Collins, Colorado

Pet Peeve 24: Misspelling *etc.*

Chances are you have looked at something for years but never really *noticed* it? Many people, for example, have never really seen a very common little word. Take a look at the last word in the following sentence:

> *Before we went into the theater, we bought popcorn, Cokes, gummy bears, Junior Mints, etc.*

A very large percentage of English speakers look at that sentence and think they see the word "ect." (Look carefully. That's not what is there.) Many pronounce the word as if it were spelled "eKsetera." There are probably millions of people across America who really believe the word is "ect."

It is not. The word is pronounced "eTsetera." It is spelled *etc.*, with a "t" in the middle, not at the end.

Correct the following:

Bill got out his notebook, pen, paper, pencil, eraser, ect. Then he filled a snack table with popcorn, Coke, potato chips, a Milky Way, some red licorice, ect. He opened his chemistry book. He saw words like tellurium, palladium, mendelevium, einsteinium, ect.

He closed the book, sighed, and turned his attention to the Milky Way.

Pet Peeve 25:
Writing "The End"
at the end of a paper

Look at some newspaper articles. When an article is over, it's over. You don't see the words "The End" at the end.

Look at books or magazines. They rarely use the phrase "The End." The words in the last paragraph of the story let you know the piece is over, not the words "The End."

English teachers don't like to see the phrase "The End" at the end of a composition or report. That isn't because they are picky — although they sometimes *are* picky (but of course for good reason). They don't like to see that phrase because they know students are using it as a crutch. Instead of writing a conclusion to their papers, they plunk down the words "The End" and hope that takes care of it.

It doesn't. Skip the phrase "The End." It is almost never necessary. Instead, write a conclusion that lets the reader know your work is over.

PRACTICE

Rewrite this paragraph so that we know that it is the end of the story without seeing the words "The End."

The princess watched as the frog turned into a handsome prince. She was not that impressed. She had once seen an alligator turn into a lemon tree. Another time she saw a lily pad turn into a big bowl of split pea soup.

The End

Pet Peeve 26:
Dividing a word at the end of a line for convenience rather than dividing it at the syllable

If you write like this, you look very sill-
y. You also really aggravate the perso-
n reading what you have writte-
n.

    You wouldn't think that anyone wou-
ld ever do this, but English teachers s-
e it all the time.

    If you have reached the end of a line and you run out of room, it's fine to divide a word and put part of it on the next line — *if* you are dividing the word at a syllable. You must also use a hyphen (-) to show that the word is divided.

    Don't divide a word when you have only one letter left to put on the next line. Of course, it is also impossible to divide one-syllable words.

    If in doubt about where to divide a word, check a dictionary. Dictionaries always divide words into syllables for you.

PRACTICE

Correct the following:

My mother planned my slumber party. I didn't want her to, but she did it anyway. We had 100% fruit drinks — no Cokes or other sugary drinks for us. She decided that the pizzas should have stoneground whole wheat crusts, and she made them herself. She put goat cheese on top with some broccoli. "For the color," she told us.

Dessert was some carob bars she made herself. I don't know what carob is exactly, but I don't think I want to know.

She rented videos for us, too. "I think the girls will get a kick out of these old Fred Astaire and Ginger Rogers musicals," she said.

Well, they didn't. The only good thing about the party was all the red licorice whips Jade had hidden in her sleeping bag, along with the video of *The Attack of the Mutant Androids from the Center of the Earth*. We slipped it in the VCR after Mom went to bed. "I've been to your Mom's parties before," Jade explained. Then she got out the gummy bears.

Pet Peeve 27:
Writing (or saying)
"exspecially" and "excape"

Look at the words *especially* and *escape*, which are spelled correctly in this sentence. Do you see an "x" in either of them?

No. That's because there isn't one.

Many people think that the words *especially* and *escape* are really *"eXpecially"* and *"eXcape."* They aren't. They also aren't supposed to be pronounced that way. The words should be pronounced and written with an "es" at the beginning, not an "ex."

PRACTICE

Correct the following:

Dear Grandma,

Thank you for the very interesting yellow sweater with the cocker spaniel puppies embroidered all over it. It is expecially nice. I know you made it for me to wear in gym class, so I don't catch cold, but the other guys would probably be jealous if I wore it there, and I might have to make a quick excape. That's why I'm saving it to wear at home, where I know no one will steal it.

My sister expecially likes the sweater and mentions it to me all the time. To tell you the truth, the other day I got pretty sick of hearing her mention it, so I started throwing sofa pillows at her. She tried to excape, but I got her good. Then I got in trouble, even though it was really her fault. She is expecially good at getting out of things, you know.

Well, I've got to go. Thank you again for knitting me such a unique gift.

Love,
Henry

Pet Peeve 28:
Putting a comma at the beginning of a line instead of after the word on the previous line

With the English language, many, many rules about writing have exceptions. Here's one that does not: Never start a line of writing with a comma. A comma *always* goes right next to a word, not by itself. If the word comes at the end of a line, put the comma next to it, never at the start of the next line of writing.

No: *When Jerome ordered an anchovy pizza*
        , no one else would help pay for it.

Yes: *When Jerome ordered an anchovy pizza,*
        no one else would help pay for it.

Correct the following:

Scarlett was learning to drive
, but it wasn't going well. Her
dad did not have a lot of patience.
He got mad a lot. Once when she
was trying to turn left he yelled
,"Why are you stopping in the
middle of the intersection?"

"The car stalled!" she cried.
Cars started honking at them.
Soon Scarlett was in tears and
swearing she would never drive again
, and her dad was yelling unrepeatable
things and swearing he would never
get in the car with Scarlett again.

It was not, all in all, a successful
driving lesson.

Pet Peeve 29:
Using a comma before *because*

Don't use a comma before the word *because*. It doesn't need one.

No: *She yelled, because she felt like it.*

Yes: *She yelled because she felt like it.*

(Once in a while, a writer may use a comma before the word *because* to make a long, complicated sentence a bit clearer. However, these cases are rare. If you are in doubt, don't use a comma.)

PRACTICE

Correct the following:

Dear Mr. and Mrs. Everett:

I am writing this note to you, because we are having some difficulties with your son Evan here at the Lazy Daisy Preschool. We can't get him to quiet down for nap time, because he wants to play Chutes and Ladders some more. As you may have noticed, he really, really likes Chutes and Ladders. Some of our staff members are reluctant to work with Evan any longer, because their eyes are glazing over from too many rounds of Chutes and Ladders. We are wondering if you might try playing a few more rounds of the game with him at home each day. We think that might help, because even Evan has to burn out on the game sometime.

At least we sincerely hope so.

Sincerely,
The staff at the Lazy Daisy Preschool

Pet Peeve 30:
Writing "and then I woke up" at the end of a story

If you ever grow up and become an English teacher, here's something you can be *sure* will happen: You will read dozens and dozens of stories from students, and a huge percentage of them will end with either, "And then I woke up," or "It was all a dream!"

The problem isn't that this ending is a particularly bad idea. Once in a while, in fact, it's even very effective. One example comes from television.

You may have seen reruns of the old "The Bob Newhart Show," a television series set in Chicago. Newhart played a psychiatrist, and Suzanne Pleshette played his wife. Years later, Newhart had another series. This time he was a writer running an old inn in Vermont, and Mary Frann played his wife. On the last episode of the second series, Newhart woke up with the first wife, Suzanne Pleshette, next to him on the set of the old Chicago show. "I just had the strangest dream," he said, indicating that *everything* that had taken place on the second series in Vermont over the past few years had been a dream.

The show was one of the most-watched episodes on television, ever, and people loved it. The "It was all a dream!" plot probably worked so well because it was completely unexpected. After all, the second series had been in production for eight years. No one could have imagined such an ending for the series.

For a story written in an English class, however, such an ending is pretty easy to imagine. English teachers see it all the time. If you are going to use it, at least be aware that you are probably *not* going to surprise anyone, least of all your English teacher.

PRACTICE

Write a better ending for this story:

Larissa looked out the window and saw the space ship take off with her cat Fluffykins. She cried and cried.

Then she woke up! It was all a dream!

Pet Peeve 31:
Using double subjects like "My sister, she said . . ." or "Jason, he said . . ."

Sometimes people get carried away. Instead of just saying or writing the subject of the sentence, they mention it twice. Here's an example:

My dad, he went to pick up some cinnamon rolls.

The writer needs to use either *dad* or *he*, not both words. There is no reason to use both. Either of the following would be correct:

My dad went to pick up some cinnamon rolls.
He went to pick up some cinnamon rolls.

Here are some more examples of double subjects, with corrections:

No: *Loretta, she hates the color baby blue.*
Yes: *Loretta hates the color baby blue.*

No: *The president, he really wants to outlaw pickled beets.*
Yes: *The president really wants to outlaw pickled beets.*

PRACTICE

Correct the following:

After I cracked a joke, Mrs. Sutton, she got mad and yelled at me. Then the girl in the red dress, she laughed at me for getting in trouble. I turned to yell at her, but my friend Joe, he gave me a look that said, "Just be quiet." So I was.

Then the principal, she came on the intercom to make an announcement. I couldn't help myself. I made another joke. The teacher, she got mad all over again. The girl in the red dress, she laughed at me all over again for getting in trouble. Joe, he gave me another look to warn me to be quiet.

I ignored him. Joe, he just shook his head and said, "You're hopeless."

The girl in the red dress, she laughed at me again.

The teacher, she gave me detention.

Pet Peeve 32:
Mixing up *lose* and *loose*

Two little words that people often mix up, at least when they are writing, are *lose* and *loose*. *Lose* is pronounced *looz* and is used in sentences such as, "If I lose another sock in the dryer, I'm going to scream." *Loose* is pronounced so that it rhymes with *goose*. It is used in sentences such as, "My button came loose and fell in the soup."

The easiest way to remember the difference is to remember that loose and goose look *almost* the same, except for the beginning letter, and are pronounced almost the same, except for the beginning letter. In other words, *loose* and *goose* rhyme.

PRACTICE

Correct the following:

Mrs. Persnickety was a person who believed in lots of rules. "If you *loose/lose* your pencil," she said, "you will receive a zero for the day because you won't be able to do any work."

Jeremy was a person who believed in questioning everything. "What if the strap on your backpack comes *loose/lose* and your pencil falls out?" he asked. "What if someone rips off your pencil? What if you *loose/lose* it because you lend it to someone who forgets to give it back? What if you give it to a family who has lost everything in a flood and needs to fill out an application for financial aid? What if you . . ."

"Your questions are enough to make a person *loose/lose* her mind," interrupted Mrs. Persnickety.

Pet Peeve 33: Using a colon with a list when it isn't needed

A colon is a useful punctuation mark that is used fairly rarely. It is most commonly used as a kind of "announcing" mark to introduce a list of things. It says, "I'm about to give you a list or an illustration, so be alert for it; here it comes!" It's like a drum roll, or a trumpet flourish. Here's an example:

Here's what I'm going to serve at my party: pizza, Coke, brownies, and ice cream.

Do not use a colon to introduce a list of things when the list is "woven" right into the sentence, like this:

For my party I'm going to serve pizza, Cokes, brownies, and ice cream.

The first sentence announces the list of foods. The second does not. Get a feel for the difference by looking at the following examples:

Colon needed

In my opinion, these are the four major food groups: chocolate, fast food, dessert and soft drinks.

Colon not needed

In my opinion, the four major food groups are chocolate, fast food, dessert and soft drinks.

Colon needed

These are the people selected for the committee: Alexander, Alexis, Alex, and Alexa.

Colon not needed

The people selected for the committee were Alexander, Alexis, Alex, and Alexa.

Colon needed

Here's what my mother said when I came home at 2:00 a.m.: "You are grounded until your 21st birthday."

Colon not needed

When I came home at 2:00 a.m., my mother said I was grounded until my 21st birthday.

Colon needed

I'm taking three hard subjects this year: chemistry, geometry, and world history.

Colon not needed

The three hard subjects I'm taking this year are chemistry, geometry, and world history.

PRACTICE

Correct the following:

If I win the lottery, the first things I'm going to buy are: a new car, a house on the beach, and a plane ticket to Hawaii. I'm going to build the house in one of these countries: France, Mexico, or Brazil. I will be so happy that I'll probably donate a lot of money to: the Red Cross, the Salvation Army, and the American Cancer Society. I'll buy my mom: a new dishwasher, a leather briefcase, a new computer, and a hot tub. If my brother apologizes to me before I win, I'll get him: a brand new Porsche, new skis, and a new guitar. If he doesn't, I'll get him the following: a Big Mac and an order of fries.

Pet Peeve 34:
Mixing up *whose* and *who's*

It's time to remember the Magic Apostrophe Rule again. Let's review it:

The Magic Apostrophe Rule

**Except when it is used with a person's name or a noun,
an apostrophe almost always stands for a letter that has been left out.
If nothing has been left out, you don't want an apostrophe.**

The word *who's* is short for *who is*. If you can substitute the words *who is* in the sentence, you want the word *who's*. If you can't, you want the word *whose*. Let's look at some examples:

Who's/Whose *the luckiest girl in town?*
(*Who is* the luckiest girl in town? That makes sense. We want *who's*.)

It's Mary, **who's/whose** *lottery ticket was the big winner last week.*
(It's Mary, *who is* lottery ticket was the big winner last week? That doesn't make sense. We want *whose*.)

PRACTICE

Correct the following:

"*Who's/Whose* Daddy's little girl?" asked Mr. Bleeker, the father of three-year-old Anna. "It's my little Anna-kins — the bestest little girl in the whole wide world! There's no daddy in the world *who's/whose* little angel is a cuter-wuter thing than my adorable little angel!" He gave little Anna a kiss. "And *who's/whose* going to take his little angel out for an ice cweam cone? Yes — it's Daddy!"

Mr. and Mrs. Markuson looked at each other and rolled their eyes. "And *who's/whose* daddy makes everyone want to throw up when he talks to his daughter?" Mr. Markuson muttered.

"Anna-kins' daddy!" his wife muttered back to him.

Pet Peeve 35: Writing "I'am"

I'm stands for *I am.* The apostrophe stands for the missing "a."

"I'am" is not a word. No letters have been left out, so the apostrophe doesn't make any sense at all.

Write either *I am* or *I'm.* Don't write "I'am." It is not a word and is never correct.

PRACTICE

Correct the following:

"I'am going to ask Sophie to marry me," said Samuel. "I am going to ask her by renting a billboard. On the billboard, I'm going to write, 'I'am in love with you, Sophie Padelowski. Will you marry me?'"

"I'am not sure that's a good idea," said Garth. "She eloped yesterday with Manfred Carbunkle."

Pet Peeve 36:
Separating two sentences with a comma

Periods are strong. Exclamation points are strong. Question marks are strong.

Commas are not.

Writers who don't remember these punctuation personality traits often make a very common error: using a comma to separate two complete sentences. Here's an example of what *not* to do:

> *Dylan generally won't eat anything at all that is green, he makes an exception for lime Jello.*

A comma is considered weak. (You might even think of it as looking a bit like a cane.) If you're going to use it between two sentences, you need back up: the words *and, but, or, for, nor, yet,* or *so.* The sentence above could be correctly written like this:

> *Dylan generally won't eat anything at all that is green, but he makes an exception for lime Jello.*

Of course, another solution would be just to use a period, like this:

> *Dylan generally won't eat anything at all that is green. He makes an exception for lime Jello.*

All this seems simple enough. The problem is that some people remember just part of the rule. They remember that commas are weak and need backup. They forget which words are acceptable as backup. Here they are again: *and, but, or, for, nor, yet* and *so*. These are words that can be used with a comma to connect two complete sentences (sometimes called independent clauses).

Let's look at some more examples:

No: *The flight attendant pointed out the exits, she also pointed out the restrooms at the front and rear of the cabin.*

Yes: *The flight attendant pointed out the exits, and she also pointed out the restrooms at the front and rear of the cabin.*

No: *The restroom at the front of the cabin didn't do us any good, it was for first class passengers only.*

Yes: *The restroom at the front of the cabin didn't do us any good, for it was for first class passengers only.*

No: *The flight attendant addressed the passengers, she said, "In case you have been living in a cave since 1952, let me show you how to fasten a seat belt."*

Yes: *The flight attendant addressed the passengers. She said, "In case you have been living in a cave since 1952, let me show you how to fasten a seat belt."*

Correct the following:

The pilot came on the intercom, he tried to speak in a calm voice. He said, "I don't want to alarm anyone, but please fasten your seatbelts immediately. Don't even think about getting up to use the restroom right now, don't even think about getting a refill on your drink. Get ready to grab your oxygen mask, also be sure and review those rules about opening the door if you are seated at an exit. Finally, remember what the stewardess told you about the seat cushion being used as a flotation device in the event of an emergency? Well, get ready to see how well that works.

"Again, I don't want to alarm anyone, please stay calm and try to think clearly. By the way, I would like to take this opportunity to thank you for flying Sky Prince Airlines."

Pet Peeve 37:
Mixing up *lead* and *led*

People often mix up the two verbs *lead* and *led*. They use *lead* when they should use *led*. This sentence should help you keep the two straight:

Ed led the parade.

In this sentence, the word *led* is pronounced to rhyme with *Ed.* It's also spelled almost the same way. Whenever the verb you need rhymes with *Ed,* use *led.* If it doesn't rhyme with Ed, use *lead.* Here is an example of a sentence that uses *lead:*

Ed is going to lead the parade tomorrow.

Warning: If you are writing about what we call the material in a pencil, or what a pipe is sometimes made of, forget all of the above. The word you need then— not a verb — is *lead*, even though it still rhymes with Ed.

Let's review:

You might *lead* a marching band every night after school.
You *led* a marching band yesterday.
You might *lead* a marching band tomorrow, using a *lead* pencil as your baton.

Pet Peeves ©2001 Cottonwood Press, Inc. • www.cottonwoodpress.com • 800-864-4297 • Fort Collins, Colorado

PRACTICE !

Choose **lead** or **led** in the sentences below:

Lila looked at her **lead/led** pencil and wondered, "Why do they call this a Number Two pencil? Why do we have to use it on standardized tests? What if we used a Number 48 pencil instead? Would we fail? Do they even make Number 48 pencils?"

Lila often wondered about things. In history class she wondered, "What if George Washington had been a woman? I wonder if he would have **lead/led** the troops in the Revolutionary War. I wonder if he liked to **lead/led**. Maybe he really liked to **lead/led** but would rather have **lead/led** a big corporation or a university."

In math class she worked on a story problem about six plumbers, 18 feet of **lead/led** pipe, and a train traveling at 70 miles per hour, driven by a brother twice as old as his sister was two years ago. The problem made no sense to Lila. She went back to thinking about George Washington.

"He was good," she thought, "but I'll bet a woman would have been just as good. I think it's time a woman became president. Maybe I'll do it. I could **lead/led** the country really well, I'll bet. Plenty of other women have **lead/led** countries around the world." With that, she licked the point of her **lead/led** pencil and started outlining her campaign.

Pet Peeve 38:
Dropping a "quote bomb"
in the middle of a paragraph

Quote bombs are quotations you drop into a paragraph without attributing the quotation. *Attributing* means telling who is responsible for the quotation.

Here is a paragraph that contains a quote bomb:

> *Tortured Can Openers has been a popular band in the United States for several years now. "Tortured Can Openers sells out every concert in less than ten minutes." The group's latest single has topped the charts now for three months.*

It's easy to fix a paragraph with a quote bomb. Simply tell who is responsible for the quotation. Here's one way to fix the quote bomb above:

> *Tortured Can Openers has been a popular band in the United States for several years now. According to the group's publicist, "Tortured Can Openers sells out every concert in less than ten minutes." The group's latest single has topped the charts now for three months.*

Here's another paragraph with a quote bomb:

"Nine out of ten children drink too many soft drinks." Many parents are worrying about the problems caused by too much sugar in their children's diets.

Here is one way to fix the quote bomb:

According to a report by the National Watchdog Association, "Nine out of ten children drink too many soft drinks." Many parents are worrying about the problems caused by too much sugar in their children's diets.

Let's look at one more paragraph with a quote bomb:

In the final scene of the play, Penelope finally speaks up when her opinionated boss gives her one too many pieces of advice. "That's absolutely the dumbest thing I've ever heard in my life!"

Here is one way to fix the quote bomb:

In the final scene of the play, Penelope finally speaks up when her opinionated boss gives her one too many pieces of advice. She turns to him and says, "That's absolutely the dumbest thing I've ever heard in my life!"

Don't plunk a quotation into a paragraph without telling where it came from. You need to use phrases like "according to," "he said," "she thought" or "they asked."

PRACTICE

Correct the following:

Eggs can be eaten many ways. They can be hard-boiled, fried, coddled, scrambled, or poached, for example. "Some even eat eggs raw." However, it is dangerous to eat raw eggs because of the risk of contracting salmonella."

One of the most disgusting ways to eat an egg, in my opinion, is to cook it over easy. The runny egg yolk oozes over the plate and makes people looking at it feel sick to their stomachs. "I'm going to barf."

Pet Peeve 39:
Using a period too soon and turning
a perfectly good sentence into a sentence fragment

People often take a perfectly good sentence and stick a period in the middle of it, splitting it into a sentence and a sentence fragment. Here are some examples:

Yes: *I wanted to see you when I heard you were in town.*

No: *I wanted to see you. When I heard you were in town.*

Yes: *I like hot dogs, unless I think about what's in them.*

No: *I like hot dogs. Unless I think about what's in them.*

Yes: *He ate at the new restaurant, which is owned by the quarterback of the Tribecca Trout.*

No: *He ate at the new restaurant. Which is owned by the quarterback of the Tribecca Trout.*

Don't create a sentence fragment by separating a phrase or a dependent clause from the rest of the sentence.

PRACTICE

Correct the following:

"Are we there yet?" asked Michaela from the back seat.

"We are not there yet. You know that. Because you asked the same thing two minutes ago," said Ms. Rosario.

"I am sick of riding in the car. I am sick of sitting here with nothing to do. Hoping that something good will pop up on the side of the road. Like a rattlesnake farm. I think I'd like to visit a rattlesnake farm."

"We aren't going to visit a rattlesnake farm," said Ms. Rosario.

Two minutes passed.

"Are we there yet?" asked Michaela's brother Adam.

"If I hear anyone ask that question again, we're going to eat Aunt Meg's tofu and lettuce sandwiches for lunch. Instead of stopping at Burger King," yelled Mr. Rosario. "Am I making myself clear?"

"Yes," said Adam and Michaela.

Two more minutes passed.

"I need to go to the rest room," said Michaela. "We could stop at that Dairy Queen. Which I'm sure has a restroom."

"So does that Texaco station," said Mr. Rosario, gritting his teeth.

Pet Peeve 40:
Assuming that slang is acceptable for any kind of writing

One of the most important things you can ever do as a writer is to learn to step outside of yourself and imagine that you are the person reading your work. Imagine what the person would think, how the person would react.

For example, suppose that you are writing to your great grandmother, who has never before used a computer. You tell her how to get started:

First, boot up by using the power button on the tower. After your operating system loads, you will need to log on with your username and password. Once you are granted access to your system, the desktop will load on your monitor. On your desktop you will have icons, which are shortcuts to different program files. The taskbar will tell you which programs you have open. Most computers come pre-loaded with an Internet browser, but you will need to sign up with an ISP before you will be able to use the Internet or e-mail. The ISP will give you a phone number that you will dial up with your modem. You can use e-mail through your ISP or you can use a web-based e-mail program like Yahoo! or Excite!

Now that may make perfectly good sense to you, but think of your poor great grandma. What does "boot up" mean? Which part is the tower? What is a username, an icon, a browser, an ISP? If you are able to look at things through your great grandmother's eyes, you will see that you need to write differently for her than you might for your friend, who is a computer whiz.

The same thing goes for other situations. You need to pay attention to your readers and tailor your language to fit your audience. That means that, generally, you should avoid most slang.

It isn't that slang is bad. In the right circumstances it is fine. One problem with using it in writing is that its meaning often changes quickly. Think of how silly *groovy* sounds today, though it used to be a perfectly good slang word. Another problem is that communication can be lost when writers use slang. Not everyone understands every slang word or phrase. Finally, slang can often make it difficult for others to take your writing seriously.

Avoid slang in all but the most informal kinds of writing. You should *not* write a sentence like the following, except perhaps to a close friend in a note:

> *The dude was really ticked when the station started playing this cheesy music. He thought it was so lame.*

The following would generally be more appropriate:

> *The lawyer became very angry when the station started playing the Beatles' song "I Want to Hold Your Hand," recorded by a full orchestra. He thought the recording was an insult to the Beatles.*

PRACTICE

Eliminate slang from the following:

Last night Mom told us we had to go listen to this cheesy barbershop quartet my dad is in. I was all, "Mom, I'm *so* not into barbershop quartets."

Mom goes, "It will be cool, honey."

I was like, "As *if!* Who ever heard of a good barbershop quartet? Those guys are totally lame."

Mom started wigging out and was like, "The group is the best barbershop quartet in the whole county! The least you could do is go support your father!"

I rolled my eyes and was like, "Whatever, Mom. Chill out."

Things went downhill from there. I ended up getting grounded because of "disrespect."

Unfortunately, the grounding didn't start until *after* the stupid barbershop quartet concert. Bummer.

Pet Peeve 41:
Using the wrong pronoun, as in "Her and me are going to the mall" or "Mary gave it to she and I"

Would you write, "Her is going to the mall?" or "Me is going to the mall"?

Of course not. Then why write, "Her and me are going to the mall?" It just doesn't make sense.

Don't let pairs of pronouns confuse you. Just figure out what word you would use if you were writing about each person separately. Then put the two choices together. For example, you would say, "She is going to the mall" or "I am going to the mall." Put them together and you have, "She and I are going to the mall."

Look at another example: Should you write, "Mary gave it to she and I"?

No. You wouldn't say, "Mary gave it to she" or "Mary gave it to I." You would say, "Mary gave it to her" or "Mary gave it to me." Therefore, the correct way to write the sentence is, "Mary gave it to her and me."

PRACTICE

Correct the following:

"Me and Ricardo are going to win," boasted Nick. "Me and him worked on it so hard. Our science fair project is lots better than anyone else's."

"You and him are so modest," said Patricia sarcastically. "Did it ever occur to you that you might have competition from Candace and I? Or the rest of the class?"

"Nope. "You and them are not in the same league as me and Ricardo. We're going to win for sure. Our project is called 'A Comparison of the Big Mac and the Whopper in Satisfying the Hunger Pangs of the Typical Adolescent Male After an Afternoon of Playing Basketball Against a Really Good Team That We Hate from the Other Side of Town.'"

Pet Peeve 42:
Writing an entire paper
as one paragraph

The paragraph you are reading right now is going to be very confusing to you because it goes on and on and on without any breaks for your eyes or your brain. Our eyes and our brains prefer to look at things in smaller pieces, and a huge glob of writing usually looks pretty boring and is hard to sort out. If you wanted to learn about aardvarks, for example, and bought a magazine with an article on them, you would be pretty intimidated if you opened the book and saw that it consisted of one huge paragraph, seven pages long, on aardvarks. You would see all about what they eat mushed right together with where they live and what they look like. If you wanted to skim the article and find out if aardvarks are aggressive or not, it would be hard because there would be no breaks to help you see when a new subject is being addressed. Paragraphs are designed to *help* us. English teachers hate it when students turn in papers that are written as one long paragraph. Anything more than about a half a page in length should probably be divided into different paragraphs. Each paragraph should be about one thing. For example, if you were writing about aardvarks, you might have a paragraph on their eating habits. You might have another on their habitat. You might have another telling about how they raise their young. You might have another on what kind of aardvark to choose as a Mother's Day gift. Just kidding. That was a test to see if you are still reading. If you are, perhaps you have gotten the point, which is that good writing needs to be divided into paragraphs to help the reader. This paragraph, by the way, is definitely *not* an example of good writing.

PRACTICE

Rewrite the following, using paragraphs to make it easier to follow:

Robyn had three brothers. Her brother Alex dyed his hair green last week. He is thinking about adding some blue or orange highlights soon. Alex usually wears a black motorcycle jacket and blue jeans. He has a tattoo on his right hand and a nose ring in his right nostril. He works part-time at a music store, where he sells guitars. Robyn's brother Nick would never dye his hair green. He has short, neatly trimmed hair. He always wears neatly pressed white shirts, khaki pants and loafers. He is very polite to everyone and always carries a briefcase. He volunteers for Meals on Wheels, but he doesn't have a job. Robyn's brother Vince has curly red hair. He wears shorts during summer, fall, winter, and spring. That's because he is usually playing basketball or soccer, biking, hiking, rock climbing, kayaking, or practicing for a marathon. He works part-time pouring concrete. All three boys are in college, and you might be surprised at their career plans. The one who wants to be a minister is Alex. The one who plans to become a lawyer is Vince. The one who has no idea what he wants to do with his life is Nick.

Pet Peeve 43:
Writing "alright" instead of *all right*

If you finished your cereal, you might say, "All done!" You wouldn't say, "Aldone!"

If you were getting ready to go somewhere with someone, you might ask, "All set?" You wouldn't ask, "Alset?"

If you were a train conductor, you might announce, "All aboard!" You wouldn't say, "Alaboard."

Using the same logic, if you are agreeing with someone, you should write, "All right," *not* "Alright." *All right* is two words, not one. There is no such word as "alright."

PRACTICE

Correct the following:

In the last few seconds of the soccer match, Will kicked the ball and made a goal. "Alright!" he cried!

"Alright!" echoed his teammates.

Then the opposing team recovered and made a goal.

"Alright!" shouted Evan's girlfriend Madison, from the sidelines. Everyone on the team turned to stare. "Oops," she said, puzzled. "Wrong thing to say?"

"Madison isn't exactly a quick study when it comes to sports," explained Will, sighing.

Suddenly Will was lying on the ground.

"I have a black belt in karate," Madison smiled.

Pet Peeve 44:
Starting sentences with *But* or *And*

Many English teachers say, "Don't start sentences with *but* or *and*."

That is good advice.

However, many students then ask, "How come we often see sentences in books, newspapers or magazines that start with *and* or *but*?"

The answer is that sometimes, *if you know what you are doing*, it is okay to start a sentence with *and* or *but*. Until you are a very good writer, though, it is not a good idea. *And* and *but* are really conjunctions — words designed to connect things. When you start a sentence with one of these words, you aren't connecting anything. You are likely to end up with sentence fragments and weak sentences.

Try using *also* or *in addition* instead of *and*. Try using *though* or *however* instead of *but*. Another solution is to leave the *and* or *but*, add a comma and connect the sentence to the previous sentence. Here are some examples:

No: *Bethany really liked Spike a lot. But Spike didn't like her.*

Yes: *Bethany really liked Spike a lot, but Spike didn't like her.*

           Bethany really liked Spike a lot. However, Spike didn't like her.

           Bethany really liked Spike a lot. Spike didn't like her, though.

PRACTICE

Correct the following:

I went to the store. And I picked up some Pepsi and some potato chips. And some Twinkies. And then I stopped at the video store and got a couple of movies. And then I took the rest of my money and bought some new socks. But I didn't get wool ones this time. And I don't care if the new ones aren't as warm as wool because the wool itched. And drove me crazy.

I put on my new socks. And sat down in front of the TV with all my goodies. I popped in the video and settled down for a long night of munching and movies. But in only 10 minutes I was fast asleep.

Pet Peeve 45:
Writing "gotta," "gonna," or "wanna" instead of *got to* or *going to* or *want to*

"Gotta," "gonna," and "wanna" aren't really words. They are slangy, sloppy versions of *get to, going to,* and *want to.* For most situations, don't write the sloppy version.

Write out the separate words *get to, going to,* and *want to.* Examples:

No: *I'm gonna get an A in English," said Anton.*

Yes: *"I'm going to get an A in English," said Anton.*

No: *"Do you wanna bet?" replied Lena.*

Yes: *"Do you want to bet?" replied Lena.*

No: *"I've gotta go study," said Anton.*

Yes: *"I've got to go study," said Anton.*

PRACTICE

Correct the following:

"Are you gonna eat your dessert?" asked Rebecca.

"I don't know yet," answered Paul. "I gotta see if I'm full after I eat this pizza and these two hamburgers."

"I'm gonna have just a little bite of it," said Rebecca. "I really love rhubarb pie."

"Why don't you order a piece then?" asked Paul.

"Oh, I don't wanna. I'm on a diet." She stared at the pie. "How about if I take just a *little* bite?" She reached her fork across the table.

"No!" said Paul, grabbing her fork. "I'm gonna order you a piece." He called to the waitress.

"Don't be ridiculous!" said Rebecca. "I told you I don't want a dessert."

"Fine," said Paul. He dug into his French fries. When he looked up he had a tiny sliver of pie left. "I thought you didn't want any dessert!" he said.

"Oh, I don't," said Rebecca, through a mouthful of pie. "I don't wanna get fat."

Pet Peeve 46:
Using double negatives
like "I ain't got none"

Although they aren't acceptable today, double negatives — even triple or quadruple negatives — have a long history in the English language. William Shakespeare used them, for example. In his day, the more negatives you strung together, the more negative you were being. For example, if someone said, "George will not never, no how, no way, eat no peas!" people could be pretty sure that George wasn't going to be digging into a pea souffle anytime soon.

Times, however, have changed. Good writers today don't use double negatives. Words that express a negative are *not, never, none, no, isn't, wasn't, can't,* etc.

Here's an example of a sentence with a double negative:

There isn't never going to be a clear winner.

Isn't and *never* are considered negatives because they convey a negative meaning. Only one of these words should be used. Either of these versions of the sentence is acceptable:

*There **isn't** ever going to be a clear winner.*
*There is **never** going to be a clear winner.*

PRACTICE

Correct the following:

Casey opened the door and let Sasha, his golden retriever, out in the back-yard. He sat back down in the easy chair to read the paper.

In a moment, Sasha was scratching at the door.

Casey sighed, got up and let her back in. He settled back down in the chair. In a moment, Sasha was sitting at the back door, whining to go out.

Casey looked up and said, "There isn't no way I'm getting up again. You can just whine."

Soon Sasha was sitting at Casey's feet. She looked up with pleading eyes.

"Don't look for sympathy from me," said Casey. "There isn't none here."

She put her chin on Casey's leg and looked up at him imploringly. "It doesn't make no difference to me how cute you look," said Casey. "You aren't doing nothing that's going to change my mind." He went back to his paper.

Sasha just sat, patiently. There was no more whining. There were no more imploring looks.

In a moment, Casey threw down the paper, stalked to the door, and opened it. "Okay, you got me with guilt. Now go!"

Pet Peeves ©2001 Cottonwood Press, Inc. • www.cottonwoodpress.com • 800-864-4297 • Fort Collins, Colorado

Pet Peeve 47:
Using *good* as an adverb

"Good" should not be used as an adverb. (An adverb is just a word that tells how someone *did* something.) Use *well* instead of *good* to describe how someone did something, or use an adverb that gives you more specific information.

No: *He played **good**.*

*He jumped **good**.*

*He spelled **good**.*

*He did everything **good**.*

Yes: *He played **well**.*

*He spelled **correctly**. (Correctly gives you more specific information about how he spelled.)*

*He jumped **high**. (High tells you more about how he jumped.)*

*He did everything **well**.*

PRACTICE

Correct the following:

"I did good on the test!" cried Kyle. "I studied good and slept good and ate good before I came to school. Then I concentrated good and finished before the bell rang. My teacher graded the test, and I did good on all but one thing."

"What was that?" asked his friend.

"The grammar. I didn't do good on that."

Pet Peeve 48:
Writing "all of the sudden" instead of *all of a sudden*

"All of a sudden" has been an accepted English phrase for a long, long time. A strange thing has been happening in the last few years, though. Many people have started saying "All of *the* sudden." It is not clear why this is happening. It may even be that so many people will start saying it that someday it will be the accepted phrase.

Now, however, it is not. You don't see it written in newspapers or magazines or books. You only *hear* it.

Learn to write "all of *a* sudden."

Correct the following:

All of the sudden, Grant burst onto the stage, wearing a chicken costume. The audience went crazy, laughing, whistling, and applauding. Grant clucked out his song over the noise. Then, all of the sudden, he disappeared.

Pet Peeve 49:
Writing "these ones" instead of *these*

No one used to hear the phrase "these ones." People said "Look at these," not "Look at these *ones*."

Why are people saying *these ones*? It is a mystery. The word *ones* adds nothing. It is just as clear to say, "Look at these." For very complicated grammatical reasons not worth going into here, "these ones" is incorrect. So is "those ones." Use *these* or *those* instead.

No: *I want these ones.*
Yes: *I want these.*

No: *I want those ones.*
Yes: *I want those.*

PRACTICE

Correct the following:

"I want these ones and these ones and these ones," said Elena to her aunt.

"Why these ones?" asked Aunt Joyce.

"Because these ones here are the best. Those ones there are ugly."

"Oh," said Aunt Joyce. "These ones cost 16 times as much as those ones."

"They are worth it," said Elena.

"I have only $4.50," said Aunt Joyce. "I guess we can't get any."

Elena paused. "Well, these ones will do then," she said.

Pet Peeve 50:
Mixing up *quiet* and *quite*

People sometimes mix up the spellings of *quiet* and *quite*. It's easy to keep the words straight if you remember that an "e" at the end of a word is almost always silent. Here are a few examples:

kite	rate	vote	flute
bite	fate	wrote	brute
trite	hate	quote	cute

Quite fits the pattern, with an "e" that is silent. The word is, of course, pronounced "kwite," to rhyme with "kite."

The word *quiet*, however, has an "e" in the middle of it. That "e" is pronounced, making the word "kwi-ut."

If you remember to pronounce the "e" when it comes in the middle of the word, and not to pronounce it when it comes at the end, you will get the "e" in the right place.

PRACTICE

Correct the following:

Mr. Snidely had the philosophy that children should be seen and not heard. When little Poindexter whispered to his friend one afternoon, Mr. Snidely yelled, "**Quite/quiet!** I am **quite/quiet** sick of this noise. It is not **quite/quiet** time to go, so you should still be working on your assignment. It is **quite/quiet** long, and it will take you **quite/quiet** long time to complete it."

"Yes, Mr. Snidely," murmured Poindexter.

"*What?*" yelled Mr. Snidely. "I can't hear you!"

"You told me to be **quite/quiet**," said Poindexter.

"I've had **quite/quiet** enough of you for one day!" said Mr. Snidely.

Review Exercises

The activities on the next pages are filled with English teachers' pet peeves. Rewrite each, correcting all the errors you find. Choose solutions that you find most effective.

Gorillas

I am going to tell you about gorillas. Your not going to believe what I learned doing this report. Well, me and my friend Bill were supposed to choose a animal to research, so we looked thru a lot of books. We seen a lot of pictures and stuff but the pictures that looked the most interesting were the pictures of gorillas. So that's why I chose gorillas. So that's why I'am going to write about them for this report, which I no is suppose to be at least 500 words long. Irregardless of how long it turns out to bee, I know that Bill and I have learned alot of cool stuff about this awesome subject. Gorillas do not live in the United States. Except in zoos. They live in other places. I am sure alot of people could tell you where those places are, everyone who studies zoology in their college years could tell you. If you really want to know, you could ask a zoologist. Or maybe your teacher. Teachers are wise people. They know alot of stuff! Gorillas belong to the animal family, not the plant family. There very big animals. Very, very big animals. Once I saw a movie that had a gorilla in it. It, like, got lose in the city and squashed a lot of people, buildings, cars, ect. People were going, "Who let this gorilla lose? We can't have no gorilla running around the city. We need to kill it." Then they tried to kill it. But it was to hard too do. So they decide to try to tame it. They give it hot fudge sundaes and stuff. All of the sudden the gorilla was quiet friendly to people and stopped squashing things. The people lead it to the edge of town. Where it made a home at the base of a mountain and lived their quietly. It was lonely but content as long as it's supply of ice cream held out. It was a good movie. I can't remember the name of it right now, but I use to watch it alot, cuz my brother gave me the video for my birthday. I use to watch it to excape from my homework and stuff. I really don't like homework to much. Though art homework is alright. I don't draw to good. But I like drawing anyway. I am a lot happier to: watch TV, play games on the computer, play soccer, talk on the phone and stuff. My brother and I also sorta like to mess with model airplanes. My dad gave a bunch of them to he and I last Christmas. I liked his present a lot better than another one I got. My aunt, she gave me a book about why vegetables are good for you. Vegetables, by the way, are something that gorillas supposebly eat. I hope you have learned a lot about gorillas. I no me and Bill did. I think this is 500 words now.

The End.

(Note: The best way to improve this report would be to start over and actually make it *about* gorillas. However, to practice your proofreading and editing skills, go ahead and correct the paper as it is.)

A Fairy Tail

Ones upon a thyme there was a witch named Wicked Witch Winifred. One day she cot a frog named Phil hopping around next too her cauldron full of a secret potion! She thinks he is spying on her and trying to steal her famous All Purpose Potion 99! She'd had alot of, like, success with All Purpose Potion 99 and new it was worth alot of money.

"What are you doing here?" she shrieked when she saw Phil. "Your trying to steel my potion, you fiend! How dare you!"

"Huh?" said Phil. He was just hopping around trying too kill some time before going to pick up his frog date, Tiffany.

"Don't play innocent with me!" said Winifred. "Me and my sister Winona no all about frogs like ewe. You are cent by evil kings to steel are secrets. Me and Winona no how to handle spies like you, though."

"Huh?" said Phil again. "I'am not a evil spy. I'm a frog."

"A likely story." She looked around for her sister. "Winona!" she called. "Come here. I need you're help for a moment cuz there is a problem hear." She looked at Phil. "My sister, she always nose what to do."

Out of the bushes stepped Winifred's beautiful sister Winona. She wore: diamond earrings, diamond toe rings, diamond belly button rings, diamond nose rings, ect. She really sparkled. Phil was dazzled by both her beauty & her brightness.

"Wow," he said.

Pet Peeves ©2001 Cottonwood Press, Inc. • www.cottonwoodpress.com • 800-864-4297 • Fort Collins, Colorado

"Don't you flirt with me!" said Winona. She was beautiful. But she was kinda a snot. She scowled at him and stuff & then said, "What do you want to do with him, Winifred? We need to due something quickly before he, like, excapes."

Well, Winifred thought for a moment. Then said, "We could boil him in oil." Winifred had a twisted mind sometimes.

Winona shook her head. She was a snot, but she wasn't twisted. "No. That's to cruel. It's to bad we can't do the usual."

"Huh?" said Phil again. He was still dazzled, though the boiling in oil had gotten his attention. "What's the usual?"

"The usual is to turn you into a frog," she said. "It's quiet boring and ordinary, as spells go. But your already a frog, so I guess it will be alright to turn you into a human bean."

All of the sudden Phil started paying attention. "Hold on, ladies," he goes. "Sorry to rush off, but I need to get going now." He turned to go. But he was to slow.

"Alacabamma-ramma-lama-ding-dong!" shouted Winifred and Winona together. Suddenly, Phil was a prince.

He was knot happy. "How could you do this too me?" he cried. "You shouldn't never have done nothing like this! How will Tiffany ever recognize me?"

"She won't," Winona shrugged. She had a cruel streak. She didn't care about Phil's feelings.

"You coulda done something less drastic!" cried Phil. "Surely there are other curses. I seen a witch turn someone into a fish once. I wouldn't mind being a trout. In fact, Tiffany kinda likes trout. How about changing me into a trout?"

"Nope, There isn't no way we're going to do that."

All of the sudden Tiffany came by looking for Phil. "Phil!" she called. "Phil! Where are you?"

"Here!" said Phil, trying to look particularly handsome.

"Eeeeek!" she cried, seeing a prince. She started to hop away.

"Tiffany! Wait!" cried Phil.

Tiffany stopped. She was quiet puzzled. "Phil?" she said. "I here you. But I don't see you."

Then Phil stepped forward. Then Tiffany screamed again. Then she hopped off for good.

Then Phil was very angry, because he had been turned into a prince. "I hate bean a prince! I want to be a frog again!" he cried.

Winifred and Winona just ignored him, they went back to stirring the All Purpose Potion 99. While Phil yelled at them.

No one lived happily ever after.

But then it turned out it was all a dream!

The End

Answer Keys

Practice, page 16

Our trip was supposed to be a wonderful vacation for us, but when we got off the bus at Shady Beach, we couldn't do anything but stare. I started to wonder, "Where are we?" because the beach looked nothing like the one in the brochure.

"Where's our beautiful beach?" asked my brother Carlos.

"Where's our palm trees?" asked my mom.

"Where are the cute guys?" asked my sister Judy.

"Where is the travel agent?" fumed my father. "Wait until I get my hands on him!"

"Calm down, dear," said Mom. "There is probably a perfectly good explanation for our problem."

"Yes. Our travel agent is a crook!" yelled Dad.

Dad doesn't take disappointment real well.

Practice, page 19

Scientists have just discovered that a microscopic animal that lives on the human scalp is responsible for a common problem throughout the United States: bad hair days. Although the zigglebot is usually quite a friendly creature, there are times when it becomes angered at its host person and seeks revenge. That's when problems start.

Practice, page 22

"*It's* always *me* who gets blamed for everything," whined Felicity.

"You get blamed because *it's* always your fault," said her brother calmly. "For example, the car is missing **its** front bumper because you failed to notice a stop sign yesterday."

"I was putting on lipstick," cried Felicity. "*It's* not my fault. I didn't have time to do it before I left the house."

"Yes it is," said Jacob. "*It's* your fault because you slept through your alarm." He looked at her carefully. "I do see why you would be desperate, though. You look pretty bad without lipstick. You might also consider using a little more mascara. *It's* amazing what a little makeup can do for a homely person."

Felicity smacked him. Then she went looking for her make-up bag, which, unfortunately, wasn't in *its* usual place.

Practice, page 24

The members of the Melting Lemons sauntered on stage. "*You're* going to love our first song," said the lead singer, Clovis. "It's not *your* average heavy metal tune, man. It's way deeper than anything ever before created. *You're* just going to be blown away by its brilliance."

He paused. "This tune has a lot of meaning for me, and for the members of the band because it's about a subject very dear to our hearts: toenail clippers. *You're* so lucky to be here and share in the very first performance of this piece. I know *you're* going to enjoy *your* listening experience."

Practice, page 26

"We should look *to* the future when deciding who should have our vote," announced the candidate for the Senate. "It is *too* expensive for our future if you choose my opponent."

"Why?" asked Maria. "I am planning *to* vote for the other guy, and most of the rest of us here are, *too*."

"My opponent, unfortunately, is veracity-challenged. He also is less than respectful **to** his constituents and tends to alienate those with whom he has contact."

"Tell us in plain English," said Maria. "What's wrong with the guy?"

"**To** get right **to** the point, he lies," said the candidate. "He's a big jerk, **too**."

Practice, page 28

Jacob sighed. "Imagine what I **could have** done if only I'd remembered that I need to *apply* to colleges if I want to have a chance at being admitted to one."

Hallie's mother yelled at her, "You **should have** told me you were borrowing my white silk dress! You **should have** told me you spilled mustard on it. You **could have** taken it to the dry cleaner immediately, begged my forgiveness, and offered to clean the kitchen every night for the next year and a half!"

"I **would have** given you a passing grade," said Mrs. Turnblossom, "if only you had indicated in any way to me, at any time during the quarter, that you were actually conscious."

Mike thought he **could have** won the contest if he had worn his lucky skull earring and his Goofy T-shirt.

Practice, page 30

Answers will vary. Here is one example:

My little sister bugs me a lot. She is in my room a lot when I'm not home and that causes me a lot of problems. That makes me mad a lot of the time. She also giggles a lot and acts really silly a lot. Besides that, I really like her a lot.

Practice, page 33

"***There*** is no excuse for locking Fluffy and Puff in the closet," cried Mrs. Hagglemeister. "***They're*** such darling little kitties, and as my pet sitter, you were entrusted with ***their*** safety."

"They kept hissing at me," said Arnold.

"My kitties do not hiss unless ***they're*** given a good reason," said Mrs. Hagglemeister sternly. "What happened before they hissed?"

"***There*** was this ugly chewed up stuffed mouse they kept trying to drop on my head," answered Arnold. Then they wanted to climb on my shoulder and sit draped around my neck while I was watering your plants."

"And that's when they hissed?"

"No. They seemed to get ***their*** feelings hurt or something when I squirted them with the plant mister. That's when they hissed."

"So your solution was to lock them in a closet. That's unbelievable!" cried Mrs. Hagglemeister. "What kind of pet sitter are you, anyway?"

"Maybe I should have mentioned that I hate cats," confessed Arnold. "***They're*** awful."

Practice, page 36

I was walking along the beach when something moved in the water. I shielded my eyes from the sun and looked. It was the Loch Ness monster! I freaked out. What was it doing in Teal Lake? Was it hungry?

The waiter at *Le Fancy* restaurant was obnoxious. He poured hot tomato soup down my arm, and all he had to say was, "Oops." He brought our salads, but he didn't bring us forks. Then he disappeared for 20 minutes. When he finally showed up again, he brought me halibut instead of the T-bone steak I ordered. When I complained, he said, "You'll like the halibut better." Then he dripped chocolate fudge sauce on my date's white silk jacket. Finally, when I got mad and asked for the manager, he said, "Dude! Like, chill out!"

Present tense example: I sit on the park bench and eat my delicious lunch of ham and swiss on rye. I am enjoying the sunny afternoon and taking my time. A little boy is bouncing a beach ball down the sidewalk. When he sees me, he throws the beach ball right at my head! The ball knocks my wonderful sandwich on the ground and the little boy laughs. What a day I am having.

Past tense example: I sat on the park bench and ate my delicious lunch of ham and swiss on rye. I enjoyed the sunny afternoon and took my time. A little boy bounced a beach ball down the sidewalk. When he saw me, he threw the beach ball right at my head! The ball knocked my wonderful sandwich on the ground, and the little boy laughed. What a day I was having.

Practice, page 38

Dear Editor:

Because I think your article on education was so unfair, I am canceling my subscription. It is not okay to badmouth kids and teachers and schools through unfair articles like these. Because of articles like yours, people think that all schools are bad, and that, in my opinion is definitely not okay! Through the commitment of many people, including parents and other concerned people, we are trying to change the image of schools and build a positive environment for everyone because we really care about education. We're through with negative attitudes! Please shine your light on the *good* things kids are doing because then you will be helping make the world a better place.

Sincerely,

Constance Spooner

P.S. My son is selling chocolates to raise money for his school. Do you want to buy some?

Practice, page 41

"I never saw anyone with such a bad cold," said Doctor Gutting. "I saw a lady yesterday who was coughing so much it drove everyone in the waiting room crazy. Still, her cold was nothing compared to yours."

"Great," said Gregory. "I'm thrilled."

"I saw a guy once who couldn't stop sneezing. He sneezed constantly for an hour straight and used up three boxes of Kleenex. Still, his cold is not nearly as bad as yours. I never saw anyone with such red eyes and such a swollen nose. I never saw anyone with such a runny nose and such a puffy face. I never saw . . ."

"This is all very interesting," said Gregory, losing the little bit of patience he had left. He peered at the doctor through his very red eyes. "I don't really want to know how bad my cold is, though. I want you to *fix* it!"

"Oh, there's nothing you can do for a cold," said Doctor Gutting.

Practice, page 43

Maya kind of wanted to go, but, on the other hand, she kind of wanted to stay home. She thought that a quiet night watching TV might be better than a night at the mall hoping the guy she kind of liked would say "Hey!" to her like he had last Friday night. She kind of liked him, but she wasn't sure. "He's sort of weird," she confessed to her friend Allison.

"Sort of?" cried Allison. "He's the weirdest guy to set foot in the mall in the last ten years!" She saw the look on Maya's face. "I meant that in a *good* way, of course."

Practice, page 45

Here's what happened when I tried to take back the shirt I bought. There was a crabby lady at the counter and she insisted that I had to have a receipt. I didn't have a receipt. I don't keep receipts.

The lady said, "I can't give you a full-price refund without the receipt. I can only give you a refund of the sales price."

"Fine," I said. "What is the sales price?"

"Let's see. That shirt was on the 90% off rack. Here's your $2.00."

I was pretty mad. I decided it would be better to keep the shirt than get only $2.00 for it. By the way, I hope a shirt is just what you wanted for your birthday because that is what you are getting.

Practice, page 47

Answers will vary. Here is one possibility:

Why I Didn't Turn in My Report on the Battle of Bunker Hill

Our computer crashed this weekend, so I couldn't look up anything on the Internet for my report on the Battle of Bunker Hill. I decided to go to the library on Sunday, but my mom's car got a flat, and she didn't have time to change it. I called my dad to see if he could take me, but I got his answering machine. After that, I begged my mom to fix the flat and take me, and she finally said she would. She got out the jack, but she couldn't get it to work right, so she asked the neighbor boy Peter to help. He tried, but the jack slipped, and somehow he managed to cut a big gash in his hand. I ran over to get his mom because it looked pretty bad. His mom came running over and took one look at the blood and started crying because she doesn't like blood. My mom said she would drive him to the hospital, but she would have to use the neighbor's car because ours still had a flat. She did, but it took four hours in the emergency room. When she finally got home it was too late to take me to the library because it closes at 6:00 p.m. on Sundays. That's why I don't have my report finished.

Practice, page 49

Dad, Mom, my brother Sam, and I went to a hockey game. There was an awful lot of fighting going on. Mom and I didn't like it much. Dad and Sam did. They thought it was "action-packed." Mom and I thought it was bloody.

Dad said Mom and I could stay home next time.

Practice, page 51

The pizza delivery guy at the door said, "That will be $12.99."

Jill and I looked at each other. We hadn't ordered a pizza. Jill said, "You must have the wrong house."

The pizza guy said, "Nope. This is the house."

Jill said, "But we didn't order a pizza."

The pizza guy said, "I have a delivery here for 630 Break Street. You need to pay for it."

Jill and I laughed. As she shut the door, she said, "You clearly don't know the state of our finances."

Practice, page 54

Caroline and Sophie walked home after school. They ate some ice cream and cookies. After that, they watched TV and painted their toenails. They were supposed to put the roast and potatoes in the oven at 4:00 p.m., but they forgot. They were too busy listening to CDs and calling their friends.

Practice, page 56

"I used to like English," said Marvin, "but then I found out that spelling is important. My teacher pointed out that no one but me could read anything I wrote. I used to spell things however I wanted — not the way I was supposed to. I guess that wasn't a good idea. Now I have to pay attention and use a dictionary. I'm trying hard to do what I'm supposed to do.

"Things used to be a lot easier."

Practice, page 58

The bus driver supposedly warned the kids that they would be kicked off if they didn't settle down. They didn't settle down.

He stopped the bus. Supposedly, he said, "Get off at the corner now, or I'll set you down in the middle of the highway later." He had a very crazed look in his eyes. They believed him.

The driver supposedly let out an insane laugh and threw water balloons at the kids as he drove away.

Then he went to the bus station and retired.

Practice, page 60

Dear School Board:

I am writing to ask you to change your policy about the state standardized test. It is so useless and wastes all our time. We don't take it seriously, and our teachers spend way too much time teaching us to take the tests instead of helping us learn something that might be valuable to us in the future. I'm sick of this.

Sincerely,
Aaron Dimwiddie

Practice, page 63

"I won the lottery!" cried Delmont. "I won two million dollars!"

"That's nice, dear," said his mother. "I think I'll run to the grocery store now. Do you want Cocoa Puffs or Wheaties this week? Maybe I'll get some Frosted Flakes."

"Mom! Did you hear me?" Delmont asked.

"Of course I heard you," said his mother. "You are so cute when you are excited. Now, let me decide on dinner. Let's have hot dogs. I think I'll also whip up some Jello with bananas. That would be good."

Delmont shook his head. "You never hear a word I say, Mom."

"Let's invite that nice Olivia from church, too," said his mother. "She is so cute. Don't you think so, Delmont?"

Delmont shook his head as he went out the door. He was on his way to turn in his lottery ticket and buy a one-way ticket to Acapulco.

Practice, page 65

"I expect you to be home by 10:00," said Troy's dad, "regardless of when the party is over."

"I'm not going to be getting in any trouble," said Troy.

"I know you aren't. That's because you're going to be home by 10:00."

"It isn't fair," said Troy. "Everybody else gets to stay out later."

"If everybody else jumped off a cliff, would you jump off a cliff?"

"You always say that."

"That's because parents are required to say that at least once a week or so. It's in the *Rule Book for Parents, Volume I*."

Troy looked at his dad suspiciously. "Is that true?"

"Regardless of whether it's true or not, I expect you to be home by 10:00."

"But why?"

"Because I said so. That's in *Volume II*."

Practice, page 67

"I want an egg for breakfast," said Ed.

"What else?" asked his grandmother.

"An orange. Maybe an apple, too."

"Of course, dear," said Grandma. "Can I iron a shirt for you, too?"

"Sure," said Ed. "I think I want to wear an olive green one today."

"Very well. Can I give you a few dollars for lunch money?"

"Sure. An eight dollar bill would be nice."

"Sweetie, they don't make eight dollar bills."

"Oh. Sure. I knew that."

"Of course you did, dear. Those *Fs* in math were all the teacher's fault. Now — what else can I do for you before you leave? How about if I brush your teeth for you?"

"Grandma, that's going too far. You wouldn't want to spoil an excellent grandson like me now, would you?"

Practice, page 69

Bill got out his notebook, pen, paper, pencil, eraser, etc. Then he filled a snack table with popcorn, Coke, potato chips, a Milky Way, some red licorice, etc. He opened his chemistry book. He saw words like tellurium, palladium, mendelevium, einsteinium, etc.

He closed the book, sighed, and gave his attention to the Milky Way.

Practice, page 71

The princess watched as the frog turned into a handsome prince. She was not that impressed. She had once seen an alligator turn into a lemon tree. Another time she saw a lily pad turn into a big bowl of split pea soup. Though she wasn't amazed that there was a handsome prince standing in front of her, she acted surprised, just to be polite. Then she left and went back to the castle, erasing the incident from her mind completely.

Practice, page 73

My mother planned my slumber party. I didn't want her to, but she did it anyway. We had 100% fruit drinks — no Cokes or other sugary drinks for us! She decided that the pizzas should have stoneground whole wheat crusts, and she made them herself. She put goat cheese on top with some broccoli. "For the color," she told us.

Dessert was some carob bars she made herself. I don't know what carob is exactly, but I don't think I want to know.

She rented videos for us, too. "I think the girls will get a kick out of these old Fred Astaire and Ginger Rogers musicals," she said.

Well, they didn't. The only good thing about the party was all the red licorice whips Jade had hidden in her sleeping bag, along with the video of *The Attack of the Mutant Androids from the Center of the Earth*. We slipped it in the VCR after Mom went to bed. "I've been to your Mom's parties before," Jade explained. Then she got out the gummy bears.

Practice, page 75

Dear Grandma,

Thank you for the very interesting yellow sweater with the cocker spaniel puppies embroidered all over it. It is especially nice. I know you made it for me to wear in gym class so I don't catch cold, but the other guys would probably be jealous if I wore it there, and I might have to make a quick escape. That's why I'm saving it to wear at home, where I know no one will steal it.

My sister especially likes the sweater and mentions it to me all the time. To tell you the truth, the other day I got pretty sick of hearing her mention it, so I started throwing sofa pillows at her. She tried to escape, but I got her good. Then I got in trouble, even though it was really her fault. She is especially good at getting out of things, you know.

Well, I've got to go. Thank you again for knitting me such a unique gift.

Love,

Henry

Practice, page 77

Scarlett was learning to drive,
but it wasn't going well. Her
dad did not have a lot of patience.
He got mad a lot. Once when she
was trying to turn left he yelled,
"Why are you stopping in the
middle of the intersection?"

"The car stalled!" she cried.
Cars started honking at them.
Soon Scarlett was in tears and
swearing she would never drive again,
and her dad was yelling unrepeatable
things and swearing he would never
get in the car with Scarlett again.

It was not, all in all, a successful
driving lesson.

Practice, page 79

Dear Mr. and Mrs. Everett:

I am writing this note to you because we are having some difficulties with your son Evan here at the Lazy Daisy Preschool. We can't get him to quiet down for nap time because he wants to play Chutes and Ladders some more. As you may have noticed, he really, really likes Chutes and Ladders. Some of our staff members are reluctant to work with Evan any longer because their eyes are glazing over from too many rounds of Chutes and Ladders. We are wondering if you might try playing a few more rounds of the game with him at home each day. We think that might help because even Evan has to burn out on the game sometime.

At least we sincerely hope so.

Sincerely,
The staff at the Lazy Daisy Preschool

Practice, page 82

Answers will vary. One possibility:

Larissa looked out the window and saw the space ship take off with her cat Fluffykens. She cried and cried. Her sister Ruby didn't cry, though. She opened the closet door and took the secret passageway to her underground laboratory. All week she had been mixing fuel for her hyperspeed spaceship. Now all she had to do was grab the fuel and head to the treehouse, where her spaceship was waiting.

In no time at all, Ruby was floating out of the top of the treehouse. The next thing Larissa knew, a fluffy tail was brushing up against her cheek. She opened her eyes, and there stood Fluffykins. He blinked his eyes once and said, "Berap!" That, it turns out, is Martian for "meow."

Practice, page 84

After I cracked a joke, Mrs. Sutton got mad and yelled at me. Then the girl in the red dress laughed at me for getting in trouble. I turned to yell at her, but my friend Joe gave me a look that said, "Just be quiet." So I was.

Then the principal came on the intercom to make an announcement. I couldn't help myself. I made another joke. The teacher got mad all over again. The girl in the red dress laughed at me all over again for getting in trouble. Joe gave me another look to warn me to be quiet.

I ignored him. Joe just shook his head and said, "You're hopeless."

The girl in the red dress laughed at me again.

The teacher gave me detention.

Practice, page 86

Mrs. Persnickety was a person who believed in lots of rules. "If you *lose* your pencil," she said, "you will receive a zero for the day because you won't be able to do any work."

Jeremy was a person who believed in questioning everything. "What if the strap on your backpack comes *loose* and your pencil falls out?" he asked. "What if someone rips off your pencil? What if you *lose* it because you lend it to someone who forgets to give it back? What if you give it to a family who has lost everything in a flood and needs to fill out an application for financial aid? What if you . . . ."

"Your questions are enough to make a person *lose* her mind," interrupted Mrs. Persnickety.

Practice, page 87

If I win the lottery, the first things I'm going to buy are a new car, a house on the beach, and a plane ticket to Hawaii. I'm going to build the house in one of these countries: France, Mexico, or Brazil. I will be so happy that I'll probably donate a lot of money to the Red Cross, the Salvation Army, and the American Cancer Society. I'll buy my mom a new dishwasher, a leather briefcase, a new computer, and a hot tub. If my brother apologizes to me before I win, I'll get him a brand new Porsche, new skis, and a new guitar. If he doesn't, I'll get him the following: a Big Mac and an order of fries.

Practice, page 89

"***Who's*** Daddy's little girl?" asked Mr. Bleeker, the father of three-year-old Anna. "It's my little Anna-kins—the bestest little girl in the whole wide world! There's no daddy in the world ***whose*** little angel is a cuter-wuter thing than my adorable little angel!" He gave little Anna a kiss. "And ***who's*** going to take his little angel out for an ice cweam cone? Yes — it's Daddy!"

Mr. and Mrs. Markuson looked at each other and rolled their eyes. "And ***whose*** daddy makes everyone want to throw up when he talks to his daughter?" Mr. Markuson muttered.

"Anna-kins' Daddy!" his wife muttered back to him.

Practice, page 93

"I'm going to ask Sophie to marry me," said Samuel. "I am going to ask her by renting a billboard. On the billboard, I'm going to write, "I'm in love with you, Sophie Padelowski. Will you marry me?"

"I'm not sure that's a good idea," said Garth. "She eloped yesterday with Manfred Carbunkle."

Practice, page 96

The pilot came on the intercom. He tried to speak in a calm voice. He said, "I don't want to alarm anyone, but please fasten your seatbelts immediately. Don't even think about getting up to use the restroom right now, and don't even think about getting a refill on your drink. Get ready to grab your oxygen mask. Also be sure and review those rules about opening the door if you are seated at an exit. Finally, remember what the stewardess told you about the seat cushion being used as a flotation device in the event of an emergency? Well, get ready to see how well that works.

"Again, I don't want to alarm anyone. Please stay calm and try to think clearly. By the way, I would like to take this opportunity to thank you for flying Sky Prince Airlines."

Practice, page 96

Lila looked at her *lead* pencil and wondered, "Why do they call this a Number Two pencil? Why do we have to use it on standardized tests? What if we used a Number 48 pencil instead? Would we fail? Do they even make Number 48 pencils?"

Lila often wondered about things. In history class she wondered, "What if George Washington had been a woman? I wonder if he would have *led* the troops in the Revolutionary War. corporation or a university."

In math class she worked on a story problem about six plumbers, 18 feet of *lead* pipe, and a train traveling at 70 miles per hour, driven by a brother twice as old as his sister was two years ago. The problem made no sense to Lila. She went back to thinking about George Washington. "He was good," she thought, "but I'll bet a woman would have been just as good. I think it's time a woman became president. Maybe I'll do it. I could *lead* the country really well, I'll bet. Plenty of other women have *led* countries around the world." With that, she licked the point of her *lead* pencil and started outlining her campaign.

Pet Peeves ©2001 Cottonwood Press, Inc. • www.cottonwoodpress.com • 800-864-4297 • Fort Collins, Colorado

Practice, page 101

Eggs can be eaten many ways. They can be hard-boiled, fried, coddled, scrambled ,or poached, for example. "Some even eat eggs raw, though it is dangerous to do so because of the risk of contracting salmonella," said Dr. Wilkies from the Institute for Safer Eating.

One of the most disgusting ways to eat an egg, in my opinion, is to cook it over easy. The runny egg yolk oozes over the plate and makes people looking at it feel sick to their stomachs. I usually say, "I think I'm going to barf," when I see eggs like this.

Practice, page 103

"Are we there yet?" asked Michaela from the back seat.

"We are not there yet. You know that because you asked the same thing two minutes ago," said Ms. Rosario.

"I am sick of riding in the car. I am sick of sitting here with nothing to do, hoping that something good will pop up on the side of the road, like a rattlesnake farm. I think I'd like to visit a rattlesnake farm."

"We aren't going to visit a rattlesnake farm," said Ms. Rosario.

Two minutes passed.

"Are we there yet?" asked Michaela's brother Adam.

"If I hear anyone ask that question again, we're going to eat Aunt Meg's tofu and lettuce sandwiches for lunch instead of stopping at Burger King," yelled Mr. Rosario. "Am I making myself clear?"

"Yes," said Adam and Michaela.

Two more minutes passed.

"I need to go to the rest room," said Michaela. "We could stop at that Dairy Queen, which I'm sure has a restroom."

"So does that Texaco station," said Mr. Rosario, gritting his teeth.

Practice, page 106

Answers will vary. One possibility:

Last night Mom told us we had to go listen to a barbershop quartet my dad is in. I said, "Mom, I really don't like barbershop quartets."

Mom said, "You will enjoy this one, honey."

I said, "I can't imagine enjoying it. Who ever heard of a good barbershop quartet? The performers are so old-fashioned, and the music is boring."

Mom became very upset and said, "The group is the best barbershop quartet in the whole county! The least you could do is go support your father!"

I rolled my eyes and said, "I don't believe you. You don't need to get so upset, though."

Things went downhill from there. I ended up getting grounded because of "disrespect."

Unfortunately, the grounding didn't start until *after* the barbershop quartet concert. That was unfortunate because I hated it, just as I had suspected.

Practice, page 108

"Ricardo and I are going to win," boasted Nick. "He and I worked on it so hard. Our science fair project is lots better than anyone else's."

"You and he are so modest," said Patricia sarcastically. "Did it ever occur to you that you might have competition from Candace and me? Or the rest of the class?"

"Nope. "You and they are not in the same league as Ricardo and me. We're going to win for sure. Our project is called "A comparison of the Big Mac and the Whopper in Satisfying the Hunger Pangs of the Typical Adolescent Male After an Afternoon of Playing Basketball Against a Really Good Team That We Hate from the Other Side of Town."

Practice, page 111

Robyn had three brothers. Her brother Alex dyed his hair green last week. He is thinking about adding some blue or orange highlights soon. Alex usually wears a black motorcycle jacket and blue jeans. He has a tattoo on his right hand and a nose ring in his right nostril. He works part-time at a music store, where he sells guitars.

Robyn's brother Nick would never dye his hair green. He has short, neatly trimmed hair. He always wears neatly pressed white shirts, khaki pants and loafers. He is very polite to everyone and always carries a briefcase. He volunteers for Meals on Wheels, but he doesn't have a job.

Robyn's brother Vince has curly red hair. He wears shorts during summer, fall, winter, and spring. That's because he is usually playing basketball or soccer, biking, hiking, rock climbing, kayaking, or practicing for a marathon. He works part-time pouring concrete.

All three boys are in college, and you might be surprised at their career plans. The one who wants to be a minister is Alex. The one who plans to become a lawyer is Vince. The one who has no idea what he wants to do with his life is Nick.

Practice, page 113

In the last few seconds of the soccer match, Will kicked the ball and made a goal. "*All right*!" he cried!

"*All right!*" echoed his teammates.

Then the opposing team recovered and made a goal.

"*All right!*" shouted Evan's girlfriend Madison from the sidelines. Everyone on the team turned to stare. "Oops," she said, puzzled. "Wrong thing to say?"

"Madison isn't exactly a quick study when it comes to sports," explained Will, sighing.

Suddenly Will was lying on the ground.

"I have a black belt in karate," Madison smiled.

Practice, page 115

I went to the store and picked up some Pepsi, some potato chips, and some Twinkies. Then I stopped at the video store and got a couple of movies. In addition, I took the rest of my money and bought some new socks. I didn't get wool ones this time, but I don't care if the new ones aren't as warm as wool because the wool itched and drove me crazy.

I put on my new socks and sat down in front of the TV with all my goodies. I popped in the video and settled down for a long night of munching and movies, but in only 10 minutes I was fast asleep.

Practice, page 117

"Are you going to eat your dessert?" asked Rebecca.

"I don't know yet," answered Paul. "I'm going to see if I'm full after I eat this pizza and these two hamburgers."

"I'm going to have just a little bite of it," said Rebecca. "I really love rhubarb pie."

"Why don't you order a piece then?" asked Paul.

"Oh, I don't want to. I'm on a diet." She stared at the pie. "How about if I take just a *little* bite?" She reached her fork across the table.

"No!" said Paul, grabbing her fork. "I'm going to order you a piece." He called to the waitress.

"Don't be ridiculous!" said Rebecca. "I told you I don't want a dessert."

"Fine," said Paul. He dug into his French fries. When he looked up he had a tiny sliver of pie left. "I thought you didn't want any dessert!" he said.

"Oh, I don't," said Rebecca, through a mouthful of pie. "I don't want to get fat."

Practice, page 119

Casey opened the door and let Sasha, his golden retriever, out in the backyard. He sat back down in the easy chair to read the paper.

In a moment, Sasha was scratching at the door.

Casey sighed, got up and let her back in. He settled back down in the chair. In a moment, Sasha was sitting at the back door, whining to go out.

Casey looked up and said, "There is no way I'm getting up again. You can just whine."

Soon Sasha was sitting at Casey's feet. She looked up with pleading eyes.

"Don't look for sympathy from me," said Casey. "There isn't any here."

She put her chin on Casey's leg and looked up at him imploringly. "It doesn't make any difference to me how cute you look," said Casey. "You aren't doing anything that's going to change my mind." He went back to his paper.

Sasha just sat, patiently. There was no more whining. There were no more imploring looks.

In a moment, Casey threw down the paper, stalked to the door, and opened it. "Okay, you got me with guilt. Now go!"

Practice, page 121

"I did well on the test!" cried Kyle. "I studied well and slept well and ate well before I came to school. Then I concentrated well and finished before the bell rang. My teacher graded the test, and I did well on all but one thing."

"What was that?" asked his friend.

"The grammar. I didn't do well on that."

Practice, page 123

All of a sudden, Grant burst onto the stage, wearing a chicken costume. The audience went crazy, laughing, whistling and applauding. Grant clucked out his song over the noise. Then, all of a sudden, he disappeared.

Practice, page 123

"I want these and these and these," said Elena to her aunt.

"Why these?" asked Aunt Joyce.

"Because these here are the best. Those are so ugly."

"Oh," said Aunt Joyce. "These cost 16 times as much as those."

"They are worth it, " said Elena.

"I have only $4.50," said Aunt Joyce. "I guess we can't get any."

Elena paused. "Well, these will do then," she said.

Practice, page 127

Mr. Snidely had the philosophy that children should be seen and not heard. When little Poindexter whispered to his friend one afternoon, Mr. Snidely yelled, "*Quiet!* I am *quite* sick of this noise. It is not *quite* time to go, so you should still be working on your assignment. It is **quite** long, and it will take you *quite* a long time to complete it."

"Yes, Mr. Snidely," murmured Poindexter.

"*What?*" yelled Mr. Snidely. "I can't hear you!"

"You told me to be *quiet*," said Poindexter.

"I've had *quite* enough of you for one day!" said Mr. Snidely.

Review Exercises

Gorillas, page 131

The best way to correct this paper would be to rewrite it so that it is actually a paper about gorillas. However, barring that, here is one way to correct it:

Gorillas

My friend Bill and I were supposed to choose an animal to research, so we looked through a lot of books and saw a lot of pictures. The pictures that looked the most interesting were the pictures of gorillas. That's why I chose gorillas for this report, which I know is supposed to be at least 500 words. Regardless of how long it turns out to be, I know that Bill and I have learned a lot about this fascinating subject.

Gorillas do not live in the United States, except in zoos. They live in other places. I am sure that a lot of people could tell you where those places are. Everyone who studied zoology in their college years could tell you. If you really want to know, you could ask a zoologist or maybe your teacher. Teachers are wise people, and they know a lot.

Gorillas belong to the animal family, not the plant family. They are big animals — *very* big animals.

Once I saw a movie that had a gorilla in it. It got loose in the city and squashed a lot of people, buildings, cars, etc. People were saying, "Who let this gorilla loose? We can't have a gorilla running around the city. We need to kill it." They tried to kill it, but it was too hard to do. Instead, they decided to try to tame it by giving it hot fudge sundaes and chocolate shakes. All of a sudden, the gorilla was quite friendly to people and stopped squashing things. The people led it to the edge of town, where it made a home at the base of a mountain and lived there quietly. The gorilla was lonely but content as long as its supply of ice cream held out. It was a good movie. I can't remember the name of it right now, but I used to watch it a lot because my brother gave me the video for my birthday. I used to watch it to escape from my homework and my chores around the house.

I really don't like homework too much, though art homework is all right. I don't draw too well, but I like drawing anyway. I am a lot happier watching TV, playing games on the computer, playing soccer, talking on the phone and just hanging out with my brother. My brother and I also sort of like to build model airplanes. My dad gave a bunch of them to him and me last Christmas. I liked his present a lot better than another one I got. My aunt gave me a book about why vegetables are good for you. Vegetables, by the way, are something that gorillas supposedly eat.

I hope you have learned a lot about gorillas. I know Bill and I have. I think this is 500 words now.

A Fairy Tail, page 133

A Fairy Tale

Once upon a time there was a witch named Wicked Witch Winifred. One day she caught a frog named Phil hopping around next to her cauldron full of a secret potion. She thought he was spying on her and trying to steal her famous All Purpose Potion 99. She'd had a lot of success with All Purpose Potion 99 and knew it was worth a lot of money.

"What are you doing here?" she shrieked when she saw Phil. "You're trying to steal my potion, you fiend! How dare you!"

"Huh?" said Phil. He was just hopping around trying to kill some time before going to pick up his frog date, Tiffany.

"Don't play innocent with me!" said Winifred. "My sister Winona and I know all about frogs like you. You are sent by evil kings to steal our secrets. Winona and I know how to handle spies like you, though."

"Huh?" said Phil again. "I am not an evil spy. I'm a frog."

"A likely story." She looked around for her sister. "Winona!" she called. "Come here. I need your help for a moment because there is a problem here." She looked at Phil. "My sister always knows what to do."

Out of the bushes stepped Winifred's beautiful sister Winona. She wore diamond earrings, diamond toe rings, diamond belly button rings, diamond nose rings, etc. She really sparkled. Phil was dazzled by both her beauty and her brightness.

"Wow," he said.

"Don't you flirt with me!" said Winona. She was beautiful, but she was kind of a snot. She scowled at him and then said, "What do you want to do with him, Winifred? We need to do something quickly before he escapes."

Winifred thought for a moment and then said, "We could boil him in oil." Winifred had a twisted mind sometimes.

Winona shook her head. She was a snot, but she wasn't twisted. "No. That's too cruel. It's too bad we can't do the usual."

"Huh?" said Phil again. He was still dazzled, though the boiling in oil had gotten his attention. "What's the usual?"

"The usual is to turn you into a frog," she said. "It's quite boring and ordinary, as spells go. However, you're already a frog, so I guess it will be all right to turn you into a human being."

All of a sudden Phil started paying attention. "Hold on, ladies," he said. "Sorry to rush off, but I need to get going now." He turned to go, but he was too slow.

"Alacabamma-ramma-lama-ding-dong!" shouted Winifred and Winona together. Suddenly, Phil was a prince.

He was not happy. "How could you do this to me?" he cried. "You should never have done something like this! How will Tiffany ever recognize me?"

"She won't," Winona shrugged. She had a cruel streak. She didn't care about Phil's feelings.

"You could have done something less drastic!" cried Phil. "Surely there are other curses. I saw a witch turn someone into a fish once. I wouldn't mind being a trout. In fact, Tiffany kind of likes trout. How about changing me into a trout?"

"Nope. There isn't any way we're going to do that."

All of a sudden Tiffany came by looking for Phil. "Phil!" she called. "Phil! Where are you?"

"Here!" said Phil, trying to look particularly handsome.

"Eeeeek!" she cried, seeing a prince. She started to hop away.

"Tiffany! Wait!" cried Phil.

Tiffany stopped. She was quite puzzled. "Phil?" she said. "I hear you, but I don't see you."

Phil stepped forward, and Tiffany screamed again. Then she hopped off for good.

Phil was very angry because he had been turned into a prince. "I hate being a prince! I want to be a frog again!" he cried.

Winifred and Winona just ignored him. They went back to stirring the All Purpose Potion 99 while Phil yelled at them.

No one lived happily ever after.

To Order More Copies of
How to Avoid English Teachers' Pet Peeves

Please send me _____ copies of *How to Avoid English Teachers' Pet Peeves*.
I am enclosing $10.95, plus shipping and handling ($4.50 for one book, $2.00
for each additional book). Colorado residents add 33¢ sales tax per book. Total
amount $_____.

Name _____

School _____
(Include only if using school address.)

Address _____

City _____ State _____ Zip Code _____

Method of Payment:

❏ Payment enclosed   ❏ Visa/MC/Discover   ❏ Purchase Order

Credit Card# _____Expiration Date _____

Signature _____

Send to:

Cottonwood Press, Inc.
107 Cameron Drive
Fort Collins, CO 80525
1-800-864-4297 • **www.cottonwoodpress.com**

Or call for a free catalog of practical materials
for English and language arts, grades 5–12.

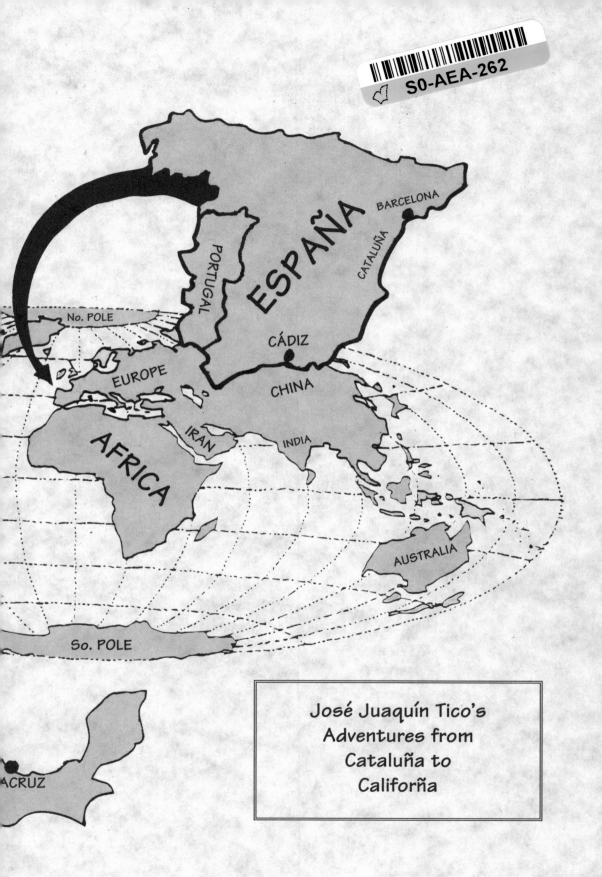

José Juaquín Tico's
Adventures from
Cataluña to
Califorña

PROMISES! PROMISES!

REVIEWS

"...Vivid descriptions of the soldiers and their families...Based on fact...Based on research of an actual family, early California comes to life for the reader...Rich in language...The reader has a clear picture of the day-to-day existence of the early settlers in California, and of the soldiers, their families, and the bureaucracy that affected all their lives.

"Written in a unique style with Spanish/Mexican words inserted in the text and explained as footnotes, readers of all ages learn word origins and meanings without losing the thread of the story. The timeline, notes, maps, as well as an English glossary, provide expanded information valuable to the teacher as lesson plans and helpful to the student reader in gaining a better understanding of life in early California.

"Much of California history focuses on the missions. This book expands on the lives of one family with vivid details of their day-to-day experiences.

"Thank you for sharing your delightful book with me." Linda Shephard, Arroyo Grande, California: **Educator.**

"After reading this wonderful history aloud to our ten-year-old son, Jefferson, I would highly recommend it for all fourth and fifth grade teachers in California. This account of the life of Juan Tico and his parents brings alive the turn-of-the-century mission days when California was being settled by the colonists from Spain and Mexico. Engaging and Fun." Cheryl P. Bruckner, Ventura, California: **Instructor of Spanish, Westlake High School.**

"A delightful read as well as a rich educational experience for any reader interested in learning about the Spanish culture and early California history." Patricia L. Fry, Ojai, California: **Author** of _The Ojai Valley; An Illustrated History_ and _Nordhoff Cemetery_.

"Most books on early California are written in English. Britton's unique book reminds us that Spanish was the dominant language in California until Statehood! This is a must for every California library." Kit Willis, **Youth Librarian**, Ojai Library, Ojai, CA.

PROMISES! PROMISES!

ADVENTURES OF SARGENTO TICO
CATALUÑA TO CALIFORÑA
1766 - 1802

Betty Louise Middleton Britton

Illustrations by Chris Martinez

JUANEZ BOOKS, 323 E. Matilija St., No 110-251, Ojai, CA 93023

ISBN Number 0-9655914-0-9

Library of Congress Catalog Card Number 96-95504

Britton, Betty Louise Middleton
   "Promises! Promises!"
   Adventures of Sargento Tico
   Cataluña to Califorña 1766-1802

Appendix: Notes, Historical Reference; English glossary; Bibliography; Reviews; Acknowledgments; Colophon; Index; etc.

Spanish Glossary: On each page where Spanish/Mexican words are used.

Young Adults/Adults

Researched Biography/History

1.Soldier Colonists
3.Spain — Catalan Volunteers; Bureaucracy
5.Vancouver Island — Nootka

2.Customs
4.Mexico — Sonoran War; Jesuit Departure
6.Alta Califorña: Presidio San Francisco; Presidio Monterey; Yerba Buena

Cover and Illustrations: Chris Martinez

First Edition   First printing 1997
Printed in Carpinteria, California, U.S.A.

JUANEZ BOOKS, 323 E. Matilija St., No 110-251, Ojai, CA 93023

DEDICATED TO LA FAMILIA TICO

AND THEIR DESCENDANTS

CONTENTS

MAPS

WORLD MAP MAY BE FOUND ON REVERSE SIDE OF FRONT
AND BACK COVERS

SMALL DRAWINGS SEPARATE THE NARRATIVE AND SPANISH
GLOSSARY THROUGHOUT THE STORY

ILLUSTRATIONS

PREFACE

Promises! Promises! came into being because of a
research project given to me when I became a docent at the
Ventura County Museum of History and Art and had chosen
to work in the library. The project was to locate sites and
ownership of land grants in Ventura County during the
Spanish and Mexican eras in California. The grant I was
asked to research belonged to California-born *Fernando Tico*.

In 1837, *Fernando Tico* received a Mexican land grant
for 17,719 acres in the upper and lower Ojai Valleys, where I
live, as well as twenty-nine acres of ex-mission land in *San
Buenaventura* (city of Ventura). As my research unfolded I
began to find material about *Fernando Tico's* father, as well.
As I learned more about the first *Tico* family members to
come to California, it seemed natural to first write about
them — why they came and their experiences after they left
the established Spanish colony of *Nueva España* (Mexico).

Spanish military records and genealogical charts reveal
that Sergeant *José Joaquín Tico* came from *Cataluña,* Spain,
participated in two major military campaigns while serving in
Nueva España (Mexico), and that he and his family came to
Alta Califorña in 1796. Since there is no written record
available about the lives of his Mexican-born wife, *Juana
Carrera de Tico*, and his son, *Juan Nepomucino Tico* — other
than approximate birth dates and the marriage of *Juana* to
José Joaquín — we learn about them exclusively through
the sergeant's experiences.

Most "Mexican" women of the 1700's could neither read
nor write, therefore we do not have personal diaries or letters
for references. We can only imagine *Juana's* courage in
leaving her family and friends behind to go to *Alta Califorña.*
Juana's love for her soldier-husband must have been great

enough to overshadow doubts she might have had about such a permanent move.

Juan grew up on the *Alta Califorña* frontier and had to assume adult responsibilities at an early age. Like his brother, *Fernando,* he was a survivor of political changes in the struggling province.

I am gratefully indebted to Juanita Callender for her support; Suzanne Paquette Lawrence for her critical analysis; Yetive Hendricks who encouraged me in the early stages of writing; Linda Shephard for her comments based on a background of many years in education; Cheryl Bruckner for her help with the Spanish glossary; Patricia Fry, who took time from her own writing, to read the manuscript; Youth Librarian, Kit Willis, who read and liked the book. To all who helped bring **Promises! Promises!** to publication, many thanks. B.L.M.B.

INTRODUCTION

In 1850, a thirty-first star was added to the flag of the United States of America — that of California. English speaking individuals were not the first, second, or even the third peoples to have lived in the territory now known as the "new state."

It is believed that the first "Californians" were nomadic people who crossed from Europe over a natural land bridge to "Alaska," then drifted south over a period of many centuries. We can only try to imagine how difficult it was for them to travel on foot and to find their accustomed food. They spoke many dialects but had no written alphabet.

Russian-speaking people came next, crossing the Bering Sea to the northernmost tip of the Pacific coast. They came to hunt and buy pelts from the Indians for the fur trade in Europe, paying with colorful beads. Many were near starvation during extended winters.

After Spain's conquest of "Mexico" in 1521, Spanish ships traveled along the Pacific coast to "Alaska," introducing the Spanish language to the area by naming many sites along the way. However, the Spanish government did not occupy any of the places those explorers named until two hundred fifty years later; by that time, it was too late to claim most of them for Spain. The lack of interest on the part of the Spanish government, plus the cost of colonizing, prevented exploration and occupation of the land. Later, some areas formerly claimed by Spain were also lost due to treaties made with England.

The Spanish government tried to maintain a fort on "Vancouver Island" because the Russians wanted the island and were a threat. By the time Spain gave up the island to the English, Russians were content to stay mainly in "Alaska." Today you will find Spanish names of straits and islands around Vancouver Island which read like signs saying "Spanish was spoken here."

By 1769, "California" no longer stretched from one end of the Pacific coast to the other. Spain had to rethink the boundaries of its claims, and as a result, "San Francisco Bay" became its northernmost frontier. In that same year, *Padre Serra* from *Baja Califorña* and Lieutenant *Pedro Fages* of the Second Company of Catalonian Volunteers, among others, came to *Alta Califorña.*

Indian dialects then were heard everywhere. But the Spanish language soon dominated in Indian territory as soldiers, missionaries, and "Mexican" colonists arrived with their families.

Indians had resolved their food problems long ago, but how were the new Spanish-speaking colonists going to find their accustomed food?

Until the missions and presidios could plant their own gardens and fields and pasture their cattle. All seeds and farm animals were brought from "Mexico." Since no commercial businesses were begun, the colonists had to depend on ships to bring everything they needed, from furnishings for their huts and *adobes* to farm implements.

Indians tried to keep their tribal culture separate from that of the new colonists, but it soon became apparent that both must at least learn some words of the other's language. It was especially necessary in the missions where many Indians lived and worked.

◆

The English language was seldom spoken anywhere in *Alta Califorña,* except by a few trappers and hunters who came through the Rocky Mountains and by ship captains and crews from New England who sailed around Cape Horn to buy hides and tallow from missions along the Pacific coast. That changed somewhat, at least in the northern part of the province, when in 1849, both Yankees and Europeans traveled in droves and shiploads to San Francisco to seek their fortunes, upon hearing that gold had been discovered there. That same year the American Colonel, John C. Fremont, and his Yankee soldiers marched the length of *Alta Califorña* advising Spanish-speaking colonists that *Alta Califorña* was now an American possession. However, it took many years before those who remained after the goldrush to venture south. There was nothing to attract them, and besides, they were not able to speak with the people they met in the small, scattered Spanish/Mexican *pueblos.*

On learning of the "new state," wagon trains of families began the dangerous trip through the Rocky Mountains to become the new colonists. Schools began to spring up and many Spanish-speaking families sent their children. Indian dialects were seldom heard and Spanish was becoming a secondary language; *Alta Califorña* was now California and English became the predominant language spoken.

CHAPTER ONE

TEPIC, NUEVA ESPAÑA A.D. 1795
EL SARGENTO TICO MEETS HIS SON

Juan Nepomucino Tico doesn't usually sit hunched over on the steps of his grandmother's house with his head down. But today his eyes are tightly closed, and his chin is firmly planted in the wedge of his bent knees. Six-year-old *Juan* has shut out the world.

"*Buenos días, Juan*," calls out twelve-year-old *Manuel* from his perch on top of his sleepy *burro*, *Torpe*.

It is *Manuel's* custom to pass the *adobe* of *Juan's* grandmother, *la señora Carrera*, on his way to the open-air market each day with fruit from his father's garden. Today *los melones* fill *las canastas* hanging over *Torpe's* ribs.

Juan doesn't look up or answer. This worries *Manuel*, but before he can stop, a horsefly buzzing around settles on *Torpe's* head. *Torpe* shakes his head, snorts, kicks the air, then suddenly lurches forward. *Manuel* scrambles to keep his grip on the rope reins, and at the same time manages to grab hold of a basket. Regaining his balance, *Manuel* presses his knees hard into *Torpe's* sides to keep from sliding off his back.

In spite of *Manuel* shouting at the donkey and

"*Buenos días, Juan*," - "Good morning, John"; ***Juan*** (Whan) - John; ***burro*** - donkey; ***Torpe*** (donkey's name) - "Sleepy"; ***adobe*** - house of adobe bricks (see Notes); ***la señora Carrera*** - Mrs. Carrera; ***los melones*** - melons; ***las canastas*** - wide baskets.

pulling hard on the reins, the runaway slips and slides crazily over the cobblestones, zigzagging up *la Calle de Soldado* with his ears laid back, braying loudly.
Melons fly out of *las canastas,* smashing apart on the cobblestones and leaving a trail of yellow, orange and green squashed pulp and rind everywhere. Yesterday, *Juan* would have been out on the street chasing after his friend and the rolling *melones*, but today, he is so angry and confused, he neither wants to see nor hear any of it.

    Mamá had said many times, "Some day your *papá* will come home — you'll see. For now, *papá* has to guard the king's land and protect *los rancheros y las misiones* from *los indios.*"

    Papá had to go away before *Juan* was born. Neither he nor his mother could believe that, at last, *José Joaquín Tico, el sargento primero de la primera compañía de los Voluntarios Franca de Cataluña*, would soon be knocking on the door. *Juan* had been waiting for this special day ever since he could remember.

    When the knock came, he suddenly became frightened, remembering unhappy stories some boys told about their soldier fathers who had returned to their families. Running to the back of the room, he grasped *la abuela Carrera's* hand. Leaning over, she had whispered, "He is a very kind man, you will like him."

la Calle de Soldado - Soldier Street; *mamá* - mama; *papá* - papa; *los rancheros y las misiones* - ranchers and missions; *los indios* - Indians; *José Joaquín Tico, el sargento primero de la primera compañía de los Voluntarios Franca de Cataluña* - Joseph Joaquin Tico (Teeco), First Sergeant, First Company of Free Catalonian Volunteers.

Still, his feet wouldn't move when *mamá*, laughing and crying at the same time, called him to come and meet his father. *La abuela* had given him a little shove and whispered, "Go on, *chico*, don't be shy. He's your *papá!*"

It had been a big relief from all the hugging and kissing when they sat down for *el desayuno*. He had sat across the table from his father, watching and listening.

His father's *bigote*, spreading across his upper lip, was the most beautiful he'd ever seen. When his father leaned over, he could see a cowlick on top of his wavy dark-brown hair — the same as he had. *Papá* had a kindly voice. When he laughed, his eyes squinted at the corners and dimples creased his cheeks.

His family was together. It had felt good. Then everything changed and he no longer liked his father. It had happened when *mamá y la abuela* began making a big fuss over his *papá*.

"Have some more chocolate, *Joaquín*. Would you like *más fruta o más queso, Joaquín?*"

Couldn't they see that his plate was full? Then his father had moved his chair close to his mother, put his arm around her and whispered in her ear. When they kissed, he had felt really terrible! No one had noticed when he mumbled *perdóneme* and slipped away from the table to go outside.

"I wish he would go away!" *Juan* says, in a loud voice.

la abuela - grandmother; *chico* - boy; *el desayuno* - breakfast; *bigote* - mustache; *más fruta o más queso* - more fruit or more cheese; *perdóneme* - excuse me.

Tears begin to creep from under his closed eyelids and slowly slip down his cheeks. Putting his head on his knees again, *Juan* sighs in tearful despair.

Huddled over and feeling sorry for himself, he doesn't hear the footsteps or see the shadow falling over him. It is only after hearing his name called the second time that he recognizes his father's voice. Although he knows that it's rude, *Juan* keeps his head down and his teary eyes closed.

"*Juan, hijo*, look at me. I have wanted to be with all of you for such a long time. *La abuela Carrera* is my long-time friend; I knew her many years before I married your mother. The three of us had so much to tell each other, but now you and I can be together.

"You were six-months-old before I knew you were born. I was in a faraway place called *Nootka*, and it took all that time for a soldier from *Tepic* to bring me the news. When I told my soldier friends that your *mamá's* cousin, *Jaime*, had written about you, they all helped me celebrate the birth of my first son."

Juan slowly raises his head and looks up at the smiling face. *El sargento Tico* reaches out and lifts him up. His strong arms encircle his son in a bear hug so strong *Juan* feels that his ribs will break. After setting him down again, his father wipes away tears from his son's cheeks with his rough soldier-hands, making *Juan* wince.

"*Hijo*, let's go somewhere and talk. I want to know all about you, right now! Where shall we go?"

La abuela Carrera - *grandmother Carrera;* **Juan** (Whan) - John; **hijo** - son; **Nootka** - (see Notes); **Tepíc** - on west coast of Mexico; **Jaime** (Himay) - James.

Juan hesitates and looks down at his sandals. He's not sure if he's ready to be friends. Until now his father had talked only with *la abuela y mamá*. Still, something within tells *Juan* that his father really likes him. Without a word, he points up the street toward *la plaza*.

El sargento Tico holds out his hand where his son can see it, even with his head down. His father notices that *Juan* has a cowlick in his dark-brown hair, like his. *Juan* slowly lifts his hand. *El sargento Tico* closes his hand gently over *Juan's,* and a smiling father and serious son make their way up *la Calle de Soldado*.

"I wonder where these *melones* came from. We'll have to watch where we walk — they are everywhere!" says *el sargento Tico*, as they detour around squashed melons on the cobblestone street.

"They must have bounced *de las canastas* when *un burro* passed by," answers *Juan*.

When they arrive at *la plaza, Juan* leads the way to a bench under the shade of a *jacarandá* tree. Before they sit, he brushes the violet-blue blossoms off the seat. Then they quietly watch *unas palomas* congregating at their feet. After a few minutes, *el sargento Tico* asks, "What do you usually do each day, *Juan*?"

"Well, like everybody else, I get up when *el Padre García* rings the church bells the first time, but I hear the old rooster crow before that. Before the bells ring

la abuela y mamá - grandmother and mother; *la plaza* - town square; *la Calle de Soldado* - Soldier Street; *de las canastas* - from the wide baskets; *un burro* - a donkey; *jacarandá* - similar in English; *unas palomas* - some pigeons; *el Padre García* - Father Garcia (a priest).

the second time, I'm ready to go with *mamá y la abuela* for morning prayers over there," he says, pointing to the cathedral at the far end of *la plaza.*

"Then what do you do?"

"We go home and have *el desayuno.* Then I help with chores."

"Chores? What are your chores?" asks his father.

"*La abuela y mamá* keep me busy. Every day I have to make sure there is plenty of wood piled up for cooking. I move the chairs and lift the table so *la muchacha, Amparo,* can sweep underneath. Almost every day I have to sweep leaves off the steps and from under the big tree in the back. And I sometimes go on errands.

"When *mamá, Amparo, y la abuela* go to the well, I go with them and carry *una jarra de agua* back home by myself," he says proudly.

"Do you go to school?" asks his father.

"*Sí, voy a la escuela. El Padre García* teaches us about the church."

"What about reading and writing?"

"*El Padre García* says that when he finds more boys my age, he will start a class. For now I sit in the back of the room and listen to the older boys recite their lessons. *El Padre* is very strict. Everyone has to recite the church rules perfectly — things like that — or get switched; that's when I keep my hands over my

el desayuno - breakfast; **la muchacha, Amparo** - girl (servant), Amparo; **mamá, Amparo y la abuela** - mama, Amparo and grandmother; **una jarra de agua** - a jug of water. **Sí, voy a la escuela.** - Yes, I go to school.

ears and shut my eyes! All the boys are afraid of *el Padre García* and his switch."

"Hmmm," says his father, nodding. "That's the way it was in *Cataluña* when I was a boy."

Conversation is interrupted when *las palomas* rise noisily to snatch *pedazos de tortilla* that a woman on a nearby bench tosses into the air.

When the birds settle again, his father says, "Would you like me to teach you how to write your name?"

"You mean you're going to stay in *Tepíc* for a while?" asks *Juan*.

"I'm going to be at the barracks in *Tepíc* at least a month, then you, your *mamá* and I are going away together. There will be lots of time for me to help you."

Before *Juan* can think of a reply, his father says, "Let's go back to your grandmother's house. *Después del almuerzo y siesta,* we can have another talk. Your mother will be glad to have us out of the house; she and *la abuela* are preparing for *una fiesta esta noche.*"

Otra sorpresa, no one told *Juan* about a party!

"Your mother planned the party last month, but because she didn't want to disappoint you if my plans suddenly changed, she didn't say anything," explains *el sargento Tico.*

Juan feels better now that he understands. His father rests his hand on *Juan's* shoulder as they make

Cataluña - province of Spain; **las palomas** - the pigeons; **pedazos de tortilla** - pieces of thin, round bread; **Tepíc** - mountain village in Nayarit, Mexico; **después del almuerzo y siesta** - after lunch and quiet-time; **una fiesta esta noche** - a party tonight; **otra sorpresa** - another surprise.

their way down *la Calle de Soldado,* dodging squashed *melones.*

After *siesta, Juan* takes his father for a walk around the *pueblo.* When they come to an *adobe* with bricks and straw showing through around the open front entrance, *Juan* says, "Here is where I buy *los huevos para la abuela.*"

At that moment, four squawking chickens fly out the open door, followed by a woman with a broom in her hand shouting, *"¡Fuera!"*

When *Juan* calls out, "*Buenas tardes, señora Rojas,*" she lowers her broom and waves to him.

At the end of the village, *Juan* points to a small hut with a corral in the back.

"That's where I get *la leche* so *abuela* can make *flan y champurrado. La señora Mendoza* fills my pitcher as she milks the goat or the cow, depending on what *la abuela* needs."

Continuing their tour of the old *pueblo, Juan* describes the places along the way and proudly introduces his father to neighbors and friends. The afternoon slips away; long shadows remind them that they should begin walking back to *la abuela Carrera's* house.

At the corner of his grandmother's street, Juan says, "Listen, I hear music. Do you think it's *la fiesta?*"

siesta - a quiet time after lunch during the hottest hours of the day. After 4:00 p.m. people go back to work or to other activities. Dinner is about 10:00 p.m.; **pueblo** - village, town; **los huevos para abuela** - eggs for grandmother; **"Fuera!"** - "Out!"; **"Buenas tardes"** - "Good afternoon"; **señora Rojas** - Mrs. Rojas (Rohas); **la leche** - milk; **flan y champurrado** - custard and a thick chocolate (see Notes); **La señora Mendoza** - Mrs. Mendoza.

"It seems too soon," says his father, who is accustomed to parties beginning after ten o'clock at night.

Laughter, chatter and someone tuning a screeching violin announces that, indeed, the party has started. Mouth-watering whiffs of *carne y pollo* cooking over an open fire lead *Juan* and his father straight to *la abuela Carrera's* house.

Juan runs to the sizzling grill in the outdoor kitchen. His *gata blanca y su gatito negro* are there waiting for a handout, and almost trip him as they rub against his legs. As soon as the meat is ready, *Pepe*, the man who has come to help cook, hands *Juan* some chicken and a piece of flat round bread. *Juan* tosses the chicken skin to his cats, then quickly eats *un pedazo de pollo churrasqueado y una tortilla*; he is anxious to join the party.

Juan catches up with his father and mother near the big tree and walks beside them greeting guests.

La abuela Carrera tells *Amparo*, "Now that the wind has died down, hang the red and yellow lanterns on the side of the house and light the candles on the long table, then bring out the food."

Amparo, in soft *zapatillas*, scuffles from kitchen to table across the hard ground, balancing platters and bowls on her arms. *Juan* recognizes most of the dishes as she sets them down: *garbanzos* (chickpeas), *pollo cocido* (cooked chicken), *ensalada de papas* (potato salad), *calabaza* (squash), *zanahorias* (carrots),

carne y pollo - meat and chicken; *gata blanca y su gatito negro* - white cat and her black kitten; *pedazo de pollo churrasqueado y una tortilla* - piece of barbecued chicken and a flat, round piece of bread; *zapatillas* - soft shoes or slippers.

carne (meat), *salsa*, and freshly made *tortillas de harina y tortillas de maiz* (rounds of flat bread, some made with white flour and others from corn flour).

La señora Carrera invites everyone to take seats at the long table under the large tree. *Juan*, having already eaten, sits close to his father on a small bench where he can hear conversation at the table and watch the musicians move about *tocando las mandolinas y los violines.* As hard as he tries to stay awake, voices and music begin to fade away.

Amparo sees *Juan's* head fall to his chest and comes to his side, just before he slips off the bench. Gently lifting the sleeping boy, she carries him to bed.

It is good that *Juan* has gone to sleep. He very likely would have become confused and worried at hearing the conversation around the table about his family's impending move. *Juan* knows only that they are going away together.

So many things have happened to him during the day, *Juan* hasn't had time to think about asking questions. In the morning he will learn that he and his parents are going on a long sea voyage to *Presidio San Francisco* in *Alta California, Nueva España's* northernmost frontier army post.

tocando las mandolinas y los violines - playing mandolins (see Notes) and violins; **Presidio San Francisco** - Military headquarters (a rectangular wall enclosing homes of officers and soldiers; chapel; stables; and an open space for assemblies or other activities.); **Alta California** - upper California (see Notes and Map); **Nueva España** - New Spain - (Mexico) (see Notes and Map).

CHAPTER TWO

FRIENDS TELL THE *TICOS* NOT TO GO

Dinner now over, *el sargento Tico* motions to the musicians to stop playing. After finishing their song, the men lay down their instruments, bow to the applauding guests and disappear into the shadows near the outdoor *cocina*.

Instead of gathering to talk in separate groups of men and women as they usually do, everyone remains seated at the table, *y la muchacha, Amparo,* brings *las frutas y los dulces.* *Los hombres y las mujeres* settle back in their chairs *fumando cigarros y cigarrillos* and sipping small drinks. *El sargento Tico,* rising from his chair, lifts his glass in a toast to all at the table: his military friends, and the friends and many relatives of his wife, *la señora Juana Carrera de Tico.* In turn, the guests toast the health of their hosts, especially *el sargento,* who has returned safe and well.

Después del brindis, Jaime, el primo de la señora Juana de Tico, says to *el sargento Tico,* "*José Joaquín,* I'm sorry that you and *Juana* are going so far away from us. Since you are getting close to retiring from the military, I expected you would stay here."

"*Jaime,* I may never have such an opportunity as this again. In *Nueva España* I couldn't hope to have

cocina - kitchen; ***las frutas y los dulces*** - fruits and sweets; ***los hombres y las mujeres*** - men and women; ***fumando cigarros y cigarrillos*** - smoking cigars and cigarettes; ***después del brindis*** - after the toast (a greeting); ***Jaime, el primo de la señora Juana de Tico*** - James, Juana Tico's cousin.

the amount of land that is promised to me in *Alta California.*"

El señor Rodríguez, a distinguished-looking white-haired friend of the family, says, "From what I've heard, there is plenty of grazing land in that large frontier to raise *ganado.* It won't be an easy life, and there are many *indios.* But if this won't bother you — well then, I wish you good fortune."

The white-haired *caballero* continues, "Surely the military isn't sending you all that way just to show you the land you're going to get when you retire. There must be some other reason soldiers are going north."

"Naturally," says *el sargento Tico.* "The king wants to stop *los rusos* from coming to our Spanish islands to hunt seals from their kayaks, and from establishing trading posts in *Alta California.*

"There is another problem: *El Rey Carlos* worries that *barcos de guerra* from other countries will claim *las dos Californias,* and even *Nueva España,* for their kings. Foreign ships have been sighted sailing along the coasts. These are dangerous years for Spanish colonies; all coasts must be protected."

El señor Rodríguez says, "The king needs several hundred soldiers to keep foreigners from invading. I wonder if it is possible to defend such a long coastline."

"There really isn't much choice," says *el sargento*

ganado - cattle;   **indios** - Indians;   **caballero** - a gentleman; **los rusos** - Russians;   **El Rey Carlos (IV)** - King Charles (the Fourth) of Spain (see Real People and Places);   **barcos de guerra** - warships;   **las dos Californias (Alta y Baja)** - the two Californias, upper and lower (see Notes & Map).

Tico. "We have to make an effort. But one thing I am sure of from my experiences in *Sonora* and *Nootka, los Voluntarios de Cataluña* are the best soldiers anywhere in *Nueva España.* And this time they will have more to protect than a mission, port or *presidio:* they will be defending their homeland.

"*El teniente-coronel Pedro de Alberni,* our commander, is taking only the best soldiers — those with families, who also have good military records, are healthy, and who don't drink or gamble too much."

"How many Volunteers are going?" asks *el señor Rodríguez.*

"Seventy-two will go in separate companies to *Presidio Monterey, Presidio San Francisco, y Presidio San Diego.* Perhaps later, a few will go to *Presidio Santa Barbara,*" says *el Sargento Tico.*

"Do you know to which *presidio* you will be assigned?" asks *el señor Rodríguez.*

"*Presidio San Francisco.*"

Jaime, la señora Tico's cousin, has been listening to the conversation and says, "I know the Catalonian Volunteers have a good reputation, but with all due apologies, *don José,* I worry that the poorly equipped *presidio* soldiers, along with seventy-two poorly equipped *Voluntarios* will not be able to defend *Alta California* from a fleet of foreign warships. Let us pray

Sonora - northwest Mexico, New Mexico, Texas and Southern Arizona; **Nootka** - (see Map) a place on Vancouver Island; **los Voluntarios de Cataluña** - the Volunteers from Catalonia, Spain; **el teniente-coronel Pedro de Alberni** - Lieutenant-Colonel Peter Alberni; **Presidio Monterey, Presidio San Francisco, Presidio San Diego y Presidio Santa Barbara** - Major military headquarters in *Alta California*; **don** - a term of respect.

they don't come to our shores! By the way, where is the ranch you expect to have when you retire?"

"*En un pueblo que se llama Villa Branciforte.* Governor *Borica* established it near *Presidio Monterey*, across the river from *la Misión Santa Cruz.* *El coronel Alberni* says there is plenty of good land and water to grow grain and raise cattle; a granary is already under construction. We're told that workers will build our houses and out-buildings. And colonists will get an allowance in the beginning."

La señora Carrera's neighbor, a retired soldier, speaks. "*Sargento Tico*, I don't want to discourage you, but you must remember that *los reyes españoles* have always needed soldiers and sailors to sail uncharted seas to protect Spanish possessions in the New World. How did they get them to leave their homes and familiar shores? They promised land, gold and silver. The government has found ways, many times, not to keep those promises."

As an afterthought, he adds, "*Cristóbal Colón* had to make such a promise to get sailors to go with him on his voyages."

There was laughter around the table.

"*Sí, sí*, that is a fact!" says the old soldier, "Nothing has changed for centuries!"

In a quiet voice, he says, "I have a story to tell you about myself. I was once a proud *ranchero* not far from *la Ciudad de Méjico.* The government gave the

En un pueblo que se llama Villa Branciforte - In a town called Villa Branciforte - "Villa" signifies a town with special privileges; **los reyes españoles** - Spanish kings; **Cristóbol Colón** - Christopher Columbus; **Sí, sí** - yes, yes; **ranchero** - rancher.

land to me when I retired. Then, two years later, a
new viceroy came to the Capital. He wanted my land
for someone else. Believe me, it changed my life.

"I will never forget that day. I was tending
mi ganado when *el virrey's* soldiers came to tell me I
must give back the land immediately. I had to sell all
my livestock in a hurry and very cheaply. Now my wife
and I must live with my daughter and son-in-law, a
shopkeeper, and I don't have enough *pesetas* to buy
más de una cabra."

"*Sí, señor, yo lo entiendo,*" says *sargento* Tico. "I am
truly sorry that this terrible thing happened to you,
but that was many years ago; things are different
now."

The retired soldier begins to say something more,
then changes his mind, shrugs his shoulders, and sits
back in his chair. However this is not the end of the
conversation; another guest has been patiently
waiting.

El señor López, also a military man and friend of
the family, begins, "*Lo siento mucho* to be the bearer of
malas noticias, sargento Tico, but I must say something about that *pueblo, Villa Branciforte.* The government wants to place retired soldiers, settlers and tribal
chiefs as neighbors! I heard it from *mi primo* who
works in another office. Personally, I believe they are
dreaming in *la Ciudad de Méjico* when they think to

la Ciudad de Mexico - Mexico City; **mi ganado** - my cattle; **el
virrey** - the viceroy; **pesetas** - Spanish money; **más de una
cabra** - more than a goat; **Sí, señor, yo lo entiendo** - yes, sir, I
understand that; **lo siento mucho** - I am very sorry; **malas
noticias** - bad news; **mi primo** - my cousin.

make happy neighbors of the *gente de razón y
los indios*. As everyone knows, they are two different
cultures. Besides, *los indios* are horse thieves and
have a taste for *los caballos* — since they aren't
permitted to ride them, they serve them for dinner.
Las escoltas at *la Misión Santa Cruz* must guard their
horses night and day."

 El sargento Tico trusts his commander and old
friend, and says, "*Alberni* wouldn't lie to his soldiers
about such an important matter. He's sure that
Villa Branciforte is the place."

 "Mark my word," says *el señor López*, "*Alberni* will
learn it is a bad plan. *La señora Carrera's* neighbor is
right about broken promises; you must keep an open
mind about living there."

 "Think about this, *José Joaquín*," begins *José
Gómez*, a friend from the barracks. "If *el señor López*
is right, and for some reason you find there are no
ranches waiting for *los Voluntarios*, what happens
next? You know that all the land belongs to the king.
But remember, *los misioneros* at *las misiones* are using
most of it and will complain no matter where the government wants to put another *pueblo* and more cattle.
They will remind the viceroy that *Alta California*
belongs to *los indios* and will be given to them when
they are civilized enough to become colonists. In the
meantime, they will say the land is needed for their
own large herds of cattle and fields of corn and grain.

gente de razón y los indios - the Spanish and the Indians (see
Notes); **los caballos** - horses; **las escoltas** - mission guards;
los Voluntarios - the (Catalan) Volunteers; **los misioneros** -
missionaries.

"There might be four or five *gente de razón* who have ranches in *Alta California*. Some did favors for the king and he rewarded them with gifts of land; others married Christianized native women making it possible for them to have land — but only as long as they keep it under cultivation. Getting your promised ranch is a different matter."

El sargento Tico closes his mind to more talk against the move. But when *Juana's* best friend, *Graciela*, begins to speak, he feels he must listen. And *Juana Tico*, already unhappy at what the men have said about the place she would be calling home, is not cheered by what she hears her friend say.

"*Juana, Alta California* is a desolate place; life is hard at the frontier! Have you thought about that? If you're lucky, a ship will come from *San Blas* twice a year with supplies. There is nothing there you are used to — only mountains, trees, wild animals, *indios*, and a few strangers. Your house will be made of straw and sticks. There are neither lovely *plazas* nor large *iglesias*. Even *médicos* aren't interested in going; you will probably have only native herbalists. *Juana*, it is *primitivo!*"

Suddenly *Graciela* realizes she is almost shouting. Lowering her voice, she continues, "Like your cousin, *Jaime*, I hoped that you and *José Joaquín* would stay here with us — with your family and old friends."

It is *el sargento Tico* who speaks up.

"*Si, Graciela*, I left my mother, two brothers —

San Blas - on western coast of Mexico (see Map); **plazas** - town squares; **iglesias** - churches; **médicos** - doctors; **primitivo** - primitive.

Antonio and *Pedro*, and sister *María* back in the old country, and I want you to know that I am truly happy to have you all as my family here in *Nueva España*. But you see, there is something more. When my older brother, *Antonio*, inherited my father's farm in *Pueblo de Sedo*, I decided to join the king's colonial army instead of working on the farm for him.

"I was seventeen and it didn't occur to me that I might have land of my own, too. It was only after I enlisted that I heard the good news — the promise that I could expect to be a landowner some day.

"*Graciela*, have you ever been to *Alta California*?"

Graciela shakes her head.

José Joaquín continues, "You are right about the country being *primitivo*. And it is true, there are few *gente de razón*. But now that our government is serious about colonizing, there will be more emigrants from *Nueva España* who want to make a new life for themselves."

Smiling and teasing her, he says, "I wouldn't be surprised to see you there some time; come for a visit."

Graciela laughs and says, "¡*Qué tontería!*"

Having heard how *Graciela* feels about *Alta California*, everyone laughs, too.

El sargento Tico continues.

"I was in *Alta California* for a short time several years ago. I almost died with *la pulmonía y la disentería* the first winter our unit was at the fort in *Nootka*, and *el teniente-coronel Alberni* shipped me off

¡Que tontería! - What a joke! **la pulmonía y la disentería** - pneumonia and the dysentery.

on *La Princesa* to a hospital at *Presidio Monterey* along with other sick soldiers.

"When we felt strong enough, three of us got on horses and rode from *Presidio Monterey* to *Presidio San Francisco* and back. We scared up hundreds of rabbits and quail. And the noise of the horses crashing through the underbrush kept the bears and wildcats away; rivers and streams were full of fish.

"*Los indios* were no problem. Whenever we passed *rancherias*, the women scurried into their stick houses, and the men stopped whatever they were doing and just watched us. But seeing the countryside *llena de ganado* with *vaqueros* from some mission guarding them was a sight I'll never forget. There wasn't a fence in sight."

Then he paused, not sure if he should tell them.

"I must admit, houses in *los presidios* needed new roofs, but that was six years ago. Surely, by this time, more living quarters have been constructed and old ones repaired."

Ending on a happier note, he says, "At both of the *presidios, los soldados y sus familias* were *muy simpáticos*. I think we'll all get along *magnificamente*."

During *el sargento Tico's* conversation with *Graciela, Juana* has had time to compose her thoughts.

"*Sí, sí, Graciela,* you are right, I will miss my friends very much. But there will be other women on

rancherias - Indian villages; ***llena de ganado*** - full of cattle; ***vaqueros*** - cowboys; ***los soldados y sus familias*** - the soldiers and their families; ***muy simpáticos*** - very congenial; ***magnificamente*** - magnificently.

the ship who are leaving families and friends for the first time — probably forever — as I am. We are going to need each other."

Then, smiling at her sad friend, she says, "I've heard that the water and clean air in *Alta California* is especially good for raising children. I have also heard there are so many native servants, one for each child! I'm sure that *Juan* will do well."

Then, a little shyly, she adds, "*Gracias a Dios* that we may be blessed *con más niños*."

Graciela just shakes her head.

"*Graciela*," says *Juana*, "I know that in the beginning it won't be easy, but other women have learned to live there. Besides, some things will be the same. There will be the same church *celebraciones* as here. Mass, *las fiestas, las bodas, los bautismos, y los días de santo* will help me feel at home. And *José Joaquín* knows all about getting things from ships' stores, missions, and the *presidio* store."

Everyone stares at the tablecloth in front of them when el *señor López*, once again, rises to his feet. After pushing his metal-rimmed eyeglasses back in place, he begins to speak. It is evident from his first remarks that he has something on his mind other than *Juana Tico's* adjustment to life in *Alta California*.

"Have any of you thought about this? Not one Spanish king has ever visited his colonies in the New World. Wouldn't you think the king would like to see

Gracias a Dios - thanks to God; *con más niños* - with more children; *celebraciones* - celebrations; *Mass (Eng.)* - church service in the Catholic church; *las fiestas* - parties; *las bodas* - weddings; *los bautismos* - baptisms; *los días de santo* - saints days, a celebration of the Catholic church.

the progress colonists have made? Of course he has
his representative, the viceroy, to report to him, but
that makes everything so impersonal. I would like to
see a king come here — what a *fiesta* that would be!

"For two hundred fifty years, our Spanish kings
have cared only about what they can take out of our
colony. They have used *los indios* to mine gold, silver,
and other valuable minerals. And for all that trouble,
the royal court wastes the gold on religious and
territorial wars in Europe — not to mention the gold
pieces spent for their fancy dresses and suits of silk,
satin, and lace."

Lowering his voice, he says, "I hear secret
discussions in my office at *Tepíc* military
headquarters. Not all soldiers and citizens are loyal to
the king and his government. No one dares to
complain openly, but many officers feel neglected."

"What does that have to do with *José Joaquín*
going to *Alta California* with his family?" asks *la
señora Carrera*.

"Just this," says *el señor López*. "I object to the
king forgetting about us *ciudadanos de Nueva España*
until he needs us to save this rich colonial possession.
The same countries' warships — from Russia, England
and Portugal — frighten him now as frightened him
twenty-nine years ago, in 1769. At that time he sent
*Gaspar Portolá, el teniente-coronel Fages, el Padre
Serra*, and others to *Alta California* to establish
presidios for guarding the province, missions to feed

ciudadanos de Nueva España - citizens of New Spain; **Gaspar
Portolá, teniente-coronel Fages, el Padre Serra** - Gasper
Portolá, Lieutenant - Colonel Fages and Father Serra - (see Real
People & Places).

everyone, and missionaries to convert *los indios* to the Spanish religion. And what an expense all that was!"

He pauses a moment and everyone expects *el señor López* to sit down. Instead, he looks over the top of his crooked glasses at *el sargento Tico.*

"I believe that was about the time you came from *Cataluña.*"

José Joaquín nods his head.

El señor López continues, "Were you with *el teniente Fages* and the second company of Catalonian Volunteers when the *Serra* trek to *Alta California* took place in 1769?"

"*No, señor,* I was in *Sonora* with a unit of *fusileros* fighting *los indios* alongside *la primera compañia de los Voluntarios.*"

Returning to his complaints, *el señor López* says, "My friends, had the king colonized *Alta California* two centuries before the *Serra* trek, we would not have this heavy price to pay now."

"Are you saying we will have to pay for *José's* voyage to *Alta California*?" asks Graciela.

"*¡Seguro! España* pays for very little, if anything! We who live in *Nueva España* will pay the bill for this latest expedition to protect our coasts, just as we paid the bill twenty-seven years ago when *Serra y Fages* marched north. Whenever *el gobierno* moves the troops and supplies their food, uniforms and transport, it means an extra burden of taxation for us."

---

fusileros - shooters, infantrymen; **la primera compañia de los Voluntarios** - the First Company of (Catalan) Volunteers; **¡Seguro!** - sure; **España** - Spain; **el gobierno** - the government.

Looking directly at *el sargento Tico*, as though it was all his fault, he says, "This move of yours, *Tico*, affects all of us in some way. The extra taxation to come angers me. I find it impossible to have hope of better times for anyone!"

El sargento Tico is speechless after this depressing and seemingly uncalled-for tirade by *el señor López*.

Juana comes to the rescue when she says, "We can't help the extra taxes; that sort of thing is always out of our hands."

Looking around the table at each guest, she says, "I know that in spite of your warnings, and your efforts to convince *José* to find some way to remain here, we must go. Don't you see what is most important? No matter what awaits us, we're going to be together as a family for the first time, even if it has to be in faraway *Alta California*."

No one says a word.

El sargento Tico, taking advantage of the momentary quiet, claps his hands. *La muchacha, Amparo*, comes from the kitchen to see what he wants.

"Call the musicians; we're ready to dance!"

Guests push themselves away from the long table and *el sargento Tico* tosses corn meal over the hard-packed dirt, making it easier for the dancers to move about. The musicians take up *las mandolinas y los violines*. Their nimble fingers fly over the strings as they concentrate on entertaining everyone. Slow and familiar tunes fill the air from the mother country,

las mandolinas (see Notes) **y los violines** - mandolins & violins.

Vieja España, as well as livelier ones from
los diferentes distritos de Nueva España.

The men and women weave gracefully in and out
in time to the music. Sometimes they join in a circle;
other times they dance individually, or in couples —
stepping and clapping through the intricate steps of
el joropo and other dances.

All step forward and take their places in a familiar
pattern when the musicians strike up a piece from
Cataluña. It is always a favorite. But to those few,
like *el sargento Tico*, who actually came from there,
la sardana brings back sentimental memories of their
youth in small *pueblos* along the shores of the
Mediterranean Sea.

The violinist lowers his instrument occasionally
and sings tender ballads that everyone knows.

Surprising them all, *el señor López* sings along in
a pleasant tenor voice. He knows all the words to
popular love songs, from *Veracruz* and *Guadalajara.*

For many hours romantic songs fill the air, and
heels stomp in staccato rhythm over the hard-packed
ground. No one leaves until *el sargento Tico* tells the
tired musicians to stop playing.

As the soldiers ride out of the *pueblo* and back to
their barracks in the dark hours before dawn, their
shouting and singing echoes throughout the valley,
causing a pack of wild dogs to howl and roosters to
crow. Neighbors reluctantly leave next. But relatives
of *la señora Carrera* and *Juana* don't return to their

Vieja España - Old Spain; **los diferentes distritos de Nueva
España** - different districts of New Spain; **el joropo** - name of a
dance; **la sardana** - name of a dance from Catalonia (see Notes).

homes for a week. Although *Juana's* relatives have
known *José Joaquín* only a short time, they have
accepted him as part of the family and want to be
together with *José Joaquín* and *Juana* as long as
possible. This is the last *fiesta* they will all have
together.

As soon as everyone wishes *los Ticos* a safe
journey, and the small house no longer overflows *con
las tías, los tíos, los primos, las primas, y los bebés,
Juana* begins preparing for the long voyage and her
new life in *Alta California.*

con las tías - with aunts; **los tíos** - uncles; **los primos** - male
cousins; **las primas** - female cousins; **los bebés** - babies.

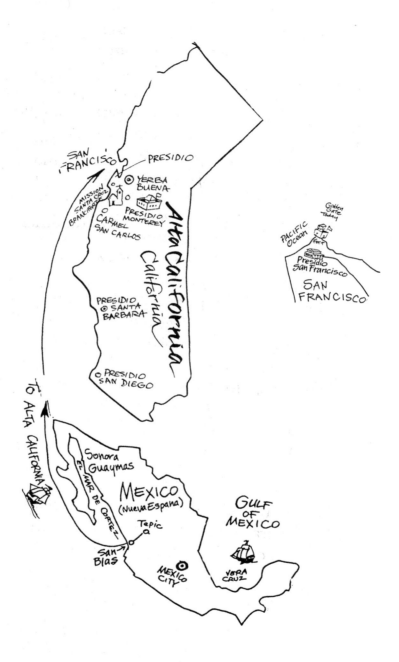

"The Tico Family's voyage to Presidio San Francisco in 1796"

CHAPTER THREE

JUANA HAS A LOT TO DO

Juan, with a bean *tortilla* in one hand and a piece of sticky *dulce de calabaza* in the other, sits in his hideaway made of tall brush and branches tied together. *Juan* has lived with his grandmother, *la señora Carrera*, all of his six years, and knowing that he won't be seeing her much longer because he's going away, he stays home now more than usual. Not far from *Juan's* hideaway, his grandmother, mother, and their friend, *Graciela,* sit in the shade of the large tree.

Gently moving her brightly painted silk fan back and forth in the still air, *la señora Carrera* listens as her daughter and *Graciela* talk.

"*Juana*, I'm really sorry I spoke so pessimistically about your move to *Alta California*. We've been such good friends, I just don't want to think of you going away," says *Graciela*.

"I hadn't thought about what it would mean to leave here until you spoke. Let's try to cheer up and forget the sad part," says *Juana*, putting her arm around her friend's shoulder and giving her a squeeze.

Realizing the time is drawing near when her only child and grandchild will be leaving her, teary-eyed *la señora Carrera* reaches for her glass of *limonada*. After a few sips, she regains her composure enough to say to *Graciela*, "At the party, you reminded me that

dulce de calabaza - candied squash or pumpkin (see Notes):
limonada -lemonade.

Juana won't find *médicos* at the frontier."

Then, looking at *Juana*, she says, "I'll tell you about the teas and poultices we have always used in our family."

"That's a good place to start," says *Juana*, mentally making a list as her mother names the remedies. She is familiar with many of them.

"I think you should attend to this matter today, *Juana*," says *la señora Carrera*."

"Then turning to *Graciela*, she asks, "Do you know the herbalist, *la señora Flora*?"

"No, I don't. I would like to go with *Juana* and meet her."

"*La señora Flora* lives in a valley east of *el pueblo*. *Jaime* can take both of you."

While *Juana's* cousin, *Jaime*, goes to his friend who has a cart and donkey for hire, *Juana* asks *Juan*, "Do you want to go in *la carreta* to get herbs with us?"

"No, *mamá*, I'll stay here *con la abuela*."

Juana leans over and plants a kiss on his sticky cheek, then she joins *Graciela* in the front of the house.

Soon *Jaime* returns in a wobbly cart with a large donkey pulling it.

"It's the only one he had today," says *Jaime*. "I'm sorry the *carreta* is so bad, but at least the donkey is strong."

As the *carreta* rumbles and sways out of the *pueblo* onto a narrow dirt road, a cloud of thick gray dust rises from the donkey's hooves and the crooked

médicos - doctors; **la señora Flora** - Mrs. Flower; **la carreta** - cart; **con la abuela** - with grandmother.

carreta wheels, making it hard to breathe. *Juana* and *Graciela* pull their shawls around their faces.

"*Jaime*, are you sure you know the way?" asks *Juana* in a muffled voice.

"*¡Por supuesto, chica!* I'm following your mother's directions. All we have to do is continue east until we find a post with a green leaf painted on it."

After bumping along in the jiggly cart for another half-mile, the three riders finally see the large green leaf on a post. It is at the entrance to a narrow path. *Jaime* reins in, ties the donkey to the post, then helps *Juana* and *Graciela* alight.

The long lane ends at a large open space surrounded by trees and the three stop —not sure where to go next. Here and there are plots with stocky bushes dividing straight rows of seedlings. In the center, a low white fence surrounds a group of tender plants with tiny pale yellow and pink flowers.

Then *Juana*, seeing a small gray house beyond, says, "I think we have found *la señora Flora*."

A black and white dog sleeping peacefully on one of the unpainted steps hears the visitors approach. He lazily stretches, then comes to greet them with a grin on his face and his tail wagging.

Juana calls out, "*¡Hola, señora Flora!*"

A short, slender woman with a long salt-and-pepper braid hanging down her back comes to the door.

"I'm *la señora Carrera's* daughter and have come for herbs and remedies," explains *Juana*.

"Por supuesto, chica!" - "Of course, girl!" **"Hola, señora Flora!"** - "Hello, Mrs. Flower!"

"*Por supuesto*," the herb lady says, smiling. "I remember your mother very well."

Juana introduces *Graciela* and *Jaime*.

"You have come to the right place; come inside. I have many plants. You saw some of them as you came to the door. What do you need?" she asks.

While naming them off from memory, *Juana* marvels at the number of jars full of dried berries, seeds and leaves that sit on a high shelf. *La señora Flora* selects from several jars and wraps up the herbs and seeds. She tells *Juana* their names and uses, as she marks each package with a symbol.

"These leaves and berries are well-known *para resfriados, dolor de cabeza, la diarrea* and other common ailments."

When *Juana* tells the herb lady that she is going to *Alta California, la señora Flora* stops to think for a moment.

"You would be wise to take other remedies with you, too. Come outside. I have special plants and trees with bark and leaves that make stronger teas *para los otros problemas.*"

"How did you find out the uses for all these plants?" asks *Graciela*.

"My people were here before *los españoles* came; they knew about the many uses *para las hierbas, las semillas, los bulbos, las hojas, y la corteza de árboles.*

por supuesto - of course; **para resfriados** - for colds; **dolor de cabeza** - headache; **la diarrea** - diarrhea; **para los otros problemas** - for other problems; **los españoles** - the Spaniards; **para las hierbas** (grasses), **las semillas** (seeds), **los bulbos** (bulbs), **las hojas** (leaves), **y la corteza de árboles** (and bark from trees).

Although we have always advised soldiers what to do about arrow poison, it is the women and *los Padres* who want to know about many more remedies."

While *Juana* and *Graciela* are talking to *la señora Flora*, *Jaime* has been walking around the large herb garden with the friendly dog at his heels. Just as they get comfortable under a shady tree, he hears, "*Jaime, venga, por favor.*"

Juana had given her cousin some money for safekeeping before they left, so he is not surprised when she calls him to pay for the herbs. With the dog loping along behind, *Jaime* walks toward the ladies. He counts out the necessary number of coins and hands them to the herb lady. *Juana* gathers up her packages and the three turn to go.

La señora Flora grasps *Juana's* hand, "*¡Tenga cuidado con los medicastros y los curanderos!*"

Halfway down the path to the waiting donkey, they hear *la señora Flora* call out, "*Vaya con Dios.*" *Juana* turns and waves to the kind lady and her smiling dog.

"After *Jaime* takes us back, will you walk to the *tienda* with me?" asks *Juana*, "I want to look at silk material."

"What would you use *seda* for? That's for special-occasion clothes. Remember, you're going to a wild and primitive place — you'll need sturdy things," says *Graciela*.

"*Jaime, venga, por favor.*" - "James, come here please;" *cuidado con los medicastros y los curanderos* - be careful of the "quack" doctors, and pretenders; *Vaga con Dios* - go with God; *tienda* - store; *seda* - silk (Spain established a silk industry in earlier times importing cocoons from China).

"I should think there would be an occasion for a party dress where there is a *presidio*, even in *Alta California*," says *Juana*.

A familiar figure is waiting for them as they turn onto *la Calle de Soldado*. *Jaime* stops the donkey, and *Juan* climbs into the cart. When his mother and her friend get out at *la abuela Carrera*'s house, *Juan* decides to go with *Jaime* to return *el burro y la carreta*.

"I see you found *la señora Flora*," says *Juana's* mother, as her daughter places several packets of remedies on the table."

"With your good directions, we found her easily," says *Juana*.

"She is a very friendly lady," says *Graciela*.

"She told us how the women of each generation in her family have shared their knowledge of herbs and remedies with their daughters, beginning before *los españoles* conquered *Nueva España* two hundred fifty years ago. I'm glad I went there with *Juana*; since her house is not difficult to find, I know I shall visit her again."

After more conversation about their dusty trip, *Juana* says, "Now that I have the herbs and remedies, it's time to do the next important thing: *Graciela* and I are going shopping. *José Joaquín* finally got his army pay and has given me a few *pesos* to spend on things for our move. He agrees that I should take something elegant to wear *en las fiestas*."

In the shop, *Juana* finds beautiful silks from

el burro y la carreta - donkey and cart; **pesos** - Spanish money; **en las fiestas** - for parties.

China brought to *Nueva España* in *los galleones* from *Manila*. She also examines the Spanish silks the merchant has imported from *Cádiz, España*.

"This red material from China is so pretty."

Then, with a sigh, she says, "But I'll get more use from the black."

"*Graciela* agrees, and pointing to laces at the front of the store, says, "Why don't you get a shawl? There is a beautiful one with red roses throughout; that will change it into a festive party dress."

Juana counts her money once more and decides to buy the shawl — when would she have another opportunity to find something so beautiful? Now that material for her party dress has been purchased, she and *Graciela* leave the store.

As they make their way up the narrow street, *Juana* says, "I'll ask mother to cut out the dress, and if you have the time, *Graciela*, I'd like you to help sew it."

"Indeed, I would like to help," says her friend.

Approaching the cobbler's shop, *Juana* says, "Let's see if he has a pair of dress shoes and a pair of sturdy ones already made up in my size. I heard that *los indios* at *las misiones* make only sandals."

"I suppose you will need very sturdy shoes to walk through mud in winter and dust in the summertime," says *Graciela*.

"Now, now, *Graciela*, saying such things only worries me, but you're probably right. Often we have to wear them here in the mountains and countryside.

los galleones - type of ship; **Manila** - a city in the Philippine Islands; **Cadis, España** - an important Spanish port; **los indios** - Indians; **las misiones** - missions.

Maybe it won't be worse than that."

"How about petticoats, *Juana*? Do you have enough? I'm told that the wind from the north and west is very cold this time of year. You may be glad to have a few layers under your skirt at the *presidio*."

"That's true, and *José* said that it would be cold on board ship. He didn't know if the captain would give out blankets. I'll get some heavy black material — enough to make two petticoats, some skirts, and a pair of warm trousers for *Juan*."

As they pass a table of ribbons, *Juana* stops to buy a few long red, black and white pieces to cut up for trim on blouses and for hair ribbons for the whole family, since her husband and son sometimes wear their hair in a short braid.

"*Graciela*, I think I have everything I can afford. The wool for *Juan's* jacket and a heavy shawl for me has used up almost all the money. I have just enough left for these combs of carved bone. I'm glad that *José* will get what he needs through the military."

Graciela envisions *Juana*, *José* and *Juan* wrapped in blankets and huddled together on a cold, windy deck. She feels sorry that her friends have to make such an unpleasant voyage.

Juana spends her days and evenings sewing with her mother and good friend, *Graciela*, as well as gathering items together she wants to take with her.

José Joaquín comes from the barracks occasionally and tells her how plans are progressing.

"Just as I thought, we will leave later than planned. It's the usual delays: Uniforms haven't arrived at headquarters in *Guadalajara*, and the new guns and cannons haven't arrived at *San Blas*. I also heard that *Alberni* is having trouble getting his quota of soldiers to sign up for duty in *Alta California*. They want their back pay first. He had this trouble before, and his arguments with the treasury over this almost got him jailed for insubordination. I hope, for his sake, such a situation doesn't happen again."

The delay is good news to *Juana*. She has more time to get her household goods together — *almohadas y mantas para las camas; olla, cacerola y sartén* for cooking; as well as plates and utensils.

La señora Carrera has everything her daughter needs, and says, "Here, *Juana*, take these. Now that you and *Juan* are leaving, I won't need so many cooking pans. And take as many blankets as will fit into the bundles; I know you will need them."

Juana hugs her mother. The few *pesos* had been spent on clothing and other items. There is nothing left.

"I heard that some *misiones* have looms to make rough cotton material and coarse woolen blankets. I will have to get such things from them," says *Juana*.

Graciela, seeing how much thread they are using every day, decides that a useful farewell present would be a supply of sewing items — needles, thread, buttons and braid.

"There is no end to the needs of a family. Trying to plan for the future with few *pesos* is so difficult. I've heard that the wives of officers take much more — even furniture," laments *Juana*.

"You know the reason, don't you?" asks *Graciela*.

---

almohadas y mantas para las camas - pillows and blankets for the beds; **olla, cacerola y sartén** - pot, casserole and frying pan.

Without waiting for an answer, she continues, "The military lets officers' wives take more things; otherwise they wouldn't leave their comfortable homes and social events in Spanish cities, or here in *Nueva España*. They know it will be a dull and uncomfortable life for them on frontier posts like *Alta California*. Officers get more pay, too — even bonuses of all kinds, and privileges."

"I think I had better concentrate on the problem in front of me. How am I going to pack the things I have?" says *Juana*, looking at everything spread around her.

"I must get all this into bundles and one or two small bags. *Gracias a Dios, José's* uniforms and military gear will be in his trunk."

Juan and *Graciela* watch *Juana* pack her possessions. In a special *maleta* she places plates, forks, cups, dried fruit, dried meat, hemmed towels, and other small items she thinks they will need aboard ship. She places some specially wrapped items carefully in the center with the towels; they are objects very dear to her, and have been purposely left out until now: a picture of *María, la madre de Jesús*, from her small corner chapel; prayer beads; crucifixes that have hung on the wall over their beds; a candlestick and some well-wrapped candles.

La señora Carrera asks, "How will anyone know whose bags these are? *José Joaquín's* name is painted on his army trunk."

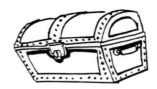

Gracias a Dios - Thank God; **maleta** - a carrying case, suitcase, bundle; **María, la madre de Jesús** - Mary the mother of Jesus.

Juana thinks for a moment, then says, "I'll sew my initials on each one."

"I'll help," says *Graciela.*

Juana hesitates to sew the letters S A N C next to her initials on the four large bags, even though they are on *José's* trunk; she doesn't know what they stand for. The question persists even after she and *Graciela* have finished adding her initials: What do those letters mean? Should she have added S A N C?

"From *Nueva España* to *Alta Califorña*"

CHAPTER FOUR

ABOARD THE *SAN CARLOS, ENERO DE* 1796

The day for which *Juana Tico* has been preparing finally arrives. Trying hard to hold back tears, she waits outside for the *carreta,* along with her husband, mother, and *Graciela*; they talk about everything except the move. All the *Ticos'* possessions, in four large bags, one trunk and a *maleta,* sit near the street.

Graciela stops talking and goes to her friend. Hugging *Juana*, she says, "I'll miss you so much."

El sargento Tico turns away as the ladies burst into tears.

Juana and her mother wrap their arms tightly around each other. It is the last time they will be together.

A neighbor joins *el sargento Tico* and then calls out to *Juan*, who is chasing his two best friends in a game of "tag," "Won't you miss your *amigos?*"

Juan calls over his shoulder, "*Sí, sí, pero mi madre dice que* there will be lots of children to play with when I get there; maybe some will be on *el barco.*"

At the sound of wheels rumbling up *la Calle de Soldado, Juan* and his friends stop their game and run to the street. A large *carreta* drawn by two strong oxen makes its way clumsily over the cobblestones and stops in front of the *adobe.* The boys go quickly to the animals. They don't often get an opportunity to look

maleta - small suitcase, bundle; *amigos* - friends; **Sí, sí, pero mi madre dice que** - Yes, but my mother says that; *el barco* - boat or ship; *adobe* - la abuela's house.

closely at the oxen's heads, and how the yoke fits over their necks.

The driver picks up the large bags to put them in the *carreta*. As he drops them heavily onto the floor of the cart, *Juana* is glad the important items are nestled safely among soft things. *El sargento Tico* helps *Juana* onto bales of hay placed on each side of the *carreta* and motions *Juan* to get in.

Juana leans over the side for last hugs.

The ladies dab at their moist eyes; mother and daughter squeeze each other's hands. Then everyone steps back when the driver shouts at the oxen, prods their sides, and the *carreta* begins to move.

Juan's friends, running alongside, shout to him as the cart moves slowly and noisily down the street. When the oxen begin to turn at the end of *la Calle de Soldado*, *el sargento Tico* tells *Juan* to say good-bye to the boys so they can go back home. *Juana* looks back and waves her handkerchief at her beloved mother, dear friends, and good neighbors who have gathered at the last minute, filling the street, waving and shouting, "*Vaya con Dios.*"

El sargento Tico raises his arm in a final salute.

As the oxen plod around the turn, everyone gasps at what they see heading toward them. A rider — head down, hunched over his donkey's neck like a jockey, shouting and whipping the animal to go faster — gets closer and closer without changing course. The speeding boy suddenly lifts his eyes, just in time to swerve around them. An empty *canasta* bounces high in the air, narrowly missing *la carreta* as the mad rider whizzes by.

"***Vaya con Dios***" - Go with God.

"*Adiós, Manuel*," shouts *Juan*.

"*Por casualidad*, would that be the same boy who scattered *los melones* along *la calle* when you and I walked to *la plaza?*" asks *el Sargento Tico*.

"*Sí, sí*, and his father switched him! But it wasn't his fault — a big fly bit *el burro*."

"The way he's riding that donkey, he may be in for another good swat when his father finds out!" says *el sargento Tico*.

In the excitement of *Manuel* racing by on the donkey, *Juan* forgets about this being the last time he will see his friends. He settles back to concentrate on the road ahead.

As the oxen pull *la carreta* slowly along the rough, winding mountain road, their hooves slide on curves and steep hills as the driver tries to hold them back; *Juan* has to hold tightly to the side of the cart.

Then peering ahead, he sees a stream flowing across the rutted path and wonders how they will make it across. But the driver knows the road and leads the oxen to the other side with only a few cold drops splashing into the cart.

If it were not for unexpected things happening along the way, *Juan* would find the two-day trip to the port of *San Blas* long and boring. He likes it when they get out to walk and his father tells him about the wild animals that hide in the woods. He stays close to *la carreta* just in case one of the hidden animals jumps out. The best stops are when his mother brings out a lunch his grandmother has packed for them.

"*Adiós, Manuel*" - "Goodbye, Manuel"; *Por casualidad* - by chance;   *la calle* - the street; *la plaza* - the town square.

When they stop for the night, *Juana* digs into the bags for blankets in which to wrap themselves while *el sargento Tico, Juan* and the driver make a large bonfire. *Juan,* rolled up in his blanket, watches the leaping orange and yellow flames until his eyes close.

The second day drags on and *Juan* looks forward to the end of the journey.

Finally reaching the port, *Juan* sees all the people and boats; suddenly he's not bored any longer. At the gated entrance, *el sargento Tico* gets out of *la carreta* and walks over to two soldiers standing guard. The guards motion the driver on, and once on the bustling dock, the driver leaves *Juana* and *Juan* alone to watch the activity around them.

"My, I haven't been to *San Blas* since your father sailed for *Nootka* seven years ago; I thought it looked better than this," she said, noticing that the warehouses badly needed paint.

"That was before I was born," says *Juan,* looking up at her.

He overhears a conversation between two men loading barrels and trunks from one of the warehouses into very large rowboats.

"Here is the list of *memorias* for the *presidio* at *Monterey;* give it to the captain of *La Concepción,*" says the man in charge.

"What are *memorias?*" *Juan* asks his mother.

"They are lists of items that people living in faraway *presidios* and *misiones* need to make their

San Blas - important port on west coast of *Nueva España* (Mexico) with financial center, barracks, storage and ship building.

lives easier. *El commandante* or the treasurer of the *presidio* makes up a list and sends it to people in *Tepíc, San Blas* or *la Ciudad de Méjico.* When those people find the things on the list, they send them here to be shipped to faraway places like *Presidio San Francisco.*"

"Can we do that if we want chocolate?" asks *Juan,* who had overheard *Graciela* talking to his mother about taking some with her.

"I hope so," says his mother.

Before *Juan* can ask more questions, *el sargento Tico,* with official papers in hand, comes over to his wife and son, and says, "We can board now."

He points to a waiting longboat. "This will take us to the ship."

Juan had noticed the large rowboat and several sailors standing next to it when they first arrived. He had hoped he would have a ride in it. Running toward the sailors, he gets into the boat and scoots across the narrow wooden seat, leaving plenty of room for his parents. Along with *Juana's* big bundles and her husband's trunk, the sailors hoist several barrels into the boat. The barrels contain *memorias* and are going to one of the ships lying at anchor.

As soon as sailors on land push the longboat away, the men inside begin rowing. *Juana* is apprehensive; this is her first boat ride. Sitting between her husband and son, she looks straight ahead and holds tightly to *Juan's* hand. The boat moves swiftly toward dim outlines of ships at anchor,

el comandante - the commander; **la Ciudad de Méjico** - Mexico City, the Capital of Mexico today.

and the three passengers soon clearly see two two-masted *paquebotes*.

At the first vessel, *el sargento Tico* points and says to his wife, "*¡Juana, mira!* It's the *San Carlos*, the same ship that took me to *Sonora!*"

Juana nods her head, and says, "Now I understand. The initials S A N C on your trunk stand for 'San Carlos.' *José*, do you think it's a good omen that we are going on the same ship now?"

El sargento Tico, not one to admit he believes in such superstition, answers, "It's probably only a coincidence. But if it is an omen, I hope it's a good one. After all, I did come back alive!"

Juana nods her head, and says, "I think it must be a good omen."

Juan sees a narrow ladder hanging down the side of the ship and cries out, "*Mamá*, do I have to climb into the ship? I can't swim. What if I slip and fall in the water?"

His mother, squeezing his hand, doesn't know what to say, since she can't swim either.

El sargento Tico, having climbed aboard before, says, "The sailors will hold our boat close to the side of the ship and help all of us climb up the ladder. You'll see, it's really not very far from the longboat to the deck."

Their boat pulls alongside the *San Carlos* and *Juan* is the first to go aboard. He bravely begins to ascend the ladder, stretching his legs to reach each rung, tightly grasping the ropes on each side to pull himself along. A sailor is right behind him until he

paquebotes - mail boats, packet boats, coastal ships; *"**Juana, mira**!"* - "Juana, look!"

reaches the top, where another sailor lifts him onto the deck. *Juan* breathes a sigh of relief and looks over the side as sailors help his mother up the ladder. Seeing the longboat bobbing on the water below, he suddenly realizes what a courageous thing he has done.

Juana, now on the noisy crowded deck, wonders where they are going to stay. A sailor seeing her come aboard with the four bundles and the *maleta*, picks up two of the large bundles and flings them over each shoulder. She watches anxiously as he makes his way through coiled ropes, masts, barrels and bales to disappear down a stairway. Returning, he motions for her and *Juan* to follow, as he lugs the last two bundles below.

Juana stoops as she starts down the few steps. At the bottom, she finds she is on the gun deck. The sailor drops her precious possessions next to the first two bundles, and returns to the top deck to help others.

After her eyes adjust to the dim light, *Juana* discovers that her family will be sitting and sleeping on bales of hay. A shiver runs over her body as she realizes this cramped area will be their bedroom and home for the next two or three months. There will be no privacy; it will be shared with strangers — soldiers and their families. She looks around to see if there is a way she can make a wall of blankets, at least on one side, but it doesn't seem possible. Holding back tears of disappointment and frustration, she sits down on a bale to think about it. Maybe they should wrap themselves in blankets and sleep on deck.

After presenting his official papers to an officer on board, *el sargento Tico* comes below. *Juan* and his parents sit on the straw beds and watch other families arriving. As *Juana* had done, they stop at the foot of the stairs to get used to the dimness, then they look around for a space to call "home." Mothers carrying babies on their hips and toddlers clinging to their skirts, make up most of the parade of humanity coming into the dimly-lit quarters. *Juan* is happy to see there are a few children his age. One of the boys in particular reminds him of a friend in *Tepíc*.

Juana turns to her husband and says with authority, "It will be so stuffy, cramped and noisy down here, we're going to stay on deck as long as possible every day! And I'm going to pray night and day for our comfort and safety."

She can only imagine how terrifying bad weather and rough seas can be. One other thing bothers her, although she doesn't mention it; she is afraid of being on the ocean, even though the *San Carlos* is much larger than the longboat.

Juana begins to search through the *maleta*. Finding her prayer beads and other religious objects, she feels more secure and hugs the bag closer to her side.

The aroma of garlic and olive oil wafting from the galley tells all aboard that the cooks have begun preparing the evening meal — which reminds *Juana* to take the tin dishes and cups from the *maleta* in case they are needed.

"I'm glad I brought the dried fruit and *charqui*, since we are only allotted two meals a day. *José*, do you think we can get more dried fruit when the captain stops to deliver *memorias*?"

charqui - dried beef.

"We'll have to see how he handles personal requests. The captain usually picks up fresh food, water, and wood for the cook each time he anchors at a *presidio* or *misión*," answers *el sargento Tico*.

"Where do we eat?" asks *Juan*.

"The same place we soldiers eat when there are no families along. When there are too many of us to eat at the same time, we have our *desayuno* and *cena* in shifts, and we eat on deck."

Juan, seemingly unaware of all the people milling about, asks his father to walk around the ship with him.

"Not now, *hijo*," says his father. "There is too much confusion."

Juan insists; there is an important reason he wants to see more of the ship. But alas, he discovers there are no outhouses on board. His father takes him to the bow and explains how to use the facilities that hang over the side.

"You mean, with all these people around? And look, *papá*, the ocean is so close!"

"Don't worry, *Juan*, you won't fall in the water, and just remember that before the voyage is over, we're all going to be one very big family, and no one will pay attention when you come here. No one can see you now. I'll be right over there," he says, pointing to the railing where *Juana* is standing.

Juan hadn't anticipated the outhouse being so out in the open — still, his father said no one is looking. Maybe it will be all right to use it after all.

As he walks back through the crowd to find his

desayuno - breakfast; **cena** - dinner; **memorias** - supplies

parents, *Juan* feels grownup. He is especially proud of his long pants, jacket, cap and new shoes. If he were back in *Tepíc*, he would be in a long shirt, like a dress, for another two years!

He finds his family at the crowded railing watching the last of the *memorias* being loaded from longboats into the *San Carlos*. Everyone can hear the loud voices of sailors working below.

"We haven't put as many barrels and trunks on board as we usually do," says one.

"That's always the way when we transport soldiers. They take up storage space," says the other, "And now they've got their families, too!"

Since it is late in the day, the *San Carlos* rides at anchor until morning. All night long, the ship gently dips and rolls in the swells. The motion lulls some to sleep, while others become seasick. Many mothers, including *Juana*, are glad they put chamber pots among household items in their bags. *El sargento Tico, Juan* and *Juana* have a bad first night at sea, and the ship is still in port!

By sunrise, everything has been made ready. Sailors raise anchors and set sails, while men, women and children scramble out of their way. As the *San Carlos* eases past the second ship at anchor, everyone at the rail is spellbound as four blindfolded mules are lifted, one by one, from a floating platform to the deck of the ship, *La Concepción*. A pulley fastened near the top of one of the masts lifts the sling placed under the mules' bellies. Sailors let down each blindfolded "flying mule" onto the ship, remove the sling, and lead it to a small corral on deck.

For that brief moment, *Juana* forgets the discomfort she has envisioned for herself during the long voyage. Then turning her eyes toward the fading coastline, she thinks about her wonderful family and friends. The thought sweeps over her: No matter how she will miss everyone, or how difficult the future years might turn out to be, she is at this moment beginning the new life for which she has been preparing.

As if to confirm her thoughts, water on each side of the ship separates and spray rolls back as the bow of the *San Carlos* cuts through the placid early-morning sea on its northward voyage to *Presidio San Francisco*. There is no turning back!

Each day after a short walk from one end of the vessel to the other for exercise, stepping around family groups and small children playing, father and son sit together on the hard wooden deck for *Juan's* lessons. *El sargento Tico* patiently shares his limited knowledge of writing with his son.

Juana sits on a bale close by, in keeping with her decision that the three of them be on deck as much as possible in the fresh air. With her large shawl enveloping her from head to toe, protecting her from the wind, she brings pink roses to bloom on a white blouse with needle and thread. Occasionally she looks proudly at her son who doesn't seem to hear the babies crying and the noisy children at play. He is concentrating on placing the *pauta* under the coarse paper so he can follow the lines and keep his work neat.

With a piece of lead his father has sharpened to a point, he slowly prints the letter "*J.*" Having few sheets of paper, *Juan* works carefully, copying the letters his father shows him. *El Padre García* had given him the lead, *pauta* and paper when he heard *Juan* was going away.

One day after lessons, while *Juan* and his father stand at the rail watching gray whales swim past on their way south to warmer waters, *Juan* asks his father, "Why are you a soldier, *papá?* Did you want to be one when you were *un niño?*"

"Let me think about that a minute; that was a long time ago," he says, laughing and ruffling his son's hair.

"*Papá*, I really want to know. When you were my age, did you think about it?"

"No, *hijo,* I didn't think about it when I was your age. It wasn't until I was older that I knew I wanted to be a soldier."

"What happened then — you know — to make you decide?" asks *Juan.*

"It's a long story. Are you sure you want to hear it?"

"Oh, yes, I like stories. Let's go back to *mamá.* She's keeping our places for us."

Sitting on the hard deck once again, with the winter sun warming them, *Juan* snuggles close to his father's arm. *El sargento Tico* begins to think about the events leading up to his becoming a soldier. Surprisingly, it all comes back so clearly. He was almost seventeen; it seems like it was just yesterday.

pauta - object placed beneath writing paper to keep straight lines; **un niño** - a child.

CHAPTER FIVE

"AN ORDINARY DAY IN 1766"

"Come on *Pedro*, let's get the kegs in first. No, no, what is the matter with you? I think you are still asleep. Here, let me finish that."

"Now, now, *José Joaquín,* you know *Pedro* isn't used to loading the cart. This is only the second time he has helped us. You will just have to be more patient."

My father is right; I need to have more patience.

Father and I lift the heavy *barriles* of wine into the cart. Thank goodness I don't have to wrestle the old pigskins any more.

"Sales are better since we switched from pigskins to small *barriles:* Men in the village like the flavor better," comments my father.

Seeing *Pedro* struggling with two large *jarras* of freshly pressed *aceite de olivo,* I run to help him.

"Here, these are too heavy for you, I'll take them."

With a jug under each arm, I walk to the cart and gently shove them back until they are three fingers from the kegs. Glancing over at *Pedro*, I see him lifting another *jarra.*

"Wait, *Pedro!*" I call out as I dash to his side — reaching him just as the jug slowly slips from his grasp.

"Why don't you wait a couple more years before you try to help?"

I look down and see tears welling up in his eyes.

Pedro (Paydro) - Peter; **barriles** - barrels; **jarras** - jugs; **aceite de olivo** - olive oil.

My little brother is trying so hard to help, and I'm only thinking of the mess there would be for me to clean up if the jug breaks, and of the loss of *pesos* from the spilled oil. What a bad start today!

"Here, *Pedro*," says father, lifting him into the back of the cart. "Take these lamb skins and place them around the kegs and *jarras* so they will stand firm during the rough ride to the quay."

Father and I watch as my young brother pushes the skins between the jugs and barrels; then I lift him down and begin to walk toward the front of the cart.

Father calls out, "Don't go yet, *José*, I have some honey and oranges in the shed."

Returning from the shed, we place the baskets of *naranjas dulces* and *naranjas agrios* on the seat of the cart, and tuck *los tarros de miel* between sheepskins in the back.

With an *abrazo* for my father and brother, I climb onto the wooden seat. The donkey's gray head, with its battle-scarred nose, rises in surprise when I slap him with the reins. With its ears twitching, and blinders flapping in the morning breeze, the old swayback donkey and I begin our journey along the dusty path, through the village and out to the even dustier road leading to *Barcelona* and the quay.

Day after day, I hitch up the old donkey, fill the cart, and go to the quay in *Barcelona* to sell the *aceite de olivo, vino,* and whichever fruits are ripe. If I return

pesos - Spanish money; **naranjas dulces** - sweet oranges; **naranjas agrios** - sour oranges; **los tarros de miel** - jars of honey; **abrazo** - hug; **Barcelona** - capital of present day Catalonia; **quay** (English) - a dockside made of stones.

early, I work in either the fields, orchard or vineyard. The next day, I fill the cart and do it over again. I have to admit that I like it once I'm at the quay. The thing that bothers me so much is all the work getting ready to go and having to follow the same dusty roads to the port.

"*Buenos días, señor Sobato,*" I call out, as I pass the coffeehouse in the *pueblo.*

El señor Sobato stops sweeping for a moment and leans on his broom, "*Buenos días, José Joaquín.* Your family is well?"

I nod my head as I flap the reins and continue on my way. No one in *Pueblo de Sedo* can remember any other family owning the coffeehouse.

It has been a week since my first time at *la tertulia* in *el señor Sobato's* place with father and *Antonio.* I thought my turn would never come. I had wanted to go since father took my brother, *Antonio,* two years ago when he was almost seventeen.

It was so smokey inside that I didn't recognize anyone at first. We found our places at my father's table with four other farmers we knew. As I watched my father's arms relax into the smoothly worn indentations on the table, I thought of all the generations of men whose arms rubbed back and forth, wearing down the table edge as they reached for cups of coffee or drew in the cards. In spite of my watering eyes, I felt proud to sit with the men in the coffeehouse.

The stranger who spoke that night had been to

aceite de olivo, vino - olive oil, wine; **Pueblo de Sedo** - the village where **el sargento José Joaquín Tico** was born and where he lived until he was seventeen; **la tertulia** - a social gathering for conversation or entertainment.

Madrid, over three hundred miles from *Pueblo de Sedo.*
Father and the others, sucking on their pipes and
sipping weak coffee, nodded in agreement each time
the traveler complained of the excessive spending by
the royal court. The king's spending didn't bother me;
I only thought about the speaker having gotten away
from some *pueblo* and was traveling; he gave me hope
of escape from my drudgery.

"Come on you old *burro,* move along! You don't
have to go to sleep. Keep going!"

Slapping the reins again across his flank, the
donkey begins to trot and I sit back to think about the
quay. I can tell we're getting there before I see the
water.

"Can you smell the sea?" I shout at the donkey.

As we get closer to the quay, a strong odor
replaces the good salt air. It is a familiar bad smell
which comes from the rancid fish oil on an Arabian
dhow's teakwood hull. Fortunately, the wind changes
direction in a few minutes, blowing the stink away.

The shifting winds bring chanteys of sailors
working the halyards, bringing down sails. Splashes
of anchors hitting the deep *aguablava* echo across the
water; a ship is here to stay for a while.

A four-masted vessel floats quietly out of the bay
with its many sails hoisted to catch the wind. I
wonder to which Mediterranean port she's headed.
Sailors told stories about those port-cities with dark-
skinned men clad all in white, and women in black
with faces covered, strolling through the cool corridors

aguablava (Catalán) - blue water

of darkened bazaars; where blue and yellow parrots screech from the shoulders of men with twisted bodies and a patch over an eye; where small monkeys reach out to passersby while clinging to the sides of bamboo cages.

Arabian dhows, and vessels from Africa, Asia, Portugal and other Spanish ports drift lazily in the quiet water. Small flags on the top of tall masts stretch out in the light breeze. In the distance, men, like strings of ants, climb down ladders that hang from sides of ships, and alight into waiting rowboats. They are probably captains with their officers and goods-dealers arriving with overdue orders of expensive cloth, specially carved furniture, and other rare goods not made in all of Spain.

Strong crewmen pull close and secure ropes into iron rings fastened between large stones along the quayside. To avoid getting their shoes wet, the captains and ships' officers gingerly step from the boats onto the wide, water-splashed stone steps. Sellers in longboats full of merchandise follow closely behind.

Canvases are raised against the sun, so displays of goods in open barrels, trunks and boxes are protected. I click to the donkey and move a little closer — not wanting to miss the haggling between buyers and sellers. Soon the flat grey stones of the quay are hidden by an assortment of items taken from longboats which continue to arrive.

Rough sailors with weathered hands gently unwrap bags and bundles. The mingling scents of an assortment of spices from *Indias Orientales* waft

Indias Orientales - India

through their wrappings, sweetening the air. Turbaned merchants from the ships display bright red and yellow, roughly woven cotton material from sunbaked African coastal cities. Sailors carefully place lined baskets overflowing with delicate lace, and painted teakwood trunks brimming with fine Chinese silks. Sturdy boxes of cobalt-blue glass ornaments blown in *Venecia*, and hand painted faience vases from *Italia*, sit next to each other.

I watch men from *Bélgica* unroll elaborate red and blue carpets with amber designs, then place gilded chairs on top. They toss finely woven wallhangings and tapestries over the chair backs.

Accountants on both sides move closer. Each has a duty to fulfill to his employer. Those from the ships speak for the turbaned merchants and captains with gestures and smiles, while those with the Spanish merchants stand aloof with their arms crossed over their chests. The men exchange short bows and a few minutes of pleasantries.

After the Spanish merchants have inspected all of the goods, the bartering begins. The bargainers from *Cataluña* are the loudest of all.

A mixture of languages rises in a gradual crescendo as the men dicker for the best prices. Finally calm prevails, and smiling faces signify that the sales are completed. Each man thinks he has made the best deal.

Spanish merchants carefully count everything

Venecia - Venice, a separate city-state during this era; faience (English) - earthenware painted with opaque glazes; *Italia* - Italy; *Bélgica* - Belgium.

before they rewrap the goods or replace the contents of opened trunks. Servants find the different shapes awkward to handle as they place large square parcels and heavy round barrels into waiting carts.

Clicking to the donkey, I move my cart out of the way, but I don't move so far that I'll miss the parade of merchants returning to their stores and sheds.

"On the way to Barcelona"

CHAPTER SIX
"MY PROBLEM"

On a quiet side of the quay, I sell the rest of the olive oil, wine and oranges to several customers before they row to their ships.

On my return to the busy side, I find that awnings have been taken down and the quay is empty of merchandise. Full carts slowly make their way across the gray stones that were hidden from sight only a few hours ago by bundles, baskets, trunks and barrels.

Wealthy merchants are leaving in covered litters — each carried away by four strong men — while a procession of carts follows, each cart bulging with parcels of expensive goods.

Men from *Nueva Castilla* — buyers for the royal family and members of the king's court — have been here for several weeks making purchases. They ride to the inn together in cushioned litters with canopies of ornately carved wood and side curtains of heavy gold damask. The king's men will leave *mañana* before dawn. Among the retinues of servants who accompany them are soldiers on horseback to guard the carriages and the long mule train during the three hundred mile return trip to *Madrid*. Sheltered from the sun by large parasols, men in bright robes walk leisurely back to their shops. Servants follow the parasols, skillfully balancing baskets full of expensive

Nueva Castilla - New Castile is a province in Spain; **Madrid** - Madrid is the capital of Spain and is in New Castile; **mañana** - tomorrow.

glassware and fine porcelain on top of their heads.   As
a driver passes me, beating his old horse, I gasp as I
see parcels swaying precariously on the back of his
cart.

A young man without either donkey or horse waits
with his small cart. The last one to be hired, he has
learned from experience that there is always a
merchant left at the quay who needs help. Today it is
a man with carpets. Putting down both gates, the
young man lifts and slides the heavy rolls wrapped in
oil-soaked canvas into the cart. He then secures the
gates, locking them in place. Standing between two
long wooden shafts, he bends at the knees and picks
up the shafts. Veins in his neck protrude as he
strains to pull the cart forward with his own strength.
Soon he gains momentum and jogs easily over the
cobblestones and along the quay toward the dusty
road.

Long before the merchants leave, captains and
men from the ships have ridden into *Barcelona*, but
not before hiding their purses somewhere deep inside
their clothing.

As the wobbly carts disappear into narrow alleys, I
begin to think of other things. My stomach tells me
it's time to eat, even before a distant church bell
across the bay tolls half past twelve. The tantalizing
aroma of barbecued lamb and freshly caught fish
cooking on small charcoal grills nearby make my
mouth water. I buy a piece of fish and some rice for a
few *centavos*. The large, sweet onion costs a little

centavos - Spanish money.

more, but I want it to go with the thick slice of bread the boy cuts from a large loaf tucked under his arm.

Now that my stomach is full, and I've given hay to the donkey, there is nothing to do at the quay until after *siesta.* Using a folded sheepskin for a pillow, I settle down for a nap.

Suddenly I'm awakened when the reins around my hand begin to tighten. Swashbucklers in black pants and shirts standing near my cart have disturbed the donkey. These men are different from the sailors I usually see at the quay. It's not their black clothes, nor their dirty bandanas covering their heads to their eyebrows that sets them off from the others. They, like most sailors, have squint lines and deep furrows etched on their leathery sunburned faces. But these men have touchy dispositions; I can tell by their calloused hands resting on carved knife handles protruding from the black sashes wrapped around their waists. I've watched them cut ropes, slice fruit, and stab chunks of meat with those long, sharp, pointed blades during daytime, but at nighttime the knives turn into weapons when pulled quickly from sashes during a drunken brawl.

If it were not for his gesturing, I probably couldn't make out what one of the sailors is saying in pidgin. Laughing, he points to long scars across his cheek and arm. He explains that he had been in an African port too long and got into a brawl. A blinding sandstorm in the desert had slowed a camel caravan carrying silks

siesta - a rest time until after 4:00 p.m. Work resumes in the cooler hours and dinner is served about 10.00 p.m.; ***pidgin*** (English) - a language made up of several languages.

and spices for his ship. Another sailor shows a long
gash on his arm from a fight on deck. He shrugs his
shoulders when asked if he had to spend time in the
brig for that one. The sailors vie with each other in
telling of great dangers they have encountered at sea
— how far off course storms have driven their ships,
how many sails were torn to ribbons and spars
cracked in half during gales and hurricanes. The
exchange of experiences suddenly takes a turn. They
speak in hushed tones of fellow sailors who went to
their graves in the black depths of the sea when giant
waves swept over the decks of their ships.

"God rest their souls," murmurs the toughest of
the lot.

Resuming their laughter and gesturing, the rough
seamen amble in a rolling gait toward a popular
taberna on the edge of town. They ignore the hawkers
waving trinkets, combs and ribbons at them, crying
out, *"¡Para su novia!"*

If their ships stay in port more than a day, the
sailors will probably get into a brawl; the tavern
keeper best take care, or his chairs and tables will
become kindling.

Would I make a daring and brave sailor? I doubt
it. A farmer-boy like me could never be like any of
those brawny men. There is no reason for me to stay
longer, so I click to the donkey, slap the reins across
his rump, and head for the dusty road back to *Pueblo
de Sedo.*

taberna - tavern; *"¡Para su novia!"* - "For your sweetheart".

As I approach the farm, I see a small form standing in the road. It's my young brother, *Pedro,* and he's crying. I rein in the donkey, get out and lift him into the cart. He can barely speak through his tears.

"Speak up, *Pedro,* what's the matter? Why are you crying?"

"*¡Papá murío!*"

Shocked, and disbelieving, I hurry to the farm and find that it is true. Father died suddenly while working in the fields with my older brother, *Antonio,* and a hired hand.

Somehow we pull ourselves together for the funeral. We dress in black, our usual church clothes. My mother — her tear-stained face shrouded in a black lace scarf — leans on *Antonio's* arm. We slowly follow the cart carrying my father's simple wooden coffin to the walled cemetery behind the old stone church. On our way home, huddled together in the jiggling cart, I realize that I will now be expected to work for *Antonio.* He's the oldest and rightfully inherits the farm.

The time has come when I must decide whether to remain with the family and work for my brother, or to leave the family farm.

"¡Papá murío! "- "Papa died."

"Going fishing"

CHAPTER SEVEN

"TO *LA SEU*"

It has been a week since we buried father, and I'm still wondering what to do. I need to talk with some-one — someone far from the farm.

Pablo, my fisherman cousin, might be just the person! He lives only a half-day's journey up the coast. Since it is *domingo*, and I don't have to go to the quay, *Antonio* lets me borrow the old donkey to pay him a visit.

"*Buenas tardes, primo*," I call out.

"*Buenas tardes, José Joaquín. Pásate.*"

After asking about the family, he says, "Are you ready to go fishing *esta noche*?"

"Tonight?"

"*Sí*, it's the best time to catch *las sardinas*."

We finish our supper and put on high boots and long jackets. He also has an extra cap for me. I feel awkward dressed in the strange clothes.

For our lunch later, *Pablo* brings a tin box of *pan, pescado en aceite de olivo y una botella de vino*, and sets it under his seat. As he pushes the boat away from the shore with an oar, I quickly jump in. Then he hands me a large lantern to hang on the stern.

Pablo continues rowing for what seems like an

Pablo - Paul; ***domingo*** - Sunday; ***"Buenas tardes, primo"*** - "Good afternoon, cousin"; ***"Buenas tardes, José Joaquín. Pásate"*** - "Good afternoon Joseph Joaquin. Come in."; **esta noche** - tonight; ***las sardinas*** - sardines, a type of fish; ***pan*** (bread), ***pescado*** (fish) ***en aceite de olivo*** (in olive oil) ***y una botella de vino*** (and a bottle of wine)

hour; I really don't like being out at sea at night, especially when there is no moon.

"We seem to be going so far out. Aren't there any fish closer to shore?"

"We really aren't far out, *José*, and it looks like we have found a school of *sardinas*. Look over there — see that silvery shine on the water? That's the food *sardinas* look for. Let's throw out the net."

There never is a right time to discuss my future — especially after we stop rowing. Immediately we are both too busy to talk.

As fast as we toss it out, the net is filled. After spilling the catch onto the bottom of the boat several times, I can no longer see my feet, but I can feel the flapping fish to the top of my boots. It is impossible to move.

I am beginning to feel miserable as the little boat rolls in the swells; how much longer can I fight off becoming seasick? After we haul in the net two more times, cousin *Pablo* says he is satisfied and heads for shore, slowly rowing the heavy boat which now is much deeper in the water.

"That was *muy rápido, José*, I usually don't have such *buena suerte* so soon. We'll have our *pescado* lunch at home."

The way I feel, it is neither the time to talk about food nor my life's work. All I want to do is return to *Pueblo de Sedo* and feel better. I'm disappointed we didn't discuss my future, but I did learn that I'm not

muy rapido - very fast; **buena suerte** - good luck; **pescado** - fish.

cut out to be a sailor or a fisherman!

My friends in *Pueblo de Sedo* who are younger sons also worry about what they will do with their lives. We agree that it's a hard decision. Two friends decide to stay and work with their older brothers on the farm. Another says he will go into the priesthood of the Spanish Catholic Church. I give that idea some thought but decide I couldn't be a *Padre*. I'm so used to wearing workpants, I don't think I could possibly wear a long brown tunic. And how could I keep a pious expression on my face when I so like to tease my sister and little brother? Besides, I would probably be given a village church — like the one in *Pueblo de Sedo* — and stay there the rest of my life!

I continue to go to the quay with the cart full of *jarras de aceite de olivo, miel, vino, y canastas de naranjas* and listen to the merchants and sailors. Surely there is something in this world I could do — something exciting that would change my monotonous life.

I sell the remaining jugs of olive oil and barrels of wine to a captain going to *Chipre*. I hear that he usually drinks all the wine during the voyage and rations the olive oil to the cook with instructions that it be used exclusively for his own special dishes.

Seeing a church spire in the distance, I get an idea. Maybe I should pray about what to do with my life. Such a big decision requires a big house of God. It is fitting that I pray in the four hundred year old

jarras de aceite de olivo (jugs of olive oil); *miel* (honey; *vino* (wine) *y canastas de naranjas* (and baskets of oranges); *Chipre* - Cyprus, an island country in the Mediterranean Sea.

cathedral, *La Seu.* Turning the cart around, I head for
la plaza de Cataluña.

Fastening the donkey to a post near the church, I
enter the dark sanctuary. Praying for ten minutes,
and feeling satisfied that I have talked it over with
God, I return to the sunshine and donkey.

There is some sort of commotion on the edge of
town; it seems too early for the sailors to be fighting.
Going to where I think the sound comes from, I rein in
the donkey and look around. There are no sailors in
sight, but troops are marching up the street — and it's
peacetime! I thought the king had ordered the
Barcelona barracks closed.

This is the first time I have seen so many soldiers
on parade, and I am spellbound by their splendid
uniforms, buttons glinting in the sunlight, black shoes
shining, and muskets resting on their shoulders. I
shiver with excitement at the sound of their strong
firm steps marching briskly over the polished bricks
and stones. A small boy at their side keeps them in
step with the beat of his drum.

Without thinking where I am, I shout, "*¡Si, si!*
That's what I want to be — *un soldado!*"

I watch the soldiers as they pass by and disappear
up the street. What would it mean to become a
soldier? I suppose I would always have a place to
sleep, food to eat, clothes to wear, money to spend —
and best of all, there would be travel and adventure!

"This must be the answer to my prayer!" I tell the
donkey.

I know what I have to do next, and go straight to

La Seu -(see Notes); **la plaza de Cataluña** - center of the old city
of Barcelona at the time; **un soldado** - a soldier.

the barracks. It is no trouble to find the recruiting officer, *Antonio Pol.* He assures me that since I am almost seventeen, I am old enough to be in the colonial army of *El Rey Carlos.* He casually mentions that the company for which he is recruiting will be going to *La Habana, Cuba.* Without thinking further about it, I enlist.

It feels good as I fill in the blanks of the recruitment form with *Antonio Pol: Barcelona, marzo de 1767, José Joaquín Tico* from *Pueblo de Sedo*, joins the *Compañia de Fusileros de Montaña, segundo regimiento de Infantería Ligera de Cataluña.*

El Rey Carlos (IV) - King Charles (the Fourth) of Spain; **La Habana, Cuba** - Havana, the Capital of the island country, Cuba, in the Gulf of Mexico; **Antonio Pol** - Anthony Pol see (Real People); **Fusileros** - shooters, riflemen; **Infantería Ligera** - light infantry.

Barcelona, March 1767, *José Joaquín Tico* from *Pueblo de Sedo*, joins the Mountain Infantry Company, Second Regiment of the Catalonian Light Infantry.

"Signing up"

CHAPTER EIGHT

"I TELL MY FAMILY"

Feeling happy, excited, and relieved that at last I know what my future life's-work will be, I'm anxious to get home to tell my family about enlisting in the army. Unhitching the donkey from in front of the recruiting office, we start out at a fast trot heading toward *Pueblo de Sedo*.

The opportunity to tell my news comes after dinner. We have the usual prayer, then eat in silence — mealtimes not being the joyous occasions they used to be before father's death. It's after the closing prayer, when everyone is still at the table, that I tell them.

"I have enlisted in the colonial army."

Instead of hearing congratulations, no one speaks. Then my mother cries out from the end of the table. With tears streaming down her weathered cheeks, she shakes her head and moans like someone grieving.

"*José Joaquín*, how could you do this to me — just after we've buried your father?"

Crying harder, she says, "I'll never see you again! What could you have been thinking? We should stay together. Don't go, please don't go!"

I'm stunned. How could I have known she would feel this way?

Mi hermano, Antonio, is also upset and says, "My dear brother, why didn't you discuss this with me?"

Mi hermano, Antonio - My brother, Anthony.

There is no point in answering him. I know he would have tried to convince me to stay.

With his hand on my shoulder, he says, "I'm sorry to see you go; we really need you here, especially since father's death. There is nothing more for me to say, since you have made your decision, except to wish you good luck, and may God be with you."

He drops his hand to his side.

Then looking at my sister who is also stunned, he says, "One of these days *María* will marry; perhaps her husband will work with us on the farm. And *Pedro* is growing so fast; it won't be long before he can take the cart to the quay."

Pedro, standing next to mother's chair with his arm around her, patting her shoulder, brightens when he hears his name mentioned. My mother doesn't stop shaking her head. Tears roll torrents down her cheeks as she wrings her hands and sways from side to side in her chair. *María* comes to her side and helps her to her room. As they leave, *Antonio* tells them, "Don't worry, it will all work out."

"I didn't mean to hurt anyone," I tell God, as I kneel at the side of my bed. "I just finally found something I really want to do with my life."

As I pull the blankets up, I think of *Antonio* telling mother not to worry, that it will all work out. Tossing and turning, I finally fall asleep mumbling, "Don't worry! Don't worry! Don't worry!"

CHAPTER NINE

JUAN QUESTIONS HIS PAPA

"*Papá*, why was everyone so sad at your leaving the farm?"

Before his father answers, his mother speaks up, "I understand very well how your grandmother *Tico* felt, *Juan*. She was losing a son. And it would be only natural that *el tío Antonio* would expect your father to help him run the farm."

El sargento Tico thinks for a moment, then says, "That part is true, but the real reason is quite different. It was peacetime."

"Peacetime!" exclaims *Juana*. "That's a very strange reason, if you ask me."

"Here's how I see it," begins *el sargento Tico*, "for centuries, practically every generation of men in our family had to take up arms against rulers, like the king and queen of *Castilla la Vieja*, who wanted to take away *catalán* freedoms. In those times, there were frequent battles between our province of *Cataluña* and people on the other side of *los Pirineos*, in the southern part of *Francia*.

"This was the first time my family had a normal life with all the children at home. My mother never thought that one of her sons would leave the farm deliberately by enlisting in the army — especially the colonial army."

el tío Antonio - Uncle Anthony; **Castilla la Vieja** - old Castile; **Catalán (s)** - what the people of *Cataluña* are called; **los Pirineos** - Pyrenees Mountains; **Francia** - France.

"Well, I'm glad you did," says *Juan*.

His father shrugs his shoulders, "I made my decision, and here I am."

"Didn't you miss your family, just a little?" asks *Juan*.

"At first, the only thing I missed was the food, since my mother and sister were such good cooks. Other than that, all the new activities kept me so busy I didn't have time to think much about the family, my friends or the village," says his father.

"What did you have to do, *papá*? Was it hard work? You know, like on the farm?"

"When I got up in the morning, instead of farm chores, I had drill practice and marched a lot. Later in the day, I learned how to use my weapons and how to care for my musket and lance. Of course, I had to make sure my uniform was neat and my cot made up. Nothing was hard to do. It was just different.

"Before I became a soldier, men learned everything about their weapons and how to use them on their way to a battle."

"When a *pueblo* was attacked, I suppose every man found some kind of weapon and immediately went out to fight the enemy," suggested *Juana*.

El sargento Tico nods and continues, "Every day I was learning more about becoming a soldier, and at all times I had to look neat."

"Did someone look after you?" asks *Juan*.

"I should say not! But I learned how other soldiers kept their uniforms looking good."

"Tell me," said *Juan*, always ready to hear more.

"I wondered why I didn't see many men polishing their shoes or brushing their coats, like I did. One day I returned to the barracks earlier than usual and

found two soldiers counting their winnings from a
gambling game. They tossed *centavos* to a poor village
boy sitting on the floor polishing their shoes and the
buttons on their uniforms. I was a new recruit and
didn't have any money to pay a boy to shine mine.
And having just left the farm, I didn't know much
about gambling, so I had to spit and polish my own
boots and buttons," says his father.

    "Did you stay long at the barracks?" asks *Juan.*

It was only a few weeks, then we left *Barcelona.*"

    "Tell me about how you came to *Nueva España.*"

    "That's *otro cuento, hijo*," says his father.

    Smiling at her husband, *Juana* says, "I think
you'd better tell us, *José Joaquín.* You have prepared
our imaginations to go with you."

    Before *el sargento Tico* can begin, a black cloud
covers the sun, and a sudden wind picks up hats,
shawls and small things from the deck, blowing them
out to sea. Everyone on the crowded deck rises at
once and runs to the stairs to get out of the
approaching storm. Fortunately *Juana* has put *Juan's*
papers into her *maleta*, which she quickly picks up
and tucks under her arm. Then gathering up her
skirts, she hurries toward the stairway, with *Juan* and
her husband following closely behind — only to wait
because of those who have already reached the
opening.

    During the rest of the day and night, the storm
rages, and giant waves sweep across the top deck,

centavos - similar to (U.S.) pennies; **otro cuento, hijo** - another
story, son.

seeping onto the deck below. *Juana,* now over her seasickness, sloshes and stumbles to the aid of women with babies and small children. The stench of sickness is everywhere; no one cares that they have missed a meal. *Juan* lies moaning on his straw bed, barely able to keep from rolling off.

In the morning, the sea is calm and the world bright. Voyagers gradually make their way out of their gloomy quarters and find places on the sparkling sea-washed deck.

By noon, *el sargento Tico* feels up to continuing his adventure to the New World.

CHAPTER TEN

"BARCELONA TO CÁDIZ ON FOOT, MAYO DE 1767"

El Rey Carlos has ordered the *Compañía de
Fusileros de Montaña* to *La Habana, Cuba,* to serve as
harbor guards. Soon, we'll begin our march to the
port of *Cádiz* where we will board ship for the New
World. Is this the adventure I've wanted? I long to tell
my family and have them see me in my uniform before
I go.

It is so elegant compared to what I wore on the
farm. Will I ever forget those hand-me-downs from *mi
hermano, Antonio*? I never had anything new, until
now. The tough old work pants often came *de me
padre, a Antonio, hasta que yo los que usé.* Father
never spent a *peseta* for clothes if he didn't have to. I
had one good thing for church and *las fiestas* —
outgrown by *Antonio* — and a change of work clothes.

A soldier calls out, "Tents come down in ten
minutes!"

I hastily put on my white shirt with its high collar
and yellow stitching, fasten the black cravat around
my neck, stretch garters over my white stockings, and
secure the white buttons on my yellow waistcoat.
After pulling up my blue breeches, I give a last spit
and polish to my black leather shoes. Then I slip my
arms into the short blue coat with the yellow collar
and yellow stitching. Looking into a small mirror, I
place the blue woolen cap on my head at a jaunty
angle.

de mi padre, a Antonio, hasta que yo los que usé - from my
father, to Anthony, until I used them; **peseta** - Spanish money.

In minutes I've packed my duffel bag with army gear and a few things from home. I'm ready to go. Tents come down, and soldiers stand around waiting for their orders to march.

Kicking up clouds of dust, a donkey cart heads toward us. Some very excited folks are waving their arms and shouting from the back of the *carreta*. As it nears the parade ground, I recognize my family crowded behind *Antonio*.

"*José Joaquín,* we're here! We're here!"

Running out to meet the cart, I hug and kiss each one as I help them down. We find a place away from the crowd of soldiers' wives, sweethearts, relatives and manservants preparing to follow the troops.

"I was afraid we'd be on the march, and I wouldn't see you again."

"We heard only yesterday that your unit was leaving," says *Antonio*.

Then looking me over, he whistles, snaps his fingers, and says, *"!Qué guapo!"*

"We're here to say good-bye," says young *Pedro* with a broad smile.

"See what *mamá* brought you," says *María*.

My mother, much more cheerful than the last time I saw her, hands me packages of dried fruit and dried meat.

"Maybe these will come in handy along the way."

"*Muchísimas gracias, mamá,* I'm sure I'll need it!" I say — hugging her, and kissing both her cheeks. As I tuck the packages into my duffel bag, I hear shouting,

"¡Qué guapo!" - "How handsome!"; *Muchísimas gracias* - many thanks.

and see the mule train and wagons start to move down the road with our tents and supplies. I want to be with my family longer, but the drummer signals it is time to leave.

Mother kisses me and gives me a long *abrazo*. Then looking deeply into my eyes, she says, "*Vaya con Dios, mi hijo.*"

I watch as she slowly makes her way through the crowd to the waiting cart. Returning to the rest of the family, I embrace my brothers and sister for the last time.

Falling into line, *los fusileros* step to the beat of the drum. My brothers and sister, with two friends who have come from *Pueblo de Sedo*, march alongside for a short distance. I suddenly feel sad when they wave and turn back.

As I concentrate on following our leaders in their long blue coats with yellow collars and large gallooned hats, I put my family out of my mind. The flowing cockade of *don Augustine Callis's* hat waves in the breeze between the plumed hats of *el subteniente Pedro de Alberni* and *el teniente Fages*.

Behind us is *un desfile* of men and women, donkeys, carts, and old horses pulling overflowing wagons laden with bedding, pots and pans. One woman, riding on the top of overhanging bundles of bedclothes, keeps kicking her donkey's ribs to keep up. Each evening until we reach *Cádiz*, soldiers and their loved ones will be together. If there is room on

abrazo - hug; "*Vaya con Dios, mi hijo.*" - "Go with God, my son."; *Pueblo de Sedo* - Sergeant Tico's village; *subteniente* - second lieutenant; *teniente* - lieutenant; *un desfile* - a parade.

the ship, the manservants will accompany officers to
Nueva España; the rest will stay behind.

Hoy es el primero de mayo; a cool breeze sweeps
over us as we tramp the ancient stones laid by Roman
slaves. The centuries-old roads will lead us through
Madrid to the port of *Cádiz.*

Children run alongside as we march through
small *pueblos.* Some villagers stop what they are
doing to watch us; others scurry around, gathering up
and hiding their chickens and small animals. As we
pass through the narrow gateway of an ancient walled-
city, a young ragamuffin sends a mud ball over our
heads.

"He probably doesn't like the king," I hear someone say.

But I know it's because *mis compañeros* have a
chicken under each arm.

Lining the roadside at entrances to *los pueblos*
and gates to *las ciudades,* men and women of the
Beggars Guild cry out with outstretched arms. A
crippled soldier in a soiled uniform, dirty rags wrapped
around his shoeless feet, leans on crudely made
crutches. With his free hand he too reaches out.
Since I don't have much money, I can't give him
anything and try not to think about his plight. But as
our commander, *Callis,* passes by, he places a few
coins in the outstretched hand.

After marching for almost four weeks, we are at a
military campground in *Madrid.* I'm told that we have

Hoy es primero de mayo - Today is May first; ***las ciudades*** -
cities; ***mis compañeros*** - my comrades.

done well to cover three hundred fifty miles in that length of time. As usual, I can hardly wait to take off my shoes and release my tired and blistered feet — even though I've had the good luck to ride on one of the wagons for a while. I'll have to repair the soles of my shoes again tonight.

"Are the chickens ready for the pot?" asks the soldier doing the cooking for my group of ten men.

Since dried meat and corn are staples while on the march, we make our meals more interesting by picking up fresh food along the way. I have never heard of a soldier paying for it.

Laughter and singing to the accompaniment of a mandolin comes from the center of the field. Soldiers, with their wives and sweethearts, sit around a blazing campfire cooking their dinner; someone in the group caught a pig during the day.

Our two-days' rest has passed quickly. Revelers of the night before quietly pack up bedding and utensils and take them to the carts that will continue to follow us.

I'm still stumbling around on stiff legs and washing up in my metal bowl when we're called to breakfast.

I make a special effort to show up for *desayuno*, since it is the first of only two meals given to us each day — unless, of course, we unexpectedly find a snack along the way. Many times I have regretted having finished, within a week of leaving *Barcelona,* the packages of food mother gave me.

As I'm finishing my saucer of coffee, the boy drums muster. Expecting to hear the usual plan of the day, I'm completely taken off guard by a surprise announcement.

"Orders have been changed. *En vez de La Habana*, troops will be sent to *el puerto de Veracruz*. Reorganization will take place in *Sevilla*."

I don't know what to make of it.

One of the older soldiers says, in a lowered voice, "You know what this means, don't you?"

No one knows.

"We're going to fight *los indios* in *Nueva España*!"

Then another soldier speaks up, "We haven't been trained to fight *los indios*!"

"They're not even on our side of the world," says another, adding, "I don't even know what they look like."

After the brief announcement, we are dismissed to break camp.

The long march is tedious and we have many more miles to cover. I wish I were going to *Cádiz* in a cart pulled by a scarred-nose donkey wearing blinders.

We've reached *Sevilla* and I'm excited about the change of orders. All the men stand "at ease" according to rank. Since I'm in the last row, I have to peer around the men in front to see what is going on. Officers sitting at a table look over papers and talk among themselves. I recognize only the men who have come with us.

Don Augustín Callis stands and announces, "There will be two companies formed from this unit. They will

en vez de La Habana - insteadof Havana; *el puerto de Veracruz* - the port of Veracruz; *Sevilla* - a city in Spain; *Nueva España* - New Spain (Mexico).

be *los Voluntarios de Cataluña,* by order of *El Rey Carlos,* and serve in *Nueva España.*

"*Los Voluntarios* will be used as trouble shooters, going wherever a military force is needed until regular troops take over.

"*El teniente Pedro Fages* will head *la segunda compañía* and *el subteniente Pedro de Alberni* will head *la primera compañía.* You will be assigned to your company at roll call."

But what's this? Roll call is almost finished and I've not heard my name. Will I still go to *La Habana* after all? I look around and see a few others with questioning looks on their faces.

After a few minutes of further consultation, *don Augustín Callis* announces that the rest of the *Compañía de Fusileros de Montaña* will join with another infantry unit going to *Nueva España.* He says that we'll keep our original name.

I'm disappointed; I had hoped to be in one of the new companies of Volunteers.

Those of us who know anything at all about writing, labor over short notes to our families telling them of the change. As I write for a soldier who comes from a small *pueblo,* I ask, "Who is going to read this to your family?"

"My father will find someone, even if he has to go into *Barcelona.*"

We'll probably be at sea by the time the couriers deliver our letters.

los Voluntarios de Cataluña - Catalonian Volunteers.

"Route of the Volunteers from Barcelona"

CHAPTER ELEVEN

"OFF TO THE NEW WORLD, *EL 27 DE MAYO 1767*"

Los Voluntarios de Cataluña move out and my unit follows. It isn't long before we reach the outskirts of *Cádiz*. In the distance, I see many buildings clustered around the port and masts silhouetted against the sky.

I remember hearing sailors talk about *Cádiz* having been in use as a port since the year 1139, before *Cristo!* They said it was a rich port, mainly due to the duties and taxes collected from privately-owned ships coming with gold and silver from *Perú, Chile, Argentina,* and *Nueva España*.

One soldier who knows more than the rest of us says that *Cristóbal Colón* had left from *Cádiz* on his second voyage to the New World.

"I'll bet the government charged *el señor Colón* plenty the second voyage to make up for his using another port the first time," says a jester in the group.

Knowing well the practice of the king to tax everything possible, and frequently, everyone laughs.

"There's the Naval College," says another, pointing to a large white building at the water's edge.

"Would you look at that!" I say, as we get closer to the king's fleet of ships.

I thought the bay at *Barcelona* was busy, but I must admit the *galleones* and smaller ships anchored in front of the Naval College are an impressive sight. With the exception of a few traders, the fleet fills the bay. There is no time to stop and look; we won't be staying in *Cádiz*.

I'm unhappy about missing shore leave. I wanted

to see first-hand the entertainments the sailors spoke about at the quay. *El capitán* and *jefe de escuadra, don Juan Antonio de la Colina* of the *Juno*, gives orders to board immediately. He wants to take advantage of the tide. The *San Juan*, our supply ship, waits nearby for the signal to depart.

As soon as the last troops climb aboard the crowded deck of the *Juno*, *el Padre* begins his prayers for the safety of the voyage, the ship, and for all on board. As he utters the last words, all rise from their knees and *don Juan Colina* signals to prepare to leave. When the shot rings out, the ship's officer shouts for the sailors to haul in the longboats, raise the anchors, and set sails. Soldiers keep out of the way of the chanting sailors as they go about their work. Judging from the activity and rhythmic chants from the supply ship, they too heard the shot.

Among barrels full of greens and fruit stowed between pens of animals and coops of chickens, most of us somehow find places at the railing. Soldiers and sailors wave and shout their last good-byes to weeping wives and sweethearts.

As loved-ones continue to wave handkerchiefs and blow kisses at the departing ships, the *Juno* and *San Juan* slowly maneuver between *galleons* and vessels bearing foreign names.   I know the adventure of my lifetime has really begun when the harbor disappears from view and we are in open sea.

El capitán and **jefe de esquadra, don Juan Antonio de la Colina** of the **Juno** - Captain and head of the squadron, Mr. John Anthony Colina of the Juno (a ship).

CHAPTER TWELVE

"LAND HO! AFTER THREE MONTHS"

A stiff breeze presses the billowing canvases into
full-blown sails as the man at the tiller bears in a
southerly direction. From the inlet, the *San Juan* and
the *Juno* smoothly sail the ninety-four kilometers to
Gibraltar, then in a southwesterly direction into open
sea.

Before Gibraltar disappears from view, a lookout
high in the rigging peers over the sea for pirate ships
which often lurk near the strait. Mainly African and
English ships wait for *los galleones* returning from the
New World with cargoes of gold and silver. I hear him
call out, "All clear; no ships in sight!"

The soldier who knows about *Cristóbal Colón*
wonders if we are following his route. The rest of us
don't care, as we struggle to get our sea legs, or hang
our heads over the railing retching up our last meal.
All the while, seasoned sailors mimic us and laugh.

We're only three days out when a storm that has
been gathering strength for an hour attacks the *Juno*
and the *San Juan* with deliberate fury. Mountainous
waves crash over the decks, confining us below like
prisoners. Sailors taking turns at the tiller lash
themselves to spars so they don't become shark food.
Sometimes I think I hear a cow bawling in the howling
wind.

As rain sheets across the bow and the *Juno* dips
and rolls for three wretched days and nights, I recall
conversations between sailors at the quay. Until now,
I hadn't realized how their nonchalant manner of
speaking hid tremendous fear.

When the *Juno* seems most at the mercy of giant-
size waves and deep troughs, murmurings of men in
prayer fill the air. Everyone knows the ship will
capsize if its ballast of sand and gravel begins to shift,
or sea water flows inside. It is then that the captain
brings out a figure of the ship's patron saint, and *el
Padre* on board hears confessions from fearful soldiers
and sailors who struggle to reach him while the ship
rolls and pitches.

Gracias a Dios, the fear-filled, nauseating days
and nights have past and sailors are bringing out fresh
sails to repair the rigging. Emerging from the hatch,
feeling weak and shaky, I make my way to a sunny
spot on deck where I make myself as comfortable as
possible. Looking across the whitecaps to the horizon,
I see the sails of the *San Juan* — and overhead, a blue,
cloudless sky. All is well.

Each day passes in the same way: much gambling, grumbling and daydreaming. I wager coins,
sometimes even buttons, on cockroach races.
Cheering and hollering fills the air as I keep pushing
my roach into line as it runs helter-skelter. Amid
shouts of "It's about time!" a sailor brings roosters on
deck for cockfights.

Many nights, I join sunburned soldiers and sailors
in singing and dancing. Those with instruments bring
out their *mandolinas*, violins, whistles and pipes and
play while the rest of us dance and sing. Whoever
doesn't know some song or dance, stomps his feet and
claps in time to the music. We sing and dance until
the musicians are exhausted.

Other nights, sailors take turns telling stories.

Even the skeptical ones among us gather around to hear the mysterious tales.

One sailor in particular likes to tell of seeing crewless ghost ships suddenly appearing, bearing names of galleons that vanished centuries ago — then, in full sail, they disappear. Another tells of a rudderless ship pitching through heavy seas with tattered sails flapping in the wind. A skeleton holds the useless tiller in his bony hand. Another, in dead-seriousness, tells of sailors who had been lost at sea coming to sit with him during his night watch.

One story often repeated, and sworn to be absolutely true, is about how whales and dolphins have led sailors to safety when their ships have been tossed off course in raging storms.

The somber storytellers slip away while their captive audience sits quietly for some minutes — not wishing to awake from their astonishment at such mysteries. I find space where I can lie back and watch twinkling stars — and think about ghost ships and friendly sea animals. Did those things really happen?

We're in the doldrums and neither the *San Juan* in the distance, nor the *Juno*, makes headway. I amuse myself the best I can, often just sitting on the hard deck and daydreaming or dozing. There is no wind or breeze, day or night. Many take this opportunity to get their hair cut by a sailor who is good at it.

I should have gotten my hair cut. The boredom and heat makes me impatient; the slightest disagreement turns into a fight. I narrowly escape time in the brig when the captain breaks up my fight with a soldier who stepped on my drying clothes. But I'm not the only one; everyone seems to be "on edge."

If it were not for the sun appearing in the morning, and the moon at night, my sense of time would disappear in the motionless days. But suddenly a miracle is happening before my eyes. Two birds fly out of nowhere and perch on a spar. The sailors say that it is definitely a rare occurrence and an omen of good luck. I wonder if the birds came from an island over the horizon.

Mis compañeros and I, bored with games, lean on the rail of the ship, watching dolphins play in the clear water. Soon a large appreciative audience hangs over the railing as more men join us. We are all hoping for a breeze to spring up.

"Do you wonder what your family is doing?" one soldier asks, while staring at the smooth, glassy sea and playful dolphins — not really speaking to anyone in particular.

"I suppose *mi esposa* is with her mother and living on her mother's pension," answers another, shrugging a shoulder. "That's the way it was when I left."

"Why even think about it? We came here to get away from all that — remember?" says another.

"Well, if *Consuelo's* husband hadn't caught me serenading his wife, I wouldn't even be here," sighs a third.

The thought of this long-haired, unshaven creature in a sweaty shirt being a "ladies man" and having to join the army to get away from an irate husband conjures up such a comical picture that we double over howling with laughter.

mis compañeros - my companions; *mi esposa* - my wife

Finding a slender strip of shade, I sit down to think about the question *el compañero* asked. Do I wonder what my family is doing now? And what about my village, *Pueblo de Sedo?* Am I sorry I left? Knowing I am having the adventure I've always wanted, I am completely satisfied to have fond memories.

It will be *hermano Antonio's* birthday soon. *Mamá* will make a large pan of *paella*. My mouth waters thinking about *arroz con pollo* cooked slowly with *langostinos o camarones y guisantes*, fresh from the garden.

María's gift will be a big bunch of flowers with a few sprigs from the flowering fruit trees tucked into the vase. She will set the flowers at *Antonio's* place at the table. I remember *María* put white pear blossoms in the bouquet on my special day. *Pedro* will bring in the plates and pull out the chairs for everyone.

With the aroma of garlic and olive oil cooking in the galley, I have to stretch my imagination to recall the sweet perfume of orange blossoms which fill the air around *Pueblo de Sedo* this time of year. I suppose old men of the village still discuss all the important matters of *el pueblo* in *la plaza*. I could always depend on seeing them each day — dressed in their black suits and hats, sitting at the same tables, sipping coffee and spirits.

I feel a shoe poking into my ribs; I must have fallen asleep thinking about home. Sailors push and

el compañero - "buddy", pal, companion; *paella* (pie-aye-ya)-a Spanish rice dish (see Notes); *arroz con pollo* - rice with chicken; *langostinos o camarones y guisantes* - lobster or shrimp and fresh peas.

shout at me to get out of the way as they rush to put
up more sails. Soldiers spread out their arms to dry
their shirts in the fresh breeze. *El capitán Colina*,
happy that his ship is moving, is on deck smiling and
talking.

"We should drop anchor at *Veracruz* within a week
or two of our expected arrival. Of course, that depends
on this wind keeping up."

We all cheer on hearing what we think is good
news.

I can't wait for the voyage to be over. Maybe then I
can get better meals; the ship's cooks have no
imagination. We mostly have *galletas, sopa* and
beans. Beans and more beans, cooked with dried pig
meat or whatever the cook can find. I miss the
vegetables and fruit that covered the deck when we left
Cádiz. In spite of eating it up as fast as we could,
much of the fresh food spoiled in the hot sun.

Every other day, the cook puts out sour oranges,
sweet oranges and lemons for us. I'm surprised there
are any left. He says these will keep us "from the
scurvy."

In pens on deck, there remain a few chickens, a
pig, two sheep, and a goat.

One of the soldiers has been in charge of feeding
the animals throughout the journey and anxiously
approaches the pens each day, fearful of finding an
animal missing. He was especially saddened when the
young cow was butchered to give us meat and soup for

galletas - crackers, hardtack; *sopa* - soup; *scurvy* - a disease
sailors suffered due to lack of fresh fruit and vegetables. It was
often fatal. Many times ships came into port with few men alive
due to the illness.

several dinners.

He's the first to tie down larger animals and get smaller ones into the hold before a storm. We all stand around anticipating the fun when he pushes the goat down the hatch. She always stops at the opening and puts up a good fight before he wrestles her down the ladder.

Although we had sighted one or two islands, the captain said there was no reason to stop, but this one coming into sight is different.

Shouts of "*Viva*" fill the air when *el capitán Colina* tells us the island has freshwater springs and we can get off the ship. Suddenly the heavy moodiness of the past few weeks disappears.

While anchors drop and sailors lower the longboats, we dash to our trunks and bundle up our dirty clothes to be washed in the fresh water. I have to wait my turn since we have to share our places in the boats with empty water barrels. I can tell when the first boatload of men arrives at the spring by the sounds of laughter, shouts and splashing that carries to the ship.

My turn finally comes to join *mis ruidosos compañeros*. A bar of soap suddenly flies through the air in my direction. Thank goodness, someone remembered to bring it.

Each time barrels are filled, a few of us reluctantly return to the ship. When it is my turn, I get into the boat with *platanos y fruto del arbol del pan* wrapped inside my wet bundle of clothes. Arriving at the ship, I

"*Viva*" - Hooray!; ***mis ruidosos compañeros*** - my boisterous, noisy pals or companions; ***platanos y fruto del arbol del pan*** - bananas and bread fruit (see Notes).

climb up the ladder and see that sailors have thrown buckets of water over the deck, trying to clean it up somewhat. Wet pants and shirts hang everywhere. After pushing a little, I make space on the railing to hang my wet clothes.

Some of the men had waded out from shore and cast nets. I don't recognize the kinds of fish they brought in, but there is plenty for everyone.

El capitán increases our small ration of *vino* and brings out hard candies. Today has been wonderful and everyone is happy. To make it complete, the captain assures us we can expect to sight *Veracruz* soon.

"Of course, that depends on the wind keeping up," he says.

"*Viva.*"

It has been a week of unrelenting humid heat. None of us can sleep. *Mis compañeros* and I are at the rail watching the sun rapidly brighten the sky. Keeping our sights on the horizon where we think *Veracruz* might be, I point to a thin dark line that seems to go on forever. At the same time, a sailor sings out that *Veracruz* has been sighted. There is shouting, dancing, and joking — so great is the relief that the long voyage is almost over.

I have been marking the days since we left *Cádiz*. The *Juno* sailed *el 27 de mayo 1767*. It is now *agosto*. We have been at sea for three months!

I wonder what *Nueva España* is like.

CHAPTER THIRTEEN

"VERACRUZ, AGOSTO DE 1767"

El Capitán Colina, looking toward *Veracruz*, remarks, "We'll have quite a reception. Everyone in *el pueblo* looks forward to our arrival. They've seen our sails. Listen!"

I still see only the dark line on the horizon, but as I listen closely, I make out the faint sound of bells coming from the direction of the port. A half hour later, nearer the shore, I hear bells tolling loudly and see small figures moving along the beach.

My elation at going ashore is suddenly checked when I hear the captain say, "I hope *Veracruz* is free of sickness. After sailing for three months, it is devastating news to hear that an epidemic of *el sarampión*, scarlet fever, or another plague has struck *el pueblo.*"

I can't help wondering what will happen if everyone in the town is sick. Will the captain find another port? I hope so.

The wind drops a little, slowing our progress into the bay. This gives all of us plenty of time to get into our uniforms. Groans rise from all sides as soldiers push their arms into hot jackets, stockings, and tight shoes for the first time in many weeks.

Now in uniform, my gear packed and at my side, I wait at the rail. Men in small boats have come out to meet the ship. *El capitán* questions the men, then satisfied there is no illness on shore, I hear him bark orders to the crew to lower the longboats and prepare to disembark.

el sarampión - measles

Los Voluntarios de Cataluña y los Fusileros de Montaña are ready to leave the *Juno* and the *San Juan* for the last time. None of us expect to return to *España*. After all, there's gold, silver and land waiting for us in the New World.

While waiting our turn to go ashore, a soldier says, "I hope this is the last time I hear an anchor drop into the sea, have to sail on a ship, or struggle into a rowboat!"

Like *el capitán* said, many people line the shore waiting to greet us. I happily step out of the boat onto the beach only to find that my legs behave like two pieces of rubber. Several children standing close by hold their hands over their faces and peer through spread fingers, politely holding back giggles. *Los indios* stop sweeping sand from a stone walkway to watch.

"I'm glad to see I have company," I remark to a soldier next to me who is also trying to find his "land legs." I must admit it is amusing to see dignified soldiers stumbling along the beach.

El capitán Colina is surrounded by men who have come to greet him — the *alcalde*, other town officials, and men in blue military uniforms. The men in blue are couriers for *el virrey*; whenever a ship is expected, they come to *Veracruz* from *la Ciudad de Méjico* carrying sealed pouches of mail for the king. The couriers exchange their pouches for others bearing the king's seal, to be taken to *el virrey*. No time is lost in the exchange; without further delay, the men in blue salute, mount their horses, and gallop off. Mail for the

alcalde - similar to a mayor (see Notes); **el virrey** - viceroy, kings representative.

king is immediately put aboard ship and locked in a secure place.

I hadn't thought how the arrival of the *San Juan* and the *Juno* would be of such importance to the colonists. They are anxious to talk with us, and have many questions. Most of them have lived in *Veracruz* for several generations. Newer arrivals think of *España* as "home," and each time a ship arrives from *Cádiz*, they hope to find that long awaited letter in the pouch.

While transfer of mail is taking place, another man from the ship with a mail pouch nervously waits while colonists begin to surround him. He's looking for the postmaster of *Veracruz*. Since the colonists have been so patient, and the postmaster is nowhere in sight, the officer opens the big leather bag, calls out names, and begins distributing packages and letters.

I see a lone man trudging along the beach toward us. When he reaches the group, I discover by his apologies that he is the postmaster. Groans from the group follow his mumbled excuse that he had trouble finding the keys to lock the post office. Since he is, after all, an important person in *Veracruz*, no one says aloud what everyone is thinking — that he'd had two-weeks and all morning to prepare for the ships' arrival!

Colonists, who have been waiting for years to hear from family or friends in Spain, don't leave until the pouch is turned upside down and shaken.

We camp in humid *Veracruz* just long enough to get rid of our sea legs. A few sick soldiers are recovering nicely and will be able to march, including two who had ignored the cook's admonition to eat fruit whenever it was served, or "get the scurvy."

"All's well"

CHAPTER FOURTEEN

JUAN BECOMES A DRUMMER BOY

"*Papá,* says *Juan,* "are we going to be in an another bad storm?"

"I can't say that we won't be getting more storms, *hijo.* It's winter and the rainy season; sometimes the wind blows hard from the north and west. Already you are wearing your jacket during the daytime. We'll just have to wait and see what each day brings. Did you hear the rain against the side of the ship last night?"

"You mean it rained last night? I didn't hear it," says *Juan.*

"You slept right through it. That's the sign of a good sailor," says *Juan's* mother.

El sargento Tico, wanting to reassure his son, says, "One thing I know, our captain and crew have taken the *San Carlos* to *Presidio San Francisco* before this voyage; I'm sure they can bring us through any kind of weather."

Juana, pulling her shawl more closely around her shoulders, changes the subject and says, "I thought it was interesting that you remembered the orange blossoms around your village. Certain flowers bring back fond memories for me, too."

"Mmmm, I can't remember any flowers that make me remember things. Which flowers remind you of something, *mamá?*" asks *Juan.*

Juana thinks a moment, then says, "Whenever I think about sunflowers, I think about my mother's garden. Roses are special, too. They remind me of your father first coming to call at *la abuela Carrera's* house before we were married."

An older boy has made his way through the crowd and stops in front of the *Ticos*.

"*Perdóneme, señor Tico. Juan* and I must practice."

"Oh, I forgot!" says *Juan*.

"Practice what?" asks his father, surprised that he hadn't been consulted about the new activity, whatever it is.

"It happened yesterday, *papá*. I thought you knew. A soldier asked *José Martínez* and me if we would be drummers. The soldier said he has two drums, and we could learn the routines on board ship. Then we'll be ready when we get to *el presidio*."

"Why, that's wonderful," says *Juan's* mother.

Then turning to her husband, she says, "Don't you think so, *José Joaquín*?"

Still a little miffed that he hadn't been asked first about his six-year-old son becoming a drummer for the soldiers, he hesitates. After they wait a while for his answer, he agrees it's all right.

"Run along, *hijo*."

Everyone on deck knows that drum practice has begun. Children of all ages gather around to watch the two proud boys learn how to summon soldiers to various duties. Eventually the boys take turns drumming the announcement of meals.

Drum lessons have changed *Juan's* life on board ship. Everyone speaks to him. He doesn't spend as much time with his parents as before, but each day there is the writing lesson and his father's story. *José*

Perdóneme, señor - excuse me, sir.

Martínez, now *un buen amigo,* is happy to be included when *el sargento Tico* continues the story of his experiences as a soldier.

After *Juan* and his father tell *José* what has happened so far, *Juan* says, "What happened next, *papá?*"

"From *Veracruz,* on the coast, we had a long march ahead of us through all kinds of weather in mountains and on flat land. I had never been in such high mountains before. The march in *España* from *Barcelona* to *Cádiz* was on bumpy old roads. They had been made by the conquering Romans, and used by chariots, farm wagons, horseback riders, and troops going to war centuries before our units marched over them. But these were not like that at all.

"We had to be on the lookout for snakes and wild animals as we followed our native guides over the rough, narrow way."

un buen amigo - a good friend.

"Drummer Boys"

CHAPTER FIFTEEN

"TWO MONTHS TO *TEPIC*"

Anxious to get away from the tropical coast, we march energetically for many miles. Then I notice we're trudging, and breathing becomes difficult in the cool mountain mist. An officer passes the word along that we have reached five thousand feet above the sea, and are making ten miles less each day than on the march to *Cádiz*.

We are always glad to stop at shelters made by *los indios*, but this one is especially welcome because of the rain. One of our men has had trouble breathing since we left the coast and is not doing well; *los indios* have been carrying him on a litter for several days.

During the night he dies. At daybreak, three men take up shovels and begin to dig his muddy grave. We wrap him well in a blanket, and as all the soldiers stand with bowed heads, he is lowered into the earth. *El Padre*, traveling with us, places a cross in the pile of dirt and stones covering the gravesite. It strikes me for the first time that it could be any one of us, for many reasons, resting under that cross.

I wonder if our commander will write to the soldier's family in Spain and let them know that he died. I'm glad when we begin our march again.

Just when I feel I can't slog through the rough paths any longer — stumbling over rocks, pushing tree branches out of my face, and fording cold mountain streams — we round a bend and the path widens. Suddenly I'm walking easily. We've come to a plateau, leaving the mountain canyons behind.

It's almost dusk by the time we reach the first

pueblo. A soldier calls out to a man leaning against a wall.

"*¿Cómo se llama este pueblo?*"

"*Puebla.*"

"*¿Cómo?*"

"*¡Puebla!*"

Marching on, out of sight of the *pueblo's* steeple and walls, we halt at an old military campsite, and proceed to set up tents. The cooks have no trouble finding chickens for dinner. Carts full of vegetables, fruits and squawking fowl have followed us since *Puebla.* After our rations of dried corn, water and jerky all the way from *Veracruz,* anything else will be a treat.

Since the *pueblo* looked interesting when we passed it, I call out to *mis tres compañeros* from the *Juno,* "What do you say, fellas? Let's go back to *Puebla* tomorrow."

"*Sí, sí, como no.*"

"That's fine with me," says another.

The third nods his head.

I return to my tent. After repairing my shoes for another day's use, I fall exhausted onto my cot and think about all the happenings since arriving at *Veracruz* — finally drifting off to sleep thinking about tomorrow.

Up early as usual, my three friends and I get permits to leave camp. Luckily, a driver with an empty *carreta* is returning to *Puebla,* saving us a long walk. On reaching the edge of town, we give the driver a few

Cómo se llama este pueblo? - What's the name of this village?; **Puebla** - name of village; **¿Como?** - What?; **"Sí, sí, como no."** - "Yes, yes, of course."

coins we've collected between the four of us, and continue on foot.

At *el mercado, los indios* are setting up their wares, laughing, and talking in their native language while proping up canvases and blankets to keep off the morning mist. Beautiful girls arrange the displays while their mothers and grandmothers, with black shawls draped around their heads, sit close by keeping an eye on them. The ladies have yarns and threads laid out, covered by a brightly striped piece of cloth until they are ready to begin their needlework for the day.

An older woman comes over to us and asks in Spanish, "Are you looking for something in particular?"

"*No, señora.*"

I explain that we just came to browse.

Accustomed to soldiers without coins in their pockets who just want to look at the pretty girls, she wastes no more time with us and returns to her yarns. Although the four of us would like to meet the girls, and say so among ourselves, we continue on, looking at the colorful displays. It isn't long before the market is full of laughter and talking between friends and vendors.

A native boy calls us to come over to his table. He pulls out some material and insists we feel the soft white fabric.

"It is a speciality of *la misión*; it makes good underwear."

If I were alone, I would have the soft material made up for myself.

Behind a display of dishes and vases on the ground, a vendor tells us to come and look closer.

"*Los hacemos como los chinos.*"

"Who told you?" I ask, doubting that anyone so far from the sea would know.

"*Ah, señor*, they were on our coasts centuries ago, and many of our people have been copying the beautiful things ever since."

I go over to tables of colorful peppers sectioned off with garlic and onions of different sizes and colors. Gray root vegetables separated with bright orange-colored carrots, their green ferns hanging over the side, fill a table. One vendor entices me to buy when she reaches out with her hands full of purple plums and green pears.

Enough of the market! I turn around and find that *mis compañeros* are nowhere in sight. They probably were bored and went off when I, a farmer's boy, came to look at the vegetables.

Walking up the main street, looking down passageways on each side, I hope to see the familiar uniforms. Two women, sitting at the entrance to one of the houses making lace, stop talking and look up when I ask if they've seen three soldiers come this way.

"*No, señor*, no one in uniform has passed by."

My heart suddenly misses a beat as I come upon a familiar sight farther on. I could be in a town square anywhere in *Cataluña*. There's the church at the end; there are *las oficinas del pueblo*; everything is in its place. I stand there amazed, until a cat surprises me when it rubs against my leg, bringing me back to the present.

Los hacemos como los chinos - We make them like the Chinese (make them). **las oficinas del pueblo** - the town offices.

Although I don't expect to find my boisterous *compañeros* in the church, I walk up the steps and enter the foyer, just to make sure.

From somewhere in the dimly-lighted interior, a voice says, "*Señor,* may I help you?"

Startled, I peer into the shadows and see a *Padre* coming toward me.

"I'm looking for three soldiers from camp who came to town with me. They've disappeared, and I thought they might have come here."

El Padre smiles.

"That would be quite unusual. We seldom see anyone in uniform, especially those passing through. Of course there are exceptions. Please, come inside."

Since my eyes have now become accustomed to the darkened interior, I can see three other people, none of them soldiers.

Since the man is so friendly, I say, "*Gracias, Padre,*" and continue on into the church, kneel, look around at the pictures on the wall and admire the large gold altar surrounded by life-size religious figures. How like the chapel in *Pueblo de Sedo!* As I rise to leave, *el Padre* is immediately at my side.

"Was it your unit that passed by *el pueblo* last evening?"

"*Sí, Padre.*"

"Do you have time to talk?" he asks.

Since *mis compañeros* have disappeared, I have lots of time.

"*Sí, Padre, como no.*"

El Padre takes me by the arm and leads me to a

"**Sí, Padre, como no.**"- "Yes, of course, Father."

chair with wide strips of leather for back and seat. Then he drags another chair from the shadows and places it across from me.

"Do you know that your campsite is on land that was used by armies over two centuries ago?" he asks.

"No," I answer.

"This is the first time I've been here."

El Padre continues, "When the Spanish *conquistador, Hernán Cortez,* came through here two hundred fifty years ago with his troops, he camped in the fields where your unit is today. He was on his way to conquer the ruler of the *aztecas* at *Tenochtitlán,* now called *la Ciudad de Méjico.*

"I believe I heard our commander say that will be our next encampment."

El Padre nods his head and continues, "*Cortez* first made friends with local natives. *Los indios* treated the soldiers very well in all ways. They provided food, and gave important information about surrounding tribes. Then they made the Spanish soldiers more comfortable by replacing their heavy armor with lightweight vests from animal skins and heavy quilted cotton; both materials resisted the natives' arrows.

"*Los indios* made friends with *los españoles;* they saw an opportunity to conquer neighboring tribes with the help of weapons much louder and more deadly than their slingshots and arrows. And above all, these men were like gods on horseback, animals *los indios* had never seen before. It would make their enemies

conquistador, Hernán Cortez - the conqueror, Hernando Cortez; **aztecas** - Aztecs.

think that an ancient prophecy was taking place before their eyes, and they would lay down their weapons."

He stops a moment, "I hope I'm not boring you. You see, I seldom have an opportunity to talk with soldiers about God or man."

I assure him that he's not boring me, and say, "Please, go on."

El Padre continues, "Of course, the chiefs who joined forces with *Cortez* didn't realize that once they conquered their enemies, *Cortez* and his followers would make slaves of them all.

"Eventually it happened, and since the conquest, *los indios* have had very hard times. Many men were separated from their families, taken from the villages and sent to work in the mines."

"*Padre*, why are you taking the side of *los indios? Aren't *la gente de razón más importante?*"

El Padre looks surprised. Then turning abruptly, says, "Excuse me, I must ring the bell, it's time for prayers. Perhaps we can talk another time. Please come again."

I nod and thank him, but as I leave I have the feeling that he purposely avoided answering my question.

As I leave the church, I see two men in familiar uniforms disappear around the corner. When I catch up, I ask, "Where did you go? You disappeared from the *mercado* in a hurry."

"Sorry about that. I guess you didn't hear us say

la gente de razón más importante - the Spanish more important (see Notes).

that we were going further into *el pueblo*. But I can tell you, there's nothing to do here! I'm ready to go back to camp and get into a game."

"And another thing," says the other soldier, frowning, "I haven't seen any gold or silver lying around. I wonder where *Antonio Pol* got that story he told us when we enlisted."

"We can't go back yet, we're missing one," I remind them.

We look everywhere for our missing *compañero*.

"Maybe he went back," I offer.

But back at camp, he does not answer roll call. A search party is sent out. When the company of soldiers returns without him, I begin to think about when and where I saw him the last time. It was at the *mercado,* and he seemed determined to meet one of the girls.

In the morning when the company of soldiers return the second time from *Puebla* without the soldier, our commander calls him a deserter and gives orders to carry on to *la Ciudad de Méjico*.

Once again we tramp slowly through mountains. Adding to the already slow pace, we carry ten soldiers on litters who are sick with diarrhea and weakened from the still unfamiliar high altitude. Reaching our campsite near the Capital, a hospital is set up immediately. Before we finish pitching the large tents, I see our commander heading in the direction of *la ciudad*.

One of the soldiers who sees him leaving, says,

mercado - market; ***la Ciudad de Méjico*** - Mexico City.

"He's going to report to *el virrey marqués de Croix*. It looks like we can relax. First he will report on the condition of the troops, who has died, how many are sick, and who has deserted. Then there will be parties with *el virrey* and his friends for a least three days."

It has been five days since we arrived and our commander has finally returned. This has been the longest rest I've had since leaving the coast, and I'm getting used to it.

We're told that in the morning we will break camp. I have repaired my shoes so many times since they were issued new in *Veracruz*, I wonder if they will make it to *Tepic*.

Marching through the mountains of *Nayarit*, we're again threading our way through narrow passes, but this time on well-used trails through dense woods. My steps get lighter with each mile as we go down the mountain.

It has taken two months to cross *Nueva España a pie*.

el virrey marqués de Croix - Viceroy Marqués de Croix; **el virrey** - the viceroy; **a pie** - on foot.

"El Padre explains about Cortez"

CHAPTER SIXTEEN

"MEETING *JUANA* FOR THE FIRST TIME, *OCTUBRE DE 1767*"

Our barracks are on the outskirts of *Tepíc viejo*. After three days' rest, I have a free day and start out for *el pueblo*. I'm going alone this time, since I can't trust *mis compañeros* to stay with me.

After a long walk, I finally come to a narrow street that I hope will lead into the oldest part of the village. From being in *Puebla*, I learned that the church spire will lead me to *la plaza*.

Approaching a group of women wringing their hands and shaking their heads, I say, "*Buenos dias, señoras.*"

They are so absorbed in conversation that instead of a greeting, I hear, "*¡Qué barbaridad!*" *¡Qué lástima!*"

Reaching *la plaza,* I am shocked; the sight before me explains why the women are so disturbed. Soldiers stand guard over haggard priests who cover the cobblestone paving in the center of the *plaza*. I walk to a bench where an old man in soldier's uniform sits watching the strange sight. He moves his cane, and motions for me to sit.

"What is going on here?" I ask.

"I heard about it a few days ago, and was as surprised as you. Jesuit priests from *Sonora* and *Baja California* are being brought to *Tepíc* to await deportation — king's orders!"

Tepíc viejo - old Tepic; "*¡Qué barbaridad! Qué lástima!*" - How barbaric; What a pity; **Sonora and Baja California** - (see Map).

"I don't know where these places are, but what could these men have done to deserve such treatment and to be sent away with very little more than what they're wearing? Are they going back to *España?*" I wonder aloud.

"You speak like someone who has just arrived here," says the soldier.

"*Sí, sí,* my unit came three days ago."

The old soldier nods his head. "You were probably somewhere in the mountains when the news came out that all Jesuit priests have to leave not only *España* but all Spanish colonies. The king thinks they have too much power and own too much land."

I can't add anything to our conversation; I don't know what it all means. As I sit beside the old soldier and continue to watch, women arrive carrying food and water for the disheveled priests. They pour water into basins they've brought and set them before the grateful men who patiently wait their turn to wash their hands and faces.

"*Buenos días, señora Carrera; buenos días, señorita Juana,*" says the old soldier to a woman carrying a bowl, and to the young girl walking with her. *La señora Carrera* returns the greeting, and *Juana* politely looks toward him, and says, "*Buenos días, señor Galindo.*"

I jump up and say, "*Buenos días, señora.* Allow me to introduce myself. *José Joaquín Tico* from *Cataluña.* My unit has just arrived."

I forget that I, like the guards, am in military

Buenos días, señora Carrera - good day (hello) Mrs. Carrera;
Buenos días, señorita Juana - good day (hello) Miss Juana.

uniform, and say, "Here, let me carry the bowl, it must be heavy."

La señora Carrera hesitates for a moment, then she hands me the bowl with *un jarro de agua* inside. I follow her and *Juana*, placing the bowl where she directs in front of the men. Although I offer to do it, she pours the water into the bowl, leaving some in the pitcher for the men to drink.

As the three of us walk back to the old soldier, *la señora Carrera* says, "Everyone in *Tepíc* is shocked that *los Padres* are treated so badly. Imagine, putting heartless soldiers to guard the priests! They are treated like common criminals! And if it weren't for the women taking pity on them, the poor men would starve to death!"

Mother and daughter say good-bye and walk toward *la Calle de Soldado,* after gathering up the empty bowl and pitcher.

It has been almost two weeks since I came to *el pueblo,* and on entering *la plaza* I find things have not changed: *El señor Galindo* sits on the same bench, while soldiers guard a new group of Jesuit priests.

un jarro de agua - a pitcher of water.

"Food and Water"

CHAPTER SEVENTEEN

JUAN QUESTIONS, *PAPA* EXPLAINS

"Did you see *mi mamá* and *la abuela* again?" asks *Juan.*

"Yes, many times, but we never had time to talk."

"Didn't you want to talk to them?" asks *Juan.*

"Of course, *hijo,* but the time was never right. There was too much to do. Remember, when I saw your mother we were taking food and water to the Jesuits, and at the barracks I was preparing to go away."

"It's hard to believe *mi mamá* was ever my age," says *Juan.* "Did you think you would marry her?"

"Oh, goodness no," says his father.

"There was a big difference in our ages then. I think your father was about eighteen, and I must have been nine-years-old," explains *Juana.*

"But I remember *mi madre* saying that your father was very polite. She usually didn't like *los soldados* because they were so rude."

José Joaquín says to his wife, "I asked the old soldier, el *señor Galindo,* if he knew your family. He said he remembered your father well; they had been guards together at the port of *San Blas.*"

"Weren't you supposed to go somewhere else, *papá?*"

"Yes, our troops came to fight *los indios,* but first we had to get to the battlefield. It was *el señor Galindo* who told me where I would be going, and when. He seemed to know about everything that was going on."

mi madre - my mother; **mi mamá** - my mama, my mother.

"At Sea"

CHAPTER EIGHTEEN

"HASTA LUEGO, JOSE JOAQUIN"

I'm talking with *el señor Galindo* when I see *la señora Carrera* and *Juana* coming up *la Calle de Soldado*. This time, *una muchacha* accompanies them carrying the bowl and pitcher, while *la señora Carrera* and *Juana* carry bowls of stew.

Going to their side, I offer to help. With a smile, la *señora Carrera* hands me her warm bowl of stew for the hungry men, then she takes the other bowl from *Juana*.

"Since I haven't seen you here for two weeks, I thought perhaps your *Compañía* had left *Tepic*," says *la señora Carrera*.

We walk together to the center of *la plaza*, and as usual *los Padres* are very grateful. *La señora Carrera* tells them that she will be back later with more food and water.

I return to the bench to talk with *el señor Galindo*.

"How long will you be in *Tepic*?" asks the old soldier.

"I didn't expect to be here this long. The government is using all ships to take the Jesuits away. I'm not sure when we'll leave."

"Once the ships are available," he asks, "Where are you going?"

"My company of *fusileros* are supposed to go to a place called *Sonora* and fight *los indios*. I must admit, I really don't know what it's all about."

"I've heard a lot about *Sonora* in recent months," says the old soldier. "Military officers are making great preparations for an attack. The natives have resisted all attempts of the *gente de razón* to settle there; they don't want to lose their homes and land, or be captured and used as slave labor in the mines — like *los indios* in the south. I fought in the desert of *Sonora* years ago against the same strong and clever tribes."

Pausing for a moment, *el señor Galindo* says, "*Señor Tico*, perhaps this may be important to you: I over-heard an officer talking about the *Sonora* campaign. He said there is a change in plans on how the troops will leave for *Guaymas* — that's the name of the port in which ships anchor when they reach *Sonora*."

The old soldier continues, "*El coronel Domingo Elizondo* is in charge of the attack and has recruited as many troops as possible throughout *Nueva España*. He plans to divide up the troops: Some of your *Compañía de Fusileros* and *los Voluntarios de Cataluña* will march through the mountains and up the coast to *Guaymas*; others will go by ship."

"I wonder why he's dividing us up?"

"Probably because of the season; it's winter here and bad storms often keep the ships from sailing," says el *señor Galindo*. "I'm sure *el señor Elizondo* is very unhappy. He has to please the viceroy who is impatient with delays. For perfect timing, all troops should have been aboard ships as soon as they arrived in *Tepic*. Then the Jesuit problem came up.

"Transporting all men by ship earlier in the season would have assured their making an early rendezvous in *Guaymas*. The weather is now the important factor. Troops marching to *Guaymas* have a better chance of

gente de razón - the Spaniards; *fusileros* - infantrymen.

getting through from here in spite of the weather. If the weather holds, the ships will be there first. Otherwise, the ships must contend with squalls and high winds on the Sea of *Cortez.*"

I wish he hadn't continued when he adds, "It's not uncommon for ships to be blown off course, sometimes for weeks at a time. And of course, we are always saddened when we hear that a ship has disappeared. But don't worry, that doesn't happen often. Captains usually find some secure haven in order to save their own lives and those of the crews."

Leaving *el señor Galindo,* I walk back to the barracks thinking about the stormy days and nights at sea when the *Juno* pitched and tossed on our way to *Veracruz.*

Back in camp, there is a great deal of activity. Preparations for our leaving go on daily. It is now the third week since I've seen *el señor Galindo, la señora Carrera* and *Juana.* I finally get away to say good-bye to my friends.

Arriving at *la plaza,* I am happy to see the old soldier is there, and the ladies of the *pueblo* are coming as usual with food and drink for the priests. However, there are fewer Jesuits in the square.

As *la señora Carrera, Juana, la muchacha* and I distribute food, *la señora Carrera* says, "We won't be coming to *la plaza* after today. This is the last group of Jesuits to be deported."

After the gaunt and exhausted men finish eating, the soldiers lead them to *carretas* for their trip down the mountain to *San Blas* where a ship will take them away.

La señora Carrera says, "Thank you for helping. If it hadn't been for the poor priests, we might never have met. Now that our Christian mission to provide food for them is over, and ships are available for the soldiers, I suppose you will be leaving. Please visit us whenever you are in *Tepíc.*"

I thank her for the invitation, kiss the back of *Juana's* hand, and turn to go.

El señor Galindo calls to me, "Have you heard how you are going to *Sonora?*"

"Soldiers began marching up the coast yesterday. I'll be going by ship."

"Have a safe voyage, *señor Tico.* I hope to see you again soon," says *la señora Carrera.*

She and *Juana* continue toward *la Calle de Soldado.* Then I hear a voice calling me. It's *Juana.*

"*Hasta luego, señor José Joaquín. Vaya con Dios.*"

"*Hasta luego, señor José Joaquín. Vaya con Dios.*" - "*See you later (or good-bye), Mr. Joseph Joaquín. Go with God.*"

CHAPTER NINETEEN

"AT *SONORA*"

For several days after my return to the barracks, we're still packing food, water, tents, and clothing into trunks, heavy bags and barrels. As fast as the animals have packs loaded on their backs, and the *carretas* are filled, the parade of mules, horses and oxen makes its slow trip down the mountain trail to the port.

Mis dos compañeros and I stay together. Our plan is to go on the same ship. But when we reach *San Blas*, my orders are to board the *San Carlos*. *Mis compañeros* board another *paquebote*, the *Laurentana*.

I'm surprised to find that the *San Carlos* is a new ship.

"Built just last year; she's got good ballast," says a sailor. "We're still looking for leaks."

I am amazed at how such a small ship can carry so many men. I hope this is a short voyage.

The *San Carlos* sets out bravely. Sailors are on deck night and day trimming sails, but strong gales blow the ship off course in spite of their efforts. After struggling against the winds for some days, the captain sails the *San Carlos* back to the safety of *San Blas*.

While we wait for favorable winds, supplies are brought aboard and leaks in the hull are caulked.

It has been one hundred five days since we set sails the first time from *San Blas*, and the *San Carlos* is finally entering the port at *Guaymas*. The *Laurentana* is already at anchor.

Mis compañeros shout and wave as the *San Carlos* makes its way into the bay. Over the soldiers' noisy greeting, a sailor on the *Laurantana* calls out, "We were blown back to *Mazatlán* and only came in last week."

He points to the shore where soldiers are running back and forth waving and shouting, and says, "It took them only fifty-eight days to get here."

Everyone is happy. We've all come through alive.

As sailors row us to shore, I ask, "Which way is better, being seasick and at the mercy of winds and tides for one hundred and five days, or marching fifty-eight days in all kinds of weather, through the muddy, insect-ridden, rough, steep trails of the *Nayarit* Mountains?"

"All I know," says the soldier beside me, "I'm a soldier and I march. If I'd wanted to sail, I would have become a sailor!"

"Maybe so," says another, "But we carried more and heavier weapons, as well as many supplies on the ship."

"Oh, I wouldn't say that makes coming by ship necessarily better," argues another. "Mule trains are slow and reliable. They carry and pull weapons and supplies, too. But more importantly, they don't roll around in a storm; they just turn their backsides to it. I definitely prefer that."

We all try to think why one way is better than the other, and in the end decide it doesn't matter, especially if the weather is good.

As I stumble out of the boat, I hear from all sides, "Where have you been? We've been waiting for you for over two months."

Needed rest in our makeshift headquarters appears to be over. Mules and horses are arriving daily from two nearby *ranchos*. Who would believe that foot soldiers would become cavalry units!

I thought *Sonora* would be a small place and the troops would charge the enemy in battle formation. I soon learn that *Sonora* covers a huge area of rough desert covered with cactus, bushes, and low-growing shrubs around half-hidden rocks, for hundreds of miles. And there is no enemy in sight.

It begins to rain turning the hard desert into a sea of mud and soft sand. We could never march in this; the horses and mules are barely able to get through. Scouts warn us to watch for flash floods.

Now in a period of dry weather, we finally begin to chase *los indios*. *El coronel Elizando* decides that we should round up the *Seri, Piatos, Yaqui, Pima, Suaqui, and Sibubapa* — notorious warriors who have evaded conquest by the military and the Jesuit missionaries for two centuries.

There are one thousand one hundred soldiers coming from all directions, attempting to drive warriors into a trap in the mountains. In spite of the broad sweep by the troops, most of the natives manage to get away, escaping inside the *Cerro Prieto* Mountains into *los cajones* they have used as hideaways before. The *coronel* is discouraged.

los cajones - boxes; hideaways in the mountain; generally composed of stone slabs, forming a box-like structure.

Suddenly our hope revives. *El teniente Alberni* and his scouts have discovered native chieftains camping with their families in *el Cajón de Palma*, a hideaway deep in the mountains. Scouts say it will be easy to take them captive. They are sitting around a fire without weapons at their sides. *El coronel Elizando* orders troops to take positions inside *el cajon* and be ready to attack at daybreak.

The first units move slowly and quietly forward in the light of a full moon. *Los Voluntarios de Cataluña* camp alongside a group of friendly natives who have been aiding the troops.

Our group makes its way slowly to a ledge above a unit from *Cataluña*. We are careful not to alert the natives at their bonfire by crackling twigs underfoot or stumbling over loose rocks. Dark shadows from the canyon sides hide soldiers already in position by the time our unit, *los Fusileros de Montaña*, catches up.

Feeling our way along the canyon wall, we take our positions. Gradually our eyes become accustomed to the darkness, and we can see the troops around us hidden away in crevices and shadows.

Suddenly I am aware that one of the *fusileros*, standing only a few feet from me, is silently raising his musket and taking careful aim across the canyon. If I try to stop him, I will alert the chieftains and doom the attack. Watching helplessly, I realize he has mistaken the friendly natives, who have been aiding us, for the enemy. He thinks the soldiers are in danger. I pray that by some miracle, he won't shoot.

The blast from the musket-shot reverberates throughout the canyon. Startled *fusileros* open fire, hitting friendly natives. The chieftains at the fire scramble for their weapons.

Instead of the planned capture by surprise attack, we are fighting the enemy hand to hand. *Los indios* get away through dark canyons, leaving their wives and children, who are rounded up and questioned.

After finding out where the warriors have fled, and angry with the troops who spoiled the attack, *el coronel Elizondo* orders us to chase them. Four hundred of us ride sixty-three miles in fifty-two hours over rough terrain with only a little water left in our canteens; supply wagons are far behind. Our mules and horses are very tired. After the long hard ride, we are called back, having been unsuccessful in finding the natives.

In a skirmish out in the open, we kill a warrior before he gets away to a nearby forest of tall cactus. Then one of our men makes the mistake of dismounting to pick up his fallen lance. When he stoops to retrieve his weapon, a well-aimed arrow flies out from the cactus forest. I hear him cry out as the arrow head finds its mark through his neck; he falls forward onto the ground — his hand still reaching for the lance.

After the Indians have disappeared, we drape the dead soldier over his horse. Solemnly we ride back to our makeshift camp and plan for a desert burial.

"The Sonoran Desert"

CHAPTER TWENTY

"1779 — CALL ME *'EL SARGENTO TICO'*"

For three years, skirmishes and battles have been going on against the native chieftains and their men. Our commander, *Domingo Elizondo*, is frustrated that the native warriors are not subdued, even with his great numbers of soldiers from *Nueva España, los Voluntarios de Cataluña*, and *los Fusileros de Montaña*, plus additional troops from *segunda compañía* who returned from their tour of duty in *Alta California* with *el teniente Pedro Fages* and *el Padre Junípero Serra*. Clever chieftains continue to evade capture and find refuge within the mountains.

El coronel Elizondo decides to cease fighting in *Sonora* when he hears reports of the *Apaches* from the north attacking settlers in *ranchos* and *pueblos* in districts nearby. He sends out a few troops to protect settlers from the native raiders. We all know the war isn't over, but there are fewer chieftains and warriors to harass the ranchers already in *Sonora*.

My company, *los Fusileros de Montaña*, is half the size it was when we started. During these three years, several soldiers retired and we have had many casualties. Some died of wounds from arrows, others from bouts of sickness.

I personally know of six deserters. They were weary of chasing the natives, fearful of possible sneak attacks, and disgusted to find scorpions in their boots every morning. They were tired of the difficult rides through the rough desert, and constant vigilance for poisonous snakes. They complained that there was not enough meat and vegetables to liven dull meals.

My unit of *fusileros* is merging with that of
el teniente Alberni, his troops also having suffered
losses. Now that I am in *Alberni's primera compañia
de los Voluntarios de Cataluña,* does this mean a raise
to sergeant for me?

After almost four years in *Sonora,* we are
beginning our march through the *Nayarit* Mountains
toward *la Ciudad de Méjico* and army headquarters in
Guadalajara.

For such an elite group as the Volunteers, my life
is as unpleasant as that of any soldier who serves in
the king's colonial army. Life is especially difficult in
frontier posts, where I am assigned most of the time.
Soldiers' quarters are often crude and uncomfortable,
and meals are simple fare, mainly due to shortages.

Everyone here is worried about the drought;
workers have not been able to grow a crop this year
because of it. There are only dregs of grain in the
storage bins, and emergency supplies are slow in
coming so far into the interior. The latest word is that
by next week there will be flour and other supplies
arriving.

My uniform is old and threadbare in many places;
I'm too cold in winter and too hot in summer. And
worst of all, my shoes are worn out. When I
complained to *el Padre,* he said conditions throughout
Nueva España were bad due to Spain not sending
supplies and money.

There is barely enough ammunition for those of us

stationed at the mission as temporary *escoltas*. The scarcity of gunsmiths and the poor condition of my flintlock, the same one I've had since I enlisted in *Barcelona*, make it risky to shoot the old musket.

As I am straightening up my side of the barracks, I hear hoofbeats pounding toward the mission. Grabbing my gun, I run out only to find a perspiring courier already dismounted and lifting a pouch from his saddle.

After the courier leaves, and *el Padre* has sorted the mail, he calls me into his office. Among the mission letters is one addressed to me with an official insignia. I ask *el Padre* to open it.

It is notification that I am now a sergeant and my new assignment is *San Blas*. I am to leave as soon as possible. What good fortune! I've finally gotten a raise in rank and I am also going to reenter civilization.

In all the years I've been in *Nueva España*, being a guard at the port of *San Blas* is the best assignment I've had. I like my barracks and the meals are better. I like my new, lighter weight uniform and new shoes. The tropical weather and the usual delay in getting paid are my only complaints.

Perhaps I can get away to visit *Tepic*. I don't suppose the old soldier is still around, and *Juana* is probably married by this time. I wonder if *la señora Carrera* still lives on *la Calle de Soldado*.

escoltas - mission guards sent from the nearest *presidio* for a period of time. Soldiers who served at missions were said to have had an easier life than those at *presidios*.

"Back to San Blas"

CHAPTER TWENTY-ONE

"*TEPIC 1780* — I TAKE *JUANA* FOR MY BRIDE"

"This is the best assignment I've ever had," I tell the soldier on guard duty with me.

"Oh, is that so?" he asks.

"*Si, si.* In the interior, there were many problems and sometimes too much excitement. In drought years, there was a scarcity of food, and supplies were slow in arriving. At any time, we could expect Indians from the north coming to raid ranches and villages. When we weren't guarding colonists and missions, we had to go to the mines and subdue uprisings by los indios.

"Life is easy here; it's like being on vacation. We have only to guard a peaceful, busy port and watch ships being built."

"You will soon get tired of it. Ships come and go; mule trains come and go. Always the same old thing," he says.

"You must admit that it's a great place to catch up on gossip from returning sailors. And what about *Tepic?* When soldiers return to *San Blas*, we always hear about the latest parties, problems, and whatever else goes on at the barracks."

"That's true, but the news is old. As for me, I'd just as soon go into el pueblo and look at pretty girls. Why should I bother my head about things I don't understand or can't change?"

"I know what you mean about things you can't change. Look over there at the goods piled up at the warehouse. There aren't enough ships to take away the pelts and hides brought in from all the *misiones*," I say.

The guard chimes in, "And that's just one of the problems. We need more ships for *memorias*, too. Ships should be taking the orders to *presidios* more often than twice a year. Well, that's what I think.

"And speaking of *memorias*, I heard that the king is going to require them to go to *Madrid* for approval. That will probably take another year."

"You mean those colonists camping out in desolate *Alta California* will have to wait even longer, and then they may only get a portion of their order?" I ask.

"I'm afraid so," says the guard. "The government is cutting down on expenses, regardless of how it affects the colonists."

"Just one shipment a year! I can't believe it! I hate to think how the colonists will live. They are completely dependent on goods sent from *España* and *Nueva España*. I hear they have shortages of almost everything now: nails, iron, tools, chocolate, coffee, spices and such things. These are what make life bearable when you are in a frontier post. I know, I've lived in such places," I say.

Shrugging his shoulders, the guard says, "See, I can't do anything about those problems and neither can you."

Then he says, "What a smell! You can always tell when the wind changes. It's the tallow and poorly tanned pelts and hides. Just one more thing we can't do anything about."

"It seems they stay in the warehouses too long. What's to become of them?" I ask the guard.

"They will go to *la Ciudad de Méjico*, into ships

going to *las Filipinas*, or even to *Nueva Inglaterra*.
Eventually all of it is sold," he answers.

"May I ask you a personal question?" I say to the
guard.

"If it isn't too personal," he answers.

"Do you have *moho* on your things?" It's on my
leather trunk."

"Everyone has it in *San Blas*; you'll get used to it.
Just keep wiping it off," he replies.

A mule train comes down from *Tepic*. As it passes
through the gates, whiffs of chocolate, spices, and
sweaty animals hang in the air. According to the bill of
lading, the heavy packs the mules carry are full of
foodstuffs, clothing, tools for a *presidio*, and religious
pictures for one of the *misiones*. The *paquebote San
Antonio* rides at anchor waiting for the supplies.

While we watch the activity from our posts, the
guard says, "Did you know that many captains are not
experienced sailors? Privileged men apply to the
Spanish government to have ships and are called
"captains," but other men on board are the
experienced officers and know how to sail the vessels."

He continues, "I talked with an old sailor who
used to be on ships going back and forth from *España*
to the New World. He said the Spanish *armada* was
defeated by *las ingleses* in 1588 because the captains
didn't know much about fighting at sea, or how to
manuever their ships into the right positions to shoot
at the enemy, nor how to avoid them."

"I heard they lost because their ships were too
old," I say.

Nueva Inglaterra - New England; *el moho* - mildew;
paquebote - packet boat. It carried mail, goods, and passengers;
armada - fleet of warships; *las ingleses* - the English.

The guard and I find all sorts of rumors and gossip to talk about as we stand guard at *San Blas*.

I'm finally free to go to *Tepīc* and am looking forward to seeing it again after many years' absence. A *carreta* driver returning to the barracks takes me to a place I had not been before.

El señor Galindo spoke about the buildings in this newer part of *el pueblo*, but I never found time to see them. Now that I'm here, they seem familiar; his descriptions were very good. This must be military headquarters, with the Spanish flag flying overhead, where he said *memorias* were approved.

Los Padres in Franciscan robes are entering and leaving another building. It must be the headquarters of the Pious Fund. El *señor Galindo* said the missionaries were always asking for money to supply religious objects and special things for churches and missionaries in *Alta California.*

The old soldier said one store charged a lot for everything because the owner had a monopoly. He wasn't sure whether the owner's uncle in the Spanish government got a special import license for his nephew, or if the merchant paid someone else to get it for him.

Here is a busy store. Soldiers and missionaries are shopping with lists in their hands. I wonder if, after thirteen years, it is the same one *el señor Galindo* spoke about.

As I step inside, I'm greeted by a confusion of

Pious Fund (English) - (see Notes.)

smells from spices, chocolate, tobacco, coffee beans, leather boots and saddles.

To one side there are a few religious relics, incense and *candeleros*. On the other side, there is fabric of fine silk and all sorts of sewing supplies.

In the center of the room are hammers, anvils, barrels of nails, and a plow. There are machetes, saws, hammers, and other metal tools, all very expensive, as *el señor Galindo* said.

Tucked in a corner are a few herbs, and varieties of seeds. This must be the place, since stores in *pueblos* I know don't usually sell such a mixture of items in one place.

Suddenly I hear church bells. Can it be time for lunch and *siesta*? I'm barely able to get out before the shopkeeper closes the door, slams down the shades, and locks the iron grillwork.

Remembering an overhanging branch heavy with apricots on my way into town, I go back to pick some of the ripe fruit. With my hands full, I return to a bench in the shade to have an apricot lunch. Unfortunately, bees are attracted by the fruit and buzz around my head, so I decide to move on.

Sauntering through the quiet *pueblo*, I recognize a street that leads into a familiar part of *Tepic*. The old town is like I remembered it — *adobe* houses, a few stores, an outdoor vegetable market, all closed until later in the day. The spire of the cathedral is not far away.

As I approach the square, I think about the sight

candeleros - candlesticks.

that greeted me when I came to *la plaza* the first time. I couldn't see the colorful stone paving; it had been covered with Jesuit priests. And women with food and water were saving the disheveled, sad men from starvation.

Still deep in thought, I enter *la plaza* and am startled to see an old soldier dozing on a bench, with his chin resting on his chest and a cane at his side. Could it be *el señor Galindo* after all these years?

Walking to the bench, I wait for him to awaken. Sensing my presence, he slowly opens his eyes. When the old soldier lifts his head, I can see he is not my old friend.

"*Perdóneme, señor*," I say. "I didn't mean to startle you. I thought you might be a soldier I met here many years ago on this same bench. His name was *el señor Galindo*."

"Ah, you knew my old friend," he says, making room on the bench. "I'm sorry to tell you that he died four years ago. How did you happen to know him?"

I tell him about the Jesuits, and how I helped *la señora Carrera*, and that *el señor Galindo* told me about *Sonora*, where I was going to fight *los indios*.

The soldier listens and nods occasionally, then says, "*Es muy amable* of you to come back to visit your friends. I'm sure *la señora Carrera* will be glad to see you. If you haven't been here for thirteen years, you won't recognize *Juana*. They still live on *la Calle de Soldado*, and there is plenty of time this afternoon to visit. The *mercado* opens soon; you can buy flowers there to take with you."

Es muy amable - it is very gracious, or kind.

I hadn't thought about visiting right away, but when the old soldier says *la señora Carrera* would be glad to see me, tells me where to buy flowers, and where to find her house, I decide I had better go this afternoon.

I'm fortunate to have money in my pocket to buy anything. Since our meals at the barracks are part of our pay, and they have been better than usual, the amount I get *es muy poco*. I wait around until the flower stall opens, then buy a few half-open pink roses. Returning to the bench, I thank the soldier, and say, "*Adiós, señor.*"

Starting up *la Calle de Soldado* with the bouquet of roses in my hand, I soon find I'm *delante de la casa*. Suddenly I feel like a timid child as I look up at the closed door. Coming to my senses, I go up the two steps, shift the bouquet to my left hand and knock.

A sleepy *muchacha* opens the door, and I ask if *la señora Carrera* is in. Before she has a chance to turn around, a lady's voice asks, "Who is it, *María?*"

Then a lovely *señorita* appears in the doorway. Can this be *Juana?* For a moment we stand looking at one another. I collect my wits and manage to ask, "Is that you, *señorita Juana?*"

"*Sí, señor.* Who are you?"

"*El sargento José Joaquín Tico.* I helped you and your mother carry food to the priests in *la plaza* many years ago."

"Who is there, *Juana?*" a woman calls out.

"Come and see!" says *Juana*. "It is *el sargento Tico.*"

---

es muy poco - it is very little; **Adiós señor** - Goodbye, Mister; **delante de la casa** - in front of the house.

As *la señora Carrera* comes to the door, I hear her say, "I should know that name, it sounds familiar."

Before *Juana* has a chance to say more, her mother appears in the doorway. After searching my face, she begins to smile in recognition and says, "*Señor Tico,* please come in."

I hand her the pink roses. She thanks me and hands the flowers to her daughter. *Juana* returns with them nicely arranged in a vase and sets it as a centerpiece on the dining table in the center of the room.

La señora Carrera says, "*José Joaquín,* you have been gone a long time. I'm sorry I didn't recognize you at first. Are you stationed nearby, or are you just passing through *Tepic* again?"

"I'm stationed at *San Blas.* This is the first time I could get away to come to *Tepic.* An old soldier at *la plaza* told me the sad news that *el señor Galindo* died. He suggested that I come to call on you and *Juana.* I hope you don't mind."

"I am so glad you came. We shared an horrendous experience at *la plaza* that year. It was a dreadful time. I can't remember anything like it before or since."

La señora Carrera motions me to a chair at the table set for four. She calls the *muchacha* and tells her to bring the food that's been prepared.

Perhaps it is the aroma of thick chocolate, or some inner voice telling him *empanaditas de calabaza* are being served, that brings a young man into the room to join us at the table. He walks directly to *la señora*

empanaditas de calabaza - small foldover pastries with a pumpkin filling (see Notes).

Carrera and holds her chair for her.

La señora Carrera says, "This is *Juana's* cousin, *Jaime*, who spends a lot of time here. *Jaime*, I want you to meet the soldier that helped me during the crisis with the *Jesuits* many years ago."

"*Con mucho gusto en conocerle,*" we say to each other.

"It is our custom *a dar un paseo* around *la plaza* when we finish eating. Will you join us *sargento Tico?*" asks *la señora Carrera.*

"I would like that," I answer. Of course I wouldn't miss it for anything. Lovely *Juana* has been sitting quietly listening to her mother and me; perhaps we will have an opportunity to get acquainted on the *paseo.*

My fondest hope comes true when we arrive at *la plaza.*

La señora Carrera says, "Perhaps you and *Juana* would like to walk with the others. I'm sure she would like to know what you have been doing all these years."

Then looking at her nephew, she says, "*Jaime*, come with me. I believe I see *la señora Fernández* at the church steps talking with *el Padre.*"

Juana and I join other couples who are talking and laughing together under the watchful eye of some family member. The custom is the same in *Cataluña.* Most everyone tries to respect the wishes of parents. No couple is supposed to be left alone until they marry. I always thought the custom came about from fear of what the community would say about a family

con mucho gusto en conocerle - glad to meet you; **a dar un paseo** - to take a walk.

that didn't watch its daughters and to keep them from
harm. Brothers are always taught to be friends with
their sisters and take care of them wherever they are.
Probably because *Juana* does not have a brother, her
cousin, *Jaime*, looks after her.

While *la señora Carrera* and *Jaime* join friends at
the other end of *la plaza*, *Juana* and I stroll quietly.

"*Sargento Tico*, the roses you brought are lovely,"
begins *Juana*. "Roses are my favorite of all flowers."

"It is my pleasure, *señorita Carrera*."

I am not sure what to say next. The last time we
met, she was a child following her mother to *la plaza*.

I blurt out, "It has been thirteen years since we
last met, and you have become a beautiful lady in that
time."

Juana, looking away, says, "*Gracias, sargento
Tico*."

"Is some lucky fellow bringing you flowers?"

"No," says *Juana*.

"May I come and see you again?"

"I'd like that," she replies.

"Call me *José Joaquín*," I say, "and I would like to
call you *Juana*."

"I would like that, too," she replies with a smile.

It is *enero de* 1780. *Juana* and I have been seeing
each other as often as I can get away. It is obvious to
all that we are in love. When we tell her mother that
we would like to marry, she kisses both of us and says
how happy she is to hear the news. The three of us

enero de 1780 - January 1780.

and *el Padre* settle on a date; *la señora Carrera* begins to make arrangements for our wedding.

El Padre posts the banns and announces our marriage more than three times before the wedding day. *Juana* asks her best friend, *Graciela*, to be a witness to our exchange of vows, and I ask a soldier from *San Blas*.

It is our wedding day and I'm nervous. After being single for so long, to get married is a very big step. But seeing my lovely bride calms me a little.

As we go through the solemn ceremony, considering thoughtfully what *el Padre* says — although he has already spoken to us in length about what marriage means — I can tell that *Juana* is nervous, too. We rise from our knees to receive the final blessing.

La señora Carrera, Juana's relatives, the soldier from *San Blas, Graciela* and *Jaime* follow as my bride and I leave the church and make our way over the cobblestones down *la Calle de Soldado*, catching flowers thrown by neighbors.

Our wedding *fiesta* at *la señora Carrera's* lasts a week. Her relatives live several miles from *Tepic* and enjoy being together as long as possible whenever someone has a birthday, wedding, baptism or funeral. But unfortunately, I have to return to my post. After only two days, I take my bride down the mountain to live in *San Blas*.

"Soldier on Guard Duty"

CHAPTER TWENTY-TWO

"1790 — I SAIL TO *NOOTKA*; *JUAN* IS BORN"

Juana and I have had the good fortune to be together at *San Blas* for nine years, when — in *diciembre de 1789* — I hear a rumor that orders have been issued for *la primera compañía*, under *el teniente Alberni*, to refortify a military base at *Nootka*.

"Does that mean you will be going?" asks *Juana*. "I never thought that our lives would change. You have been a guard here in *San Blas* since we were married."

A few weeks later, I hear that *el teniente Alberni* almost has the necessary recruits to make up his company of soldiers. Some say we will sail in *febrero*. *Juana* and I are beginning to accept my leaving and make plans.

"When you go to *Nootka*, I will go back to *mamá* in *Tepíc*," says *Juana*.

There won't be any children going with her. *Tres niñas* died at birth.

I am to remain on guard duty at the port until a replacement comes and *la primera compañía de los Voluntarios* are ready to board ship. The port is busier than usual as preparations are made. Mule trains come in with goods each day; three ships are being loaded with cannons and seemingly endless supplies.

"I've learned more about why we're going to *Nootka*," I say to the guard.

"This is an important expedition since three ships

diciembre - December; **febrero** - February; **tres niñas** - three girls.

are going. Troops will be left at *Nootka* while ships continue north as far as *Isla Unalaska* to officially reclaim territory in the far north."

"Years ago, didn't Spanish explorers claim the north territory as far as their ships could sail?"

"That's true, but the land was never occupied after the captains claimed each landing in the name of the king, planted a flag and a cross, then fired their cannon four times. Now we need to return and make sure that other countries know the land belongs to Spain."

I tell the guard that Spain is concerned because Russians are seeking to establish more fur trading colonies, especially with *los indios de Nootka*. "It seems like a race to see who gets to *Nootka* first — Russia or Spain," I add.

"What are you going to do at *Nootka*?" asks the guard. "I didn't know there was anything there."

"There's an old fort that's been neglected; I understand we'll rebuild it. And since there are *indios*, I'll no doubt have guard duty. But once cannons are in place, I don't expect we'll have trouble from them."

It is only *tres de enero*, and we are ready to sail. I'm assigned to the frigate *La Concepción*, commanded by *don Francisco Eliza*, an experienced captain in charge of explorations. On the second ship, the *San Carlos*, *Salvador Fidalgo* is *el capitán*. The third ship is *La Princesa Real* under *Manuel Quimper*.

Isla Unalaska - Alaska; **los indios de Nootka** - the Nootka Indians; **tres de enero** - January 3rd; **Nootka** - (see Locations).

This will be my first voyage on *el océano Pacifico*. I expect we will have cold winds and a strong current against us all the way. We've been supplied clothes for cold weather.

I must admit I have mixed feelings about sailing, since I become seasick on rough seas. And of course, I will miss *Juana* very much. But the thought of going with the troops is very exciting after so many years in *San Blas*.

Except for fog and a few squalls, the voyage to *Nootka* is uneventful and monotonous considering the time of year. Within sight of land most of the way, we stop several times to get more wood and supplies at *presidios* and *misiones*.

It is a cold springtime when we arrive. Coming from tropical *San Blas*, we feel the cold more than usual. *Alberni*, who is in charge at the fort, orders everyone to work. Sailors bring twenty cannons from the ships and place them around the grounds. I am working hard with a group of soldiers clearing brush and trees from around ruins of the old fortification.

It doesn't take long to see improvement. Where before there were scattered bricks and timber, there is now a rebuilt fort. Although sailors and soldiers grumble at having to work with picks and shovels, we admit the hard work doesn't hurt us. And we can't complain that there is not enough to do!

At the cove, *Alberni* works along with us as we construct barracks, sheds, and storehouses, dig wells, and plant vegetable gardens. There should be enough food for all of us, as well as for passengers and crew of any ship that might stop in need of supplies. While we're busy with work on land, one ship is exploring the strait nearby, another sails northward, and the third is anchored at the cove as added protection for the fort.

Our first spring and fall was a success, and we had few problems. But this winter has brought only trouble. I can't remember feeling so badly and have a severe cold. *Alberni* says if I'm not better soon, he will send me to the hospital at *Presidio Monterey* to recover.

Another week, and I'm not feeling any better. Now I have *pulmonia*, and have succumbed to an outbreak of dysentery. Along with thirty-two other sick soldiers, I'll be leaving for *Alta California* and *Presidio Monterey* as soon as *La Princesa* returns to the cove.

At the hospital, *los médicos* say I am lucky to be alive. Two soldiers from the ship are now buried in the mission cemetery.

After being in the hospital a month, I am feeling much stronger and am waiting for a ship to take me and others back to *Nootka*. Three of us get horses and ride from *Presidio Monterey* to *Presidio San Francisco* through forest, rivers and grazing land filled with cattle. After being confined for such a long time, it is wonderful to get away from the *presidio* hospital.

Our outing is now over and *La Princesa* has arrived. Except for three soldiers who are still too sick to travel, the rest of us board ship and look forward to returning to *Nootka*.

It is *abril de 1791*, and the vegetable garden, which proved to be such a success last year, is almost planted. I am waiting to collect more seeds from a newly arrived ship from *San Blas* when a soldier just off the ship comes up to me with an envelope. It's a letter from *Jaime, Juana's* cousin.

In a quiet moment, I read it and can hardly believe the good news. He writes that *Juana* and I have a healthy baby boy, *Juan Nepomucino*. He was born *octubre* last year. Counting the months, I find that he is now six-months-old.

The troops use the occasion of *Juan's* birth to celebrate with *una fiesta*. The timing is also right for a party because many of us have been given other assignments and we expect our replacements soon.

Alberni has delegated much authority to me since my return from the hospital. I have responsibilites of a lieutenant, but so far I have not been given the honor of such a rank. I am doing the work of two former officers; one died from pneumonia and the other was swept overboard during a storm at sea. Replacements have been appointed but they don't want to come!

I'm leaving *Nootka* and have been waiting to hear if I'm getting a raise in rank. Several others have applied for promotions because of their being in the *Nootka* expedition. *El capitán Eliza* receives a letter telling him that his application for "Captain of the Spanish Navy" is being considered. *El teniente Alberni's* application to become a lieutenant-colonel in the regular military, as well as Captain of the Volunteers, is approved.

At the same time that *Alberni* applied for himself, he also applied for officer rank for me, but there has been no reply. I remain *el primero sargento de la primera compañia de los Voluntarios de Cataluña.* I'm disappointed and indignant. Everyone agrees that I have an excellent military record.

Replacements have arrived at *Nootka.* I am returning to *Nueva España* on the same ship I came on, *La Concepción.* After spending a few days in the *Presidio Monterey* harbor to pick up passengers and goods, the ship sails on to headquarters in *Guadalajara.*

I can get to *Tepic* easily from *Guadalajara* and am looking forward to seeing my son; but I soon discover that my commander, *Alberni,* is sending me to frontiers very far from either *San Blas* or *Tepic.*

Five years later, I'm transferred back to *Tepic* and finally meet my son.

CHAPTER TWENTY-THREE

THE SAN CARLOS ENTERS THE BAY

"You know the rest of the story, *Juan*," says his father.

"You came back to *Tepíc* to get *mamá* and me, and here we are sailing to *Presidio San Francisco*," replies *Juan*.

As *José Joaquín*, *Juan* and *Juana* stand at the rail, *el sargento Tico* says, "It won't be long before we'll see the seven islands, then we're only thirty miles to the entrance of the bay. The captain says we'll probably have to anchor near one of *las islas de Farrollon* for the night."

"Why can't we just go on to the *presidio*?" asks *Juana*, eager to get off the ship.

"It's something about currents, wind and fog. When the weather is clear and the tide is right, the ship sails in," says *José Joaquín*. "If those things are not right, we have to wait."

The islands come into sight late in the afternoon, and the captain anchors at one of them. It's a long, wakeful night; all are excited at the thought of stepping onto land once more. But just after midnight, a heavy fog engulfs the ship and a moan fills the thick misty air.

Passengers, eager to get to their destination, find that time and place suddenly do not exist; efforts to see land or sky or sea are met by walls of thick fog. Their disappointment continues for two more days. They are so close to getting off the *San Carlos*, out of the stinking "prison" below deck and the filth above.

Then suddenly the fog blows east, toward shore.

The captain gives orders to lift anchors at noon. He hopes for clear weather by the time the ship arrives at the entrance to the bay. His luck holds; the wind continues and the *San Carlos* sails in with the tide.

Everyone, even small children, realize the importance of this moment and stand quietly, looking all around as the ship passes slowly through the channel. The *San Carlos*, slipping noiselessly between the hillsides is suddenly engulfed by fog once again.

All who stand near the rail are startled when they see a balsa canoe appearing out of the mist below. Curious natives paddle as close to the *San Carlos* as possible. The voyagers and *los indios* have a good look at each other.

It is *el primer día de abril 1796*, and the *San Carlos* has safely delivered its cargo of soldiers and their families to the *presidio*.

Juana, staring at the bluffs in front of her, sees this as the gateway to her future. During the past three months, she has been looking forward to getting off the ship. But now, hearing the anchors hit the water, the chants of the sailors, and the flap of the sails as they come down, she wishes time would stop. *Juana* realizes that she is really entering into her new life; it isn't a dream any longer. She thinks about her mother who won't be helping to care for her new grandchild, due to arrive in a few months.

El sargento Tico is a happy man and looks forward to his new life in *Alta California*. He thinks about the large, open pastures he saw during his ride from

primer día de abril - first day of April.

Presidio Monterey to *Presidio San Francisco* after his illness — just before he returned to *Nootka*: about the king's promise of land to soldiers. He hopes that this new assignment will finally bring him a raise in rank.

Juan and his friend, *José Martínez*, stand near the railing and drum for all to disembark. One by one, the long procession of passengers with their many bags and bundles begin to leave the ship. Crying babies and frightened children cling to sailors who carry them down the ladder to anxious mothers waiting in the longboat.

Delay caused by storms and fog now behind them, and the disembarkation from the *San Carlos* accomplished safely, the new arrivals to *Presidio San Francisco* sigh with relief as the sailors row toward shore.

At this moment, no one wants to think about what challenges might be ahead.

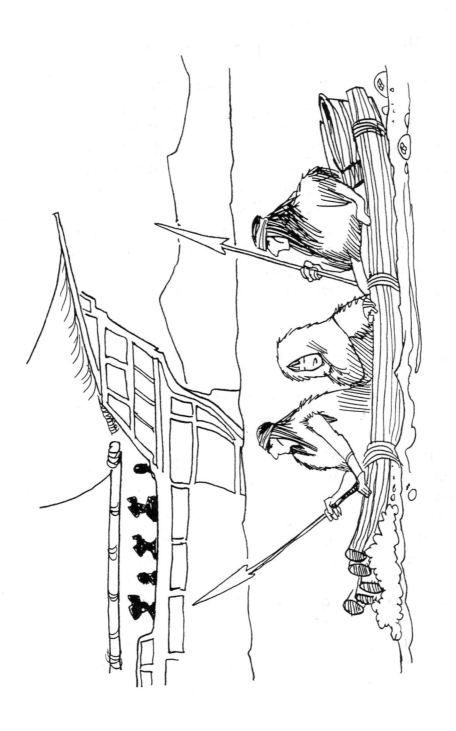

"Welcoming Committee"

CHAPTER TWENTY-FOUR

ABRIL DE 1796 — HOME SWEET HOME?

The boats reach the shore without mishap, but there remains one difficulty: The way to the *presidio* at the top of the bluff is by way of a precarious path of slippery wooden planks covering a soft, gooey bank.

When it is the *Ticos'* turn, *Juana* instinctively turns and grabs hold of *Juan's* hand. With her other hand, she not only clutches the *maleta* she has kept at her side since the start of the voyage, she must also hold her skirts up and out of the mud. It is because of *Juan's* quick action of grabbing her woolen shawl as it begins to slip from her shoulder that it is saved from falling on the slimy ground.

The new arrivals are surprised when they reach the *presidio* to find that they far outnumber the people there. All stand around in the light mist talking in groups and watch sailors from the *San Carlos* carry tents and put them up in the meadow.

In contrast to the gloomy day, those at the *presidio* are happy to see new faces and they greet the newcomers cordially. But during her conversation with one woman, *Juana* realizes that their arrival has meant a sacrifice for those at *Presidio San Francisco*; they must wait longer for *memorias* which were displaced by the human cargo of families on the *San Carlos*.

Juana didn't expect to live in a tent when she arrived, but there is obviously a tent city going up at some distance from the *presidio* wall. She's having terrible misgivings about the move.

Sargento Tico, like everyone else, would like to get out of the rain but is not concerned about being in a tent. After all, he has had to sleep in smaller ones than these, and many times he slept rolled up in a blanket on the ground.

It is the second night and the three are wrapped in blankets and wearing all the extra clothes they can put on.

"*Graciela* was right," *Juana* moans above the din of rain beating against the tent.

"*El teniente-coronel Alberni* may have assured you we won't be in tents very long, *José Joaquín*, but one more day is too long. Already the grounds are soaked. It is impossible to get to the outhouse. My shoes are caked with mud, and the hems of my petticoats and skirt are a dirty mess."

◆

After a week of bad weather, *Juana*, still finding it very hard to adjust to *presidio* life, camp style, says, "*José Joaquín*, I must talk to you. I am expecting a baby in a few months and am worried about many things. We need a better home than a tent; I must find a midwife for the delivery of the baby; I am finding it difficult to know where to get food for all of us; and I would like very much for *Juan* to write *la abuela*. He needs a teacher now that you are busy."

José had no idea so many things were bothering his wife and can only think to say, "Have patience a little longer, *Juana*. All this will change soon. It won't be long before we're settled."

All *Juana* can say is, "How much longer can it be?"

◆

Juan will miss *José Martínez*. *José's* father has been transferred to *Presidio San Diego,* approximately an eight hundred mile march away. The day they leave, *José* stands tall as he summons everyone with his drum. *Juan* watches his friend and the long line of animals, *carretas*, women, children and soldiers until they are out of sight.

Juana goes back to the tent thinking about her friends and the long distance they must travel. She prays they will make the trip safely. Fortunately, there will be a few missions along the way where they can camp and replenish supplies. *El sargento Tico* goes back to rebuilding and guarding the rundown fort overlooking the entrance to the bay.

Two weeks later, another group of soldiers and their families leave for *Presidio Monterey.* Tents are taken down and packed to be used on the journey and at their new assignment. The tent city has become much smaller, but no one has said anything about building houses for those who are still there.

It is a month later when *Juana* sees large *carretas* full of logs and thatch arrive at the *presidio* grounds. She watches with great interest *as los indios,* borrowed from *Misión Dolores*, begin the construction of huts. She is going to have a real home at last.

"I watched *los indios* put up the huts," says *Juana* to her husband. "The huts look sturdier than tents, but I miss my mother's *adobe!* It wasn't very large, but it kept the wind out. I hope these huts won't be drafty. I'll have a baby to care for soon and I want our house to be as warm as possible; *septiembre* is not far off."

"At least our housing problems are finally being

solved," says her husband. "I've been working like *un indio de la misión* rebuilding the old fort and we're not accomplishing very much. It was built twenty-two years ago, and from the looks of it, no work has been done since then. I've heard that the next project is to replace the leaking roofs of the older houses. I'm a soldier not a builder."

"How can they make you do work that's not yours to do?" asks *Juana*.

"All the soldiers are angry about it, but we have to do what we're told. And besides, to whom would we complain? If foreign trading ships were allowed to come here, then I would be doing something else besides keeping *los indios* away and building forts."

"What about the ship I saw in the channel? It looked like a foreign ship to me," says *Juana*.

"It wasn't there very long. Any ship is allowed to anchor just long enough to get necessary provisions — food, wood and water — or to make a serious repair on the ship," explains *el sargento Tico*.

"*José*, did you ever wonder why foreign ships aren't allowed in *Alta California* ports?"

"The government is afraid they are spy ships."

"Why should we be afraid of a few men looking through spyglasses at us?" asks *Juana*.

"The king doesn't want them finding out how few Spanish colonists and guards there are to defend *Alta California*. Fortunately for us, Spain has a treaty with England; their ships won't bother us."

◆

---

un indio de la misión - an Indian from the mission.

It is the fourth day of *septiembre*, and *Juana* feels her time has come to have the baby. *Juan* is sent to a friend's house for the night. When he returns the next day, he is greeted by the cries of his baby sister, *Rosalía Joaquína Josefa*. *Juana* and the baby have survived the delivery and are doing well. That night there is a small *fiesta* with the baby's *padrino, alférez Raymundo Carrillo* from the *compañía de Caballería de Monterey,* and a few friends. *Juana* wishes *Juan* could write to tell his *abuela* about *Rosalía*.

Juana has been thinking about her children's education and brings up the subject when she and her husband *dar un paseo* overlooking the entrance to the bay a few days after the birth. "The governor says we should send our children to school, but the last teacher was a sailor who didn't stay more than a month. He got right back on his ship when it came to port again."

"*Juana*, it is just a waste of money to send children to school. The boys only need to learn how to read and write, that's all they need to get along. The girls learn all they need to know from their mothers. Their husbands will take care of all business matters.

"Boys will become farmers, *soldados* or *vaqueros*. What do they need with book learning? And besides, where would books come from? Between the church and government, few books are allowed into the country and they must pass inspection. Anyway, we couldn't afford books even if they were allowed."

"*Sí sí*. All that is true," sighs *Juana*. "I'm glad

septiembre - September; *padrino* - godfather; *alférez* - second lieutenant; *Caballería* - cavalry; *dar un paseo* - take a walk.

you've taught *Juan* how to write his name and to read a few words."

After a thoughtful pause, *el Sargento Tico* says, "There is something even more important: If *Juan* learns too much from books, he will begin to think he knows more than I do and I might lose control over him. I respected my father and he respected his father. A son should honor and obey his father all his life; a father's word is law."

"Of course, *José*, *Juan* honors you. He always obeys you."

Her husband, continuing his thoughts on the subject, says, "And as for girls, they get married and have many children. I say, to fill their heads with book learning will only make them restless and troublesome. If *Juan* becomes a soldier and needs more learning to make a higher rank in the military, he can get what he needs at that time."

The *Ticos* continue their walk in silence; *Juana's* desire for her son to be able to read and write well is not shared by her husband, therefore there is no cause for further discussion.

When *José Joaquín* speaks again, it is about the land he hopes to get when he retires.

"I heard some news regarding *Villa Branciforte.*"

"I hope it's good news," says *Juana.*

"I understood *los Voluntarios* were definitely to receive land in *Villa Branciforte* when they retired. Now I'm told it had not been actually decided. *El coronel Alberni* has just petitioned *el gobernador Borica,* to grant the land to us soldiers."

"Perhaps it is only a formality between them," says *Juana.* "Didn't you say there are colonists there already?"

"Yes, there are a few, which means a settlement has actually been established."

"Well, I can't imagine that your friend, *coronel Alberni,* would lie about such a serious thing. Like I said, it must be just a formality," says *Juana.*

Borica rejects the petition. *El sargento Tico* is confused. But by the time he gets home, he's hopeful again and tells *Juana* what happened.

"The governor says he will find a more suitable site. Among other problems, drifters and derelicts from the worst sections of *Guadalajara* have been sent to *Villa Branciforte.*"

After hearing the news, *Juana* sits quietly in shock. When she's able to speak, she says, "*El señor López* and the others were right after all. They warned us about broken promises."

"It's not yet a broken promise, *Juana.* The governor said he would find a better location."

"*José Joaquín,* you are the most optimistic man I know. I hope you're right, but I can't help thinking what mother's neighbor said about the government finding ways not to keep its promises."

It is just before midnight on the eighth of *abril de 1798,* and *el sargento Tico* and *Juan* are awakened by *Juana* and the midwife. At eight o'clock in the morning on the ninth, they hear the cry of the new baby. Wrapping him in a soft blanket, the midwife lays the infant next to *Juana.* She notifies the *padrinos,* telling them the little boy is healthy and alerting them that the baptism will take place the next day.

As tiny *Fernando José María Ignacio Martín Tico* is baptized, *Manuel Martínez,* a soldier from *el sargento Tico's compañia,* and *Ramona Noriega,* wife of the cavalry sergeant at the *presidio,* listen to friar *Martín de Landaeta* instruct them of their spiritual relationship to the child and of other obligations that come with the Sacrament.

Juan stays out of the small hut as much as possible; he spends his days drumming for the soldiers and playing with other children at the *presidio.* Many times, native boys come from neighboring *rancherias* and teach the presidio children their games.

One year later, *en octubre,* another daughter is born. Her *padrinos* are different from the other childrens'. *Juan* baptizes his new sister immediately after her birth — she is not expected to live long enough to be baptized at the church. But baby *María Rafaela* survives, surprising everyone, and her baptism is celebrated at the church a few days later with *Padre Ramon Abella.*

"I heard that *Juan* very seriously accepted his obligations as *padrino* for his baby sister," says *Juana.*

"*Sí, sí,*" says *Ana María Nuñez,* who stood next to *Juan* at the baptism and celebration. "He listened very carefully to all the instructions from *el Padre.*"

"It was only yesterday you were just a boy, *Juan.* Today you have the responsibility of a man," says his mother.

"Well, *mamá,*" says *Juan,* drawing himself up to his full height, "I am nine-years-old."

padrinos - godparents; **rancherias** - Indian villages.

CHAPTER TWENTY-FIVE

1802 — THE UNFORESEEN

"We're moving to *Presidio Monterey*," announces *José Joaquín* matter-of-factly.

"You mean *Presidio San Francisco* is not to be our home after all? I've never thought about moving from here. It has taken me four years to feel at home in the frontier with all its hardships; just when I feel that the worst is over, you tell me we have to move!"

"We'll be marching as soon as possible," states her husband, who is accustomed to being ordered to leave one military post for another without questioning either the timing or the reason.

It surprises him to hear *Juana* say, "Oh, *José*, I am so happy here. Finally I feel at home and have many friends. I do wish we could stay."

"Now, *Juana*, I thought you would be aware by now that in military life there is always change. I never have the assurance that a particular place will be my real home — until I retire, of course."

Juana, disheartened at the thought, says, "I suppose we will leave like the others — in *carretas*, on horses, on *burros*, or by foot."

She remembers how tired many of the brave women looked when they left for their husbands' new assignment, especially those embarking on the long, long march to *Presidio San Diego*. She had prayed for the mothers and children. Now it is her turn.

"I'll tell the children," she says. "We'll get our things together."

"You don't have to do it today, *Juana*. It will be weeks before everything is ready. Supplies of food, water, tents, and horses will have to be collected for the trip. The *burros* and oxen will have to come from *el pueblo San José;* there are so few left here," says her husband.

Two native girls helping *Juana* at home say they will make the trip with her, but will decide whether to stay or return after they see if they are treated nicely by *los indios* at *Presidio Monterey.*

A straggly group of soldiers, women, children, native men and women, and a few animals begin their march along the well-worn rutted road. The second day, a scout rides back from *Presidio Monterey* and reports to the travelers.

"*Alberni* has arrived at the *presidio* and ordered *los indios* to begin to build huts for married couples at once."

"I thought everything would be ready for us by this time!" says *Juana.*

"*Commander Alberni* has been waiting for approval to begin construction. Now he can't wait any longer and is paying for materials with his own money."

The women, walking and talking together, gossip about news of the huts during the march. They whisper and clasp their babies a little closer when passing *rancherias*. Natives watch the procession from a distance.

Juana is grateful to have help with her two infants and little *Rosalía*, especially when they become restless and whiney. The two native women, *Juana*, and sometimes *Juan*, take turns carrying them.

At frequent rest-stops, *Juana* shakes out her clothes and uncovers the faces of the two babies who

have been sheltered from the dust by small shawls.
There are occasional wash-ups in streams along the
way to remove dust and dirt from hands and faces,
and to clean up the babies and small children. The
women are especially grateful that the leader is
considerate and gives them plenty of time to get ready
in the morning.

Tired marchers finally reach *Presidio Monterey*.
Among those greeting the travelers are many friends
from the *San Carlos*. After hot food has been offered to
the newcomers, married couples are assigned their
new homes.

"You would think they could make these places
large enough for growing families!" says *Juana*, as she
looks around the small one-room hut.

"One good thing about new huts is that they don't
come with *cucarachas* nor *ratas*," she adds, rocking
her youngest over her shoulder and wishing she had a
second room to inspect.

The native girls are shown another hut where they
will sleep at night. After finding the local natives to be
friendly, *Juana's muchachas* tell her they will stay,
news she is very happy to hear. She taught them
everything about her way of life when she arrived at
Presidio San Francisco. As before, they expect daily
bowls of beans or stew, a new dress once in a while,
and a place to sleep. Their duties are to look after the
children, wash clothes, mend and help prepare food —
grinding corn and making *tortillas* for each meal.

Juana discovers that *Presidio Monterey* is not what
she had expected; she actually likes the change. There

cucarachas nor ratas - cockroaches nor rats.

are sixty-five families here, twenty-seven more than regularly stationed at *Presidio San Francisco*. Perhaps the one thing more than any other that has made *Juana* contented and happy to be at *Presidio Monterey* is the reunion with the families who came with the *Ticos* on the *San Carlos*.

Since the governor of *Alta California* lives here, there are many more visitors and *fiestas* than at *Presidio San Francisco*. *Juana* enjoys the frequent entertainments, music and dancing that the governor shares with everyone in the plaza.

In spite of all the good things that surround her at *Presidio Monterey*, *Juana* sometimes worries that the governor has yet to find another *pueblo* for the Catalan Volunteers when they retire: *Juana* and *sargento Tico* seldom speak about it.

Captains from *San Blas*, wishing to trade in *Alta California*, must first come to *Presidio Monterey*. When their ships anchor in the bay, the customs house comes alive. Longboats filled with all sorts of goods row into shore to be inspected. It is a busy time for harbor guards like *el sargento Tico*.

The process of examining all cargoes takes several days. It involves taking everything from the ship to the customs house, an inspection, payment of taxes, and then returning goods to the ship. Captains are relieved when it's over and they have the proper clearance. It means they can visit *misiones* and *presidios* in *Alta California* to sell or trade their goods.

Few captains from *Nueva España* have trouble if they comply with the strict Spanish laws and gifts are handed out.

Gossip of the day around the wash pond, where women beat and squeeze the clothes, touches upon the governor and his visitors.

"I think it's strange that *el gobernador Borica*
keeps entertaining *los ingleses, Gorge Vancouver* and
Pedro Puget. Haven't the soldiers been teaching *los
indios* to hate the English?"

Another makes them laugh when she says, "Did
you hear that the governor spends much time with his
wife and daughter. He actually likes their company!"

"And," says another, "can you imagine this? They
have books in their house!"

On *el cuatro de mayo 1801, Juana* and *José* have
another son, *Antonio Tomás*. It is a noisy household
with three small babies demanding attention. *Rosalía*,
a pretty girl of five years, helps her mother with the
little ones.

Juan, now eleven, is becoming a good bareback
rider. He races around the countryside with his
friends. As a *vaquero* or *soldado*, his work as well as
his life, will depend on his riding skills. Many of the
girls can ride too. After all, there are only three
choices of transportation for everyone: ox carts,
horses, and walking. Native boys from a nearby
rancheria often come to play, as they did when *Juan*
lived at *Presidio San Francisco*. This time he knows
their games and can tell if there is cheating going on!

Before *Antonio Tomás* was born, and they had
been at *Presidio Monterey* less than a month, *José's*
commander, *Pedro Alberni* becomes ill. He goes to the

el cuatro de mayo - May 4th

Misión San Carlos Borromeo several times, and stays in the care of the *Padres.* Since *el sargento Tico* and his commander have been together for many years and know each other well, *José Joaquín* visits him often.

"How is *el coronel Alberni* getting on?" asks *Juana.*

"He wrote a letter to *la Ciudad de Méjico* requesting to go to *Nueva España* for treatment," says *José.* "*Padre Lasuén* says *el coronel Alberni* has come to the *misión* to rid himself of a severe melancholy which he can't shake off. He says that it is the result of an insult given him at the *presidio.*"

"I'm not surprised," says *Juana,* "He has gone through a lot since he was given full charge of creating *Villa Branciforte.* It must have been devastating for him to face his soldiers and tell them he couldn't keep his promise to get land for them."

"Perhaps the governor finds his asking bothersome and has told him so," says *José Joaquín.* "Although you would think that having been made commander of all armed forces in *Alta California* would be sufficient to cheer him."

A month goes by before *José Joaquín* has an opportunity to visit his commander again. *El coronel Alberni* is still unable to resume his duties full-time.

José reports to *Juana,* "Now *el Padre Lasuén* says *el coronel Alberni* is suffering from a severe pain in the side but may be on the road to recovery."

"What did you think about his condition when you saw him?" asks *Juana.*

"He's discouraged and wonders if his letter requesting sick leave has been lost," says *el sargento Tico.*

"It seems to me it was about three months ago that he wrote requesting leave," says *Juana.*

Several weeks go by without incident, then suddenly there is talk about a young cadet who is due to arrive at *Presidio Monterey el nueve de agosto.*

"Who is he? Is he married?" asks *Juana.*

"No, *alférez José de la Guerra* is not married. They tell me he is from Spain and came to *Nueva España* when he was about thirteen to work for an uncle who has an import business in *la Ciudad de Méjico.* Then someone convinced him to take military training. I hear he is very good with figures and will serve as *habilitado* and administrator of mail."

"My, it sounds like he will have a lot to do," says *Juana.* "I can hardly wait until he gets here. Just think of the *fiestas* there will be, especially the governor's party! There will be music, dancing, food and entertainments, and everyone will attend."

It is March 1802, and *José* has just returned from visiting his commander at the mission.

Shaking his head, *el sargento Tico* tells his wife, "*Pedro Alberni* is very sick. He told me he has made out his will and I am to be the executor."

"Oh my, that does sound serious, *José.* Do you think we both should visit him?"

"I think it would be a support to his wife, *Juana Vélez,*" says *el sargento Tico.* She was at his bedside,

alférez - military title, second lieutenant; ***el nueve de agosto*** - August 9th; ***habilitado*** - one who had charge of soldiers' affairs such as salary, housing, supplies, etc.

and when I turned to leave, she followed me out, tearfully telling me the dropsy has progressed."

"Now they say he has dropsy! I wonder if anyone knows from which illness the poor man is dying," says *Juana.* "Yes, let's go over to the mission. It must be a great strain on *Juana Vélez* to see her husband like this, and she's all alone; her only daughter died when she was only twelve-years-old, quite a few years ago."

As they ride together on *el sargento Tico's* horse to the mission, *Juana* thinks about her friend. She and *Juana Vélez* have known each other since they were young girls. *Juana Vélez* had married *Pedro Alberni,* an officer, before *José Joaquín* had returned to *Tepíc.*

The *Ticos* arrive just in time to console the grieving *Juana* as her husband dies.

The next day a notice is posted, and is also read aloud where all may hear. "*El teniente-coronel Pedro Alberni,* fifty-seven years of age, died *el undécimo de marzo* 1802, and will be buried today at *la Misión San Carlos.*"

El sargento Tico, as executor of *Alberni's* estate, arranges with *habilitado de la Guerra* to give nine thousand dollars to *la señora Alberni.* *Pedro Alberni* had set aside this money, and through his will, authorizes it to be given to his widow.

When *Juana* and *José* discuss the sadness that has befallen the *presidio,* *Juana* tells her husband, "*Juana Vélez* is going back to *Tepíc* as soon as she can make arrangements. She said she would be happy to call on *mamá* and tell her all about the children."

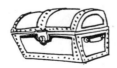

el undécimo de marzo - March 11th.

The next day, *José Joaquín* comes home early to tell *Juana* the news.

"The letter arrived today."

"The one for which *Pedro Alberni* waited a year?" asks *Juana*.

"Yes. And you won't believe what it said," says her husband. "It made all of us angry when *de la Guerra* read it aloud to us in his office."

"What did it say?" asks *Juana*.

"'*Pedro Alberni* has permission to return to *Nueva España* for treatment.' And the reason for the delay in answering was that they couldn't find a replacement for him until now!" *José Joaquín* tells her.

Juana shakes her head and says, *"¡Dios mío!"*

Alberni's funeral now over, everyone tries to get back to normal activity, but tranquility does not return to *Presidio Monterey*.

A courier brings a dispatch to the *comandante* that people are dying in three northern *pueblos* from a mysterious sickness.

When questioned further, the courier says, "No one knows how to cure the disease. People just shake their heads and say only prayer can heal it."

After each rainy season, there is always sickness, but this season could be tragic. Everyone at *Presidio Monterey* hopes and prays that the sickness from the north does not reach them.

But earnest prayers do not stop the mysterious sickness and a week later it arrives, perhaps carried by an unsuspecting visitor.

"¡Dios mío!" - "My God!"

El Sargento Tico does not feel well. Within a week he has worsened and does not respond to medicines of any kind. *Juana* has already had *el Padre* pray for her husband twice.

For the third and last time, *el Padre* is at *José Joaquín's* bedside; *Juana* stands at the foot of the bed with tears running down her cheeks.

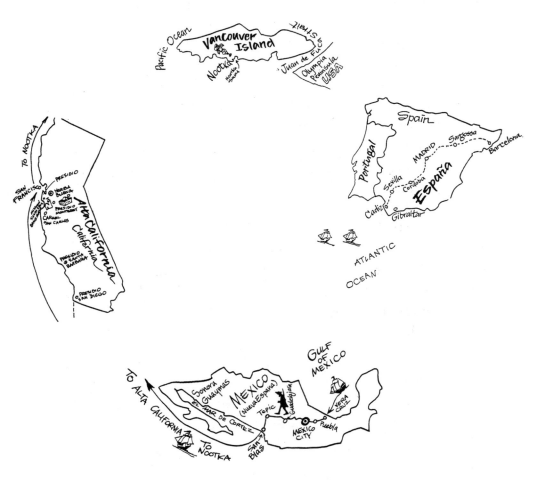

"Sargeant Tico's World"

EPILOGUE

LIFE GOES ON

Juana, alone with her thoughts, finds it impossible to understand the misery that has overtaken her so suddenly. She stares at the paper in her hands; she can't read it, but knows all too well what it says.

> El sargento primero José Joaquín Tico, nació 1750 en Pueblo de Sedo, la provincia de Cataluña, Vieja España, murió el diez y seis de mayo 1802, en el Presidio Monterey, Alta California. Fue enterrado el diez y siete de mayo de 1802 en la Misión San Carlos Borromeo de Carmelo. Tenía cincuenta y dos años.

After the children had left to stay with good friends, who had taken them into their already crowded home, she hadn't had time to think about anything but nursing her sick husband back to health. In these few quiet moments, Juana thinks about the last few days.

José Joaquín's fever didn't go down in spite of all my efforts — using all the remedies I knew. Wives at

Translation of paper: First Sergeant Joseph Joaquin Tico, born 1750 in Pueblo de Sedo, province of Catalonia, Old Spain, died May 16, 1802 at the age of fifty-two at Presidio Monterey, and was buried May 17, 1802 at Mission San Carlos Borromeo de Carmelo in Alta, California.

the *presidio* offered new remedies they had heard of from their native *muchachas*, hoping one of them might cure *José.*

Everyone at the *presidio* is in shock. They had just buried a beloved commander, *Pedro de Alberni,* and now they have suddenly lost another friend. Many of the men have been with *José Joaquín* for most of his military career.

I was up all night with those who were preparing my husband for burial. There was so little time to see him, even in death, since he had to be buried as soon as possible. I can still see the soldiers and neophytes carrying him to his final resting place.

After a brief farewell, my husband now lies in the church cemetery near the freshly covered grave of his friend, *Pedro Alberni.* Like my friend, *Juana Vélez de Alberni,* I will be dressed in black the rest of my life.

Juan, teary-eyed, sat next to me outside the church, holding my hand tightly. *Rosalía,* realizing she wouldn't be seeing her *papá* again, buried her head in my lap, sobbing. Little *María* and *Fernando,* not knowing what to make of it all, ran back and forth patting each one of us. *Juana Vélez de Alberni* walked to-and-fro with baby *Antonio Tomás* in her arms to keep him happy. She was brave to come to the funeral. I was so glad her ship had not yet arrived to take her to *San Blas.*

How can this be? Men are here to burn our hut. I had been told I must fumigate my clothes over a smoky fire, but no one said my hut would be destroyed!

Wait!" I cry out. "Wait just a few minutes more. Please, there are a few things I must get."

I run into the hut, and hastily look around the small room. *What should I take? What should I take?*

I drag out a chair, a table, two benches and some clothes. It's when I begin to drag the bed out that the men stop me.

"I'm sorry *señora Tico*, but we have orders from *el medico* to burn everything your husband used during his illness."

As they put a blazing torch to the roof, a surprised *Juan* arrives with *Fernando* on his shoulders. The three of us watch in shock as the dry wood and thatch of our home disappear in a single swoop of flame. Not until just a few charred pieces of smouldering wood remain, can we pull ourselves away from the empty place where our house once stood — the hut *Pedro Alberni* built for us with his own money only two years ago.

After scrubbing the table, benches and chair, I gratefully give them to the friends who took our children into their home. I am also staying with them for the time being, but there are just too many of us living here; I must find another place.

While still wondering where I might go, another family offers a bed in their hut. I take *Antonio Tomás* with me, since he is the youngest. *Juan* can help look after *Fernando*, *Rosalía* and *María*. The *muchachas*, who had been afraid to come near our hut for fear of getting the sickness, continue to help care for the children. Surely there is a place somewhere for us where we can all be together.

La Concepción finally arrives from *Presidio San*

Francisco on its way back to *San Blas*, and *Juana de Alberni* is ready to board. Waiting to say good-bye at the customs house, *Juana Vélez* hugs me, and says she will tell my mother about her beautiful grand-children and about *José*. I wave and watch until the tallest sail slips from view over the horizon.

A month after *Juana Vélez'* departure, I am finally notified that my children and I will be going back to *Presidio San Francisco* as soon as *habilitado de la Guerra* receives an answer from *la Ciudad de Méjico* about my widow's pension. I was told that I probably qualified for the pension because *José Joaquín* had served with the light infantry and as a Catalonian Volunteer for thirty-five years.

I couldn't resist asking a question *José* would like to have asked, "*Señor de la Guerra*, what is the reason my husband was not made an officer? Everyone says he had an excellent military record."

I wait and wait for news from *el señor de la Guerra* and finally, after many weeks, he again sends for me to come to his office.

"I am happy to tell you that a small pension is due to you, *señora Tico*. But as to the answer concerning your husband's rank, *lo siento mucho, pero no sé.* There was no reply to that question in the letter."

Of course I have to accept the fact I will not receive

lo siento mucho, pero no sé - I am sorry, but I don't know; (see Epilogue Notes)

a reply to my question; I thank him and leave his office.

The next time I'm called to *el señor de la Guerra's* office, I am told that the children and I will be leaving for *Presidio San Francisco* on the *San Antonio* presently anchored off the coast. At least now I know where we are going, but I don't know where we will stay once we get there.

The day has finally arrived and many friends are here at the customs house to say good-bye. *Las dos indias* are as excited as children; this is their first voyage on the ocean, and most importantly, they are returning home. Sailors row the eight of us to the ship and help us up the ladder. I have to get used to the motion of the sea again, and the fretful babies feel it too. However, I am extremely grateful we are not returning on *burros*. *Las dos muchachas*, so pleased to be returning to their people, are terribly seasick. I hope we all feel better tomorrow. Fortunately, the weather and seas are not stormy, and the voyage will be a short one.

Now at sea, *Juan* feels right at home, and tells his small brothers and sisters that he and his friend *José Martínez* learned to drum on a ship just like this one.

As we sail through the channel toward *Presidio San Francisco*, I recall my first voyage into the bay, and how I suddenly became fearful not knowing what

las dos indias - two Indian girls; **las dos muchachas** - two girls;

was ahead. This time, as I look at the bluffs, I know there are good friends waiting there.

The captain calls out to lower all sails and drop anchor. Then sailors work rapidly to get us from the ladder into the rowboat being tossed about by choppy waves. With lots of help, we all settle safely and the sailors row for shore. *Las indias*, frightened to be on the rough water, close their eyes and hold the youngest ones tightly, while I clasp a small hand on either side of me.

After making our way up the bluff, I'm not surprised to find we will be staying in a tent. Surely it will only be temporary, but without my husband here, I can't be sure of anything any more.

We have been here a week and I am asked to go to the office of the *habilitado*. He tells me that there is a small settlement not far from *Misión Dolores*, and that a place is available there for me and my children, since some colonists have been moved to *el pueblo San José*.

He answers my unasked questions when he says, "*Señora Tico*, a *Padre* will be returning to the mission in two days. He will take you and your family with him. The settlement, *Yerba Buena*, is on the way to *Misión Dolores*."

I return to the tent and think about the move. Having visited there before, I remember the mission very well, but *Yerba Buena* was only a fort. It's been only two years... Could there have been a settlement started in such a short time?

◆

Yerba Buena - Good Grass or Good Herbs (see Notes); **Misión Dolores** or **Misión San Francisco de Asis** - (see Notes)

Moving day is here, and the sun is burning off the fog. A large ox-drawn *carreta* filled with straw and a few blankets arrives. Neophytes from the mission who came with the *Padre* lift the children and our belongings into the high cart. We go first to the *presidio* chapel where the *Padre* and four *escoltas* are waiting for us. There is little space left, but the *Padre* manages to find room between the children and our bags. And the trip begins.

The *muchachas* walk beside the slow moving *carreta*. Three mounted *escoltas* ride ahead to lead the way, and guard us against unfriendly *indios* and wild animals. One guard, carrying his lance over his shoulder, walks behind.

Friends had packed a bulging picnic basket for us, and when the sun is directly overhead, we stop in a shady grove of trees and open it. After our lunch and a brief rest, we continue on our way until the road separates.

El Padre says, "The path to *Yerba Buena* is to the left."

As we make the turn, he motions to the right and says, "Perhaps you remember *la misión* is not far from here. I'm quite sure you will be able to walk to Mass *cada domingo*."

We begin to encounter ridge-like sand dunes, one after another, and I can see sun glinting off water in the distance. I know there are a few houses scattered around by the wisps of smoke rising from around the dunes. A solitary hut appears, then another, until we

neophytes - Christianized Indians; **escoltas** - mission guards; **cada domingo** - every Sunday.

reach the third house and the neophyte stops the
oxen.

Can this be my very own home? I suddenly feel I
have reached a patch of sunshine after stumbling
through long dark days under heavy black clouds. If
José were only here with us. Tears well up; I can
barely see to get out of the *carreta*.

Once on the ground, I look closer at our new home
and see its neglected condition. It is obvious no one
has lived here for some time. A few scraggly berry
bushes still bearing some fruit push through the dirt.
A rose bush is growing well, though north winds have
forced it to one side and its yellow blossoms press
into the soil. *María*, on seeing the roses, immediately
runs over to lift them off the ground. Before I can
reach her, she screams and backs away when sharp
thorns prick her fingers.

El Padre takes a moment to console her. Then, as
he climbs back into the cart to return to the mission,
he instructs twelve-year-old *Juan* that he is now the
man of the house, and tells all of the children to mind
their mother and come to church.

His parting words to me are, "I will send some
things from the mission."

I'm grateful *Misión Dolores* is not far away. If I
could spare the time, I would go there immediately to
sit quietly, think about broken promises, *José's*
untimely death, and how happy I am to be in my very
own *adobe* — even if it is in desolate little *Yerba
Buena*. But, alas, the children have to be fed and our
few things placed inside.

The *muchacha* is unpacking gifts from friends at
Presidio San Francisco. As she takes out a cooking pot
and looks at me, I can only shrug my shoulders;

there's no place to put it. And we have flour for *tortillas,* but there is no place to cook them. While she is doing the unpacking, I look through the basket and find enough food left from lunch to satisfy the children for tonight.

The clouds of dust that arose from our cart and horses as we came over the dirt road had not gone unnoticed. Three riders — a man, his wife and son — welcome us with a pot of stew and jugs of water, along with an invitation to come and eat with them anytime. They are new to *Yerba Buena,* too, but tell us they are almost settled.   After they leave, we all feel better about being here.

Rosalía has suffered most from our move and comes to me asking, "Are we really going to stay? Is this really our own house? Why do we have to sleep on the ground?"

I suppose I will be able to find beds somewhere, a grill and firewood. But I need a kitchen in which to cook. The broken roof and walls of the old kitchen lie in a pile of rubble in the back.

Just as the *muchachas* and I are folding blankets and placing them on the dirt floor for *Rosalía,* *Fernando* and *María,* two *carretas* arrive. We all run out and can hardly believe what we see.

Boys from the mission are bringing in a small table with four small benches, string beds with stuffed mattresses, and some wood for burning under the iron grill they lift out of the cart. *Juan* immediately goes to the horse tied to the back of the cart and takes it to a stake someone left in the ground near a patch of grass. Returning for the saddle, he takes it into the house, then makes a bale from all the hay packed in the bottom of the *carreta.* The *Padre* knew exactly what we needed.

The little ones hang onto my skirt, their eyes wide with awe and wonder at the unaccustomed activity. Basket after basket is carried into the little *adobe* from the second *carreta* which has a goat tied to it. *Juan* stakes the goat near the berry bushes which she immediately begins to eat.

Looking at the new man of the house, I say, "Now, *hijo*, your work has really begun."

As soon as the *carretas* return to the mission, *Juan* saddles up the horse and rides to our neighbors. He will ask the *ranchero* to help him build a corral, put up a sturdy roof and sides to protect the outdoor kitchen, and straighten up the leaning outhouse. While he's gone, the *muchachas* put the beds against the walls and the table in the center of the room.

When I look inside the baskets, I find dried fruit, some *garbanzos*, strings of garlic, onions, and a large yellow squash. Three live *gallinas y un gallo* with their feet tied are squawking in the corner. *Fernando* frees the chickens to find insects and seeds. The children will search for eggs once the chickens begin to lay. I remember how I helped look for nests hidden in the tall grass around the house of a friend. It was a race to get to the nests before some little animal or coyote found them. We'll have to think of some way to protect chicks when they hatch.

Las muchachas, as wide-eyed as the children, say they will stay and are prepared to even sleep on mats on the dirt floor. I am glad. How else would I handle

garbanzos - chick peas; **gallinas y un gallo** - chickens and a rooster.

all the chores and care for the little ones?

Each day brings improvements to our home; *Juan* and the neighbors finished the building work that needed to be done. Once in a while, *Rosalía* asks if men will come to burn the house down if she gets sick. We all reassure her that won't happen because she is in excellent health.

Juan hunts with his father's old gun and sets traps for squirrels, rabbits and quail. The neighbors occasionally share parts of freshly-killed deer, bear and cow. I make stew with the choice parts and hang the rest in the sun to dry. Last *domingo* after church, *el Padre,* hearing we have a corral, had a neophyte give *Juan* a sow to bring home on the end of a rope. He gave *María* a handful of flower seeds, and to *Rosalía,* a small basket full of vegetable plants. Each week the *Padre* sends dried corn; our own crop is only knee high. We hope it won't have too many worms in it when it ripens.

It isn't long before green shoots appear from the seeds *María* planted, and the carrots, squash and peas are growing, too. We'll have to wait for the pear tree to grow larger before we can pick fruit.

Everyone has a job to do, and the garden keeps us busy, especially since we have to haul water for our plants from the stream. We wash clothes and bathe in the same stream; it's a five to ten minute walk from the house.

I know *Juan* misses his father. Just last night, while cleaning his father's gun, he talked about their first meeting and getting to know him. Although he respects his father's soldier-work, he is not sure if he wants to become one. He says perhaps he will be a farmer like his Catalonian grandfather, or *un vaquero* like our neighbors.

Juan leaves us for several days when it's branding time, or when a *ranchero* needs extra help. The men tell me that he learns quickly and does everything just like they show him.

I have told neighbors that I am taking in sewing. Since my pension is so small, I accept money, food, plants or some article of clothing for the children in exchange for my work.

A soldier, who has known us from our days in *San Blas* and at *Presidio San Francisco,* stops to visit whenever he comes to *Yerba Buena* to inspect the fort. This time he brings disturbing news.

"*El virrey* at Mexico City has called back *los Voluntarios* who came here with you and *el sargento Tico*. It is not clear why the soldiers and their families are returning to *San Blas*."

Shaking my head, I say, "Surely the king hasn't broken another promise! Someone must know what is happening. I find it impossible to believe this is true."

"We are trying to make sense of the rumors," says the soldier. "Some say it is because *España* needs the money presently being spent on *los Voluntarios*, in order to pay for a war that *España* is in with *Inglaterra, Francia* or *Rusia*. No one seems to be sure which country we are at war with this time!

"The other rumor is that extra troops are needed in *Nueva España*. There is trouble there with *los*

un vaquero - a cowboy; **el virrey** - the viceroy, king's representative; **Inglaterra, Francia** or **Rusia** - England, France or Russia;

indios and rebellious citizens. I wish someone would come and tell us what is really going on," says the frustrated soldier as he gets on his horse.

"I'll let you know if I hear anything further regarding the return of the Volunteers," he says, riding off toward the *presidio*.

My first thought goes back to our farewell party in *Tepíc*, and what *el señor López* said about how unhappy many men are with the king. He explained later that part of the unhappiness is because *el rey* does not place men born in the colony in high government positions, but instead chooses to bring men born in Spain or Italy to rule *Nueva España* .

Later he confided something puzzling about French prisoners and settlers in *Chile, Perú, Argentina* and *Nueva España* spreading some treasonous ideas of men being "born free" and having "divine rights." It all seemed so unimportant at the time. After all, we were getting ready to come to *Alta California*.

But what about the women and children who must leave? How well I understand their great disappointment. Not only must they return to some crowded quarters in *Nueva España*, but imagine going on that horrible voyage again!

Eight years ago, on board the *San Carlos*, we women agreed that regardless of all the preparations we had to make to come to *Alta California*, even knowing we probably would never see our families again, we still looked forward to becoming landowners, and raising our children in the good *Alta California* air. From what my soldier friend says, there will be very

el rey - the king.

few of us left here to realize the hopes and
expectations of those early days.

   Just thinking about what these people will go
through makes my heart sink. Perhaps my life is
turning out better than I thought. I would rather stay
here.

   I don't believe for a minute that the government is
being generous by keeping us here, just thrifty. Why
bother to pay the cost of our return passage to *Nueva
España*? Maybe they think I will marry a widowed
soldier or colonist.

   We are doing fine and I'm happy that the children
are well. The same kind *Padre* who brought us here
continues to look after not only my family but everyone
here in *Yerba Buena*.

   I am sorry that *Juan* hasn't been able to get
regular schooling. It is too late now, since he is so
busy helping to keep food on our table. Perhaps
eventually a teacher will come to *Yerba Buena*. At
least *Fernando* and *José Antonio* still have an
opportunity to learn to read and write.

   Now that we're settled in our own home, and the
garden grows well, with milk and meat available, it no
longer matters to me how this all came about. I only
know that *Alta California* has gained six *Tico* colonists:
me, a widow almost forty-three-years-old; *Juan*, almost
fourteen-years-old; *Rosalía*, seven-years-old;
Fernando, five-years-old; *María*, four-years-old; and
Antonio Tomás, now two years. There are no more
promises to be broken. We just live from day to day;
life goes on.

"...men cannot take possession
of a land without that land taking
possession of them."
   S. de M. *The Three Caravels*

APPENDIX

HISTORICAL REFERENCE

CHAPTER NOTES

REAL PEOPLE, MILITARY UNITS, SHIPS

LOCATIONS MENTIONED

INDIVIDUALS CREATED FOR STORY

GLOSSARY OF ENGLISH WORDS AND
EXPRESSIONS AS USED IN THE STORY

BIBLIOGRAPHY

ACKNOWLEDGEMENTS

INDEX

COLOPHON

ORDER FORMS

Historical Reference

		Iberia/Spain	New Spain/Mexico	Alta California (& 13 Colonies)
1000s	BC	Phoenicians colonize		
c500	BC		Village life in valley	
400	BC	Carthaginian Era		
200	BC	Roman Era		
c300	AD		Indian civilizations	
400	AD	Germanic Era		
711	AD	Moorish Era		
c900	AD		Toltec Empire .... Groups of Native Americans	
1000	AD	Christian Era		
1231		Spanish Inquisition		
1479		Aragon & Castile unite		
		Final defeat of the Moors		
1492		Columbus discovers New World		
1512		Unification of Spain		
1513		Ponce de Leon claims Florida for Spain		
1519-21			Cortez claims for Spain	
1535			Antonio Mendoza first viceroy	
1542		Dominican & Franciscan friars judge at inquisitions .... Cabrillo visits CA coast		
1550		Spain controlled New Spain, Central America, nearly all of West Indies, part of what is called the southern part of the United States, and much of Western South America		

Historical Reference

Year	Iberia/Spain	New Spain/Mexico	Alta California (& 13 Colonies)
1556-98	Spanish Empire at zenith and begins its decline		
1579			Sir F. Drake visits CA coast
1588	Spanish Armada defeated by English		
1602			Viscaino visits CA coast
1609			(Jamestown settled for trade purposes)
1620			(Mayflower arrived: one half of 102 voyagers came for religious freedom)
1659	Peace of the Pyrenees ends 24 yrs. of war between Spain & France		
1692			(Witch hunts in Massachusetts: 20 executed, 150 imprisoned)
1704	Gibraltar under English control		
1750		Sergeant José Joaquín Tico born	
1760		Juana Carrera de Tico born	
1762		France ceded Louisiana to Spain	
1763	Intendencies in Spain	Intendencies in New Spain	
	Florida ceded to England		
1767		Sgt. José Joaquín Tico goes to Sonora; Jesuits expelled	

Historical Reference

	Iberia/Spain	New Spain/Mexico	Alta California (& 13 Colonies)
1769	Falkland Islands ceded to England		Presidio San Diego
1770			Mission San Diego Alcala, July 16 Presidio Monterey, Mission San Carlos Borromeo, June 3
1771		End of Sonoran War	Mission San Antonio de Padua, July 14
1772			Mission San Luis Obispo, Sept. 1 Mission San Gabriel Arcangel, Sept. 8
1773			(Boston Tea Party)
1775	Spain & England at war		
1776			(13 Colonies declare independence from England) Presidio San Francisco, Sept. 17 Mission San Francisco de Asis, Oct. 9 Mission San Juan Capistrano, Nov. 1
1777			Mission Santa Clara, Jan. 12 Civic Municipality of San Jose, Nov. 29

Historical Reference

Year	Iberia/Spain	New Spain/Mexico	Alta California (& 13 Colonies)
1780		The Ticos marry	
1781		Three groups organize to go to Alta California	Civic Municipality of Los Angeles, Sept. 4
1782			Presidio Santa Barbara Mission San Buenaventura, Nov. 31
1783	Spain regains Florida		
1786	Nootka Sound affair begins		Mission Santa Barbara, Dec. 4 (U.S. Constitution written)
1787			Mission Purisima Concepción, Dec. 8
1789			(G. Washington inaugurated)
1790		Sgt. José Joaquín Tico goes to Nootka	
1791		Juan Nepomucino Tico is born	Mission Santa Cruz, Sept. 25 Mission Nuestra Señora de la Soledad, Oct. 9
1792			(Cornerstone laid for the White House, Wash. DC)

Historical Reference

	Iberia/Spain	New Spain/Mexico	Alta California (& 13 Colonies)
1793	Spain at war with France after French Revolution		
1796			Ticos arrive at Presidio San Francisco, end of April Rosalia born Presidio San Francisco, Sept. 4
1797			Mission San Jose, June 11 Mission San Juan Bautista, June 24 Mission San Miguel Arcangel, June 25 Mission San Fernando Rey, Sept. 8
1798			Fernando Tico born Presidio San Francisco, April 9 Mission San Luis Rey de Francia, June 13
1799			
1800	Spain ceded Louisiana to France		María Tico born Presidio San Francisco, Oct. 12 (Capital Building completed, Wash. DC)

Historical Reference

	Iberia/Spain	New Spain/Mexico	Alta California (& 13 Colonies)
1801	England sinks Spanish/French fleet		Antonio Tomás Tico born Presidio Monterey, May 4
1802			Sergeant José Joaquín Tico dies, May 16, at Presidio Monterey
1803		(The United States purchased Louisiana from France)	
1804		Spain at war with England	Mission Santa Ines, Sept. 7
1805		Compulsory redemption of loans Poor citizens lose their lands	
1808		Spain seized by Napoleon	
1810		Spain rises against French occupation	
1811		Spain cedes Florida to United States	Miguel Hidalgo y Costillo begins struggle for independence from Spain	Mission San Rafael Arcangel, Dec. 14
1817		War of Independence begins against Spain	
1822		Mexico becomes a Republic	Alta California now under Mexican rule
1823			Mission San Francisco Solano, July 4
1833			Secularization of the Missions
1850			California becomes the 31st state of the United States of America

NOTES

Accent Mark. Nowhere do I find that copiests used an accent mark over the "o" in Tico, nor in military records. B.L.M.B.

Spanish Words. Spanish words in the story are used to keep the reader aware that the earliest California colonists did not speak English. Variations of Spanish and Catalán were spoken by colonial soldiers in New Spain (Mexico). "Old Spanish" spelling is used occasionally to keep the era in mind.

Catalán: Fa uns quants anys, pocs, Raimon irrompé dins la vida catalana com una veu jove, forta i sorprenentment auténtica. L'adhesió del públic fou immediata i entusiasta.

Spanish: Hace unos años, pocos, Raimon irrumpió en la vida catalana como una voz joven, fuerte y sorprendentemente auténtica. La adhesión del publico fue inmediata y entusiástica.

Examples from **100 PITFALLS IN SPANISH**

"Catalan is related to Provençal, with an admixture of harsh intonation that robs it of the soft, musical cadences of Provençal, but at the same time adds vigor and dynamism to it. Catalan is spoken from Perpignan (in Southern France near the Pyrenees) to Valencia, and with variations in the Balearic Islands. It has some affinities with French."

FODOR'S SPAIN

Fernando Tico. First California-born son of Sergeant José Joaquín Tico and Juana Carrera de Tico. Through a Mexican land grant in 1837, Fernando received the upper and lower Ojai Valleys. He was also granted acreage on ex-mission land in San

Buenaventura. Both grants became part of Ventura County when it separated from Santa Barbara in 1873.

Juan Nepomucino Tico, born in New Spain, may have been adopted — an orphan left by a relative, friend or stranger. All of these possibilities were very common. He may also have been Juana Tico's son. There are no records extant which give his exact relationship. Due to his moving around as a troubleshooting soldier, Sergeant Tico may have been away from home for many years at a time. Due to infant mortality being common, other children may not have survived during the ten-year interval between the Tico marriage and Juan's birth. For the purpose of the story, Juan is the legitimate son of José and Juana Tico.

Juana Carrera de Tico, wife of José Joaquín. Other than knowing she came from Tepíc, New Spain, nothing more is known about her prior to her marriage.

CHAPTER 1: Adobe. A name given to a house made of adobe bricks. To make the bricks, mix sandy clay or loam with water; add a small quantity of straw; place this mixture into wooden forms with partitions to form bricks; remove the bricks when they are dry and bake in the sun for ten days to two weeks. Early Mexicans and Pueblo Indians covered the bricks with mud. They are generally painted and must be protected from rain and periods of freezing and thawing or they will crumble.   **WORLD BOOK ENCYCLOPEDIA**

CHAPTER 1: Alta California. Upper California. Various records show the area was called "Nueva California" (New California) or the "Northern Province."

or becoming ill from scurvy years after sailors from other countries had solved the problem.

CHAPTER 12: Cockfights. Cruel; illegal today.

CHAPTER 13: Alcalde. A *pueblo* government official who held several offices at the same time. His duties combined those of mayor, constable, judge, and lawyer. Depending on the era in which the *alcalde* served, his authority increased or decreased.

CHAPTER 13: Couriers. Individuals who carry messages or mail. There was no other way to communicate in those days except through ships' captains, travelers, or men who rode through the country on horseback, stopping at waystations for a fresh horse periodically. Telegraph and telephone did not appear until sixty-five years later, about 1832 and 1876 respectively.

CHAPTER 15: Gente de Razon. See Ch. 2 Notes.

CHAPTER 19: The raid on the chieftains in the mountains was adapted from **SPANISH BLUECOATS.**

CHAPTER 19: Sonoran Desert. It takes in the southern part of New Mexico, Arizona and Texas, as well as parts of Sinaloa and Nayarit in western Mexico.

CHAPTER 20: Apache Raids. The nuisance of Apaches coming from the north interrupted the Sonoran War. Elizondo had no choice but to stop chasing the chieftains and send soldiers to protect the established ranchers from the raiders in Nueva Vizcaya in the direction of Chihuahua. When settlers across the Sierra Madre heard of the raids, they began to clamor for protection.   **SPANISH BLUECOATS**

CHAPTER 20: A Catalan Volunteer's Uniform.

Hat:	Black leather helmet with gold trimming; red brush.
Hair:	Worn in queue; probably powdered, although on the frontier powder was soon dispensed with.
Coat:	Dark blue; long and full; slashed below waist behind; corners in front and behind looped back and fastened with a brass button; tails faced with red.
Small roll collar:	Red.
Cuffs:	Wide and of red cloth.
Buttons:	Brass.
Waistcoat:	Red, long, reaching below waist.
Sleeves:	Buttoned up center.
Pocket:	One on each side below waistline.
Stock:	Black, high (on hat and under chin).
Breeches:	Red, tight, gartered under knees.
Leggings:	Black leather, reached above knees, buttoned up outside each leg; held up by garters under knees; fitted over black shoes with strap and tongue.
Shoulder-belt:	White leather, brass buckles, supporting black cartridge box.
Musket:	Flintlock.
Sword:	Attached to shoulder-belt at the left side.

EARLY CALIFORNIA COSTUMES

"Soldados de Cuera"

Working clothes.

Knee breeches:	Cloth.
Flap on trousers:	Narrow or wide *tapabalazo*.
Band at knee:	Fastened with buckle of metal or silver.
Vest:	*Cuera* (leather) jacket: a protection against arrows, made from seven thicknesses of antelope hide *(gamuza)*.
Shield:	Oval or heart-shaped leather *(adarga)*, oxhide doubled on the inside; loops of hide under arms.

HISTORY OF CALIFORNIA

CHAPTER 20: Weaponry. "Accoutrements were often in short supply, and commands were rarely up to strength. ...In addition to their stylish uniforms, their accoutrements were subject to the availability of supplies. As regards their weaponry, the Catalonian Volunteers used belt knives which had, typically, ten-inch blades, although officers wore sidearms. Volunteer troopers carried the *escopeta,* a type of light musket. The dimensions of the *escopeta* were —

Length: 54-55 inches.
Barrel: 39 inches, octagon taper to round decorated barrel turnings.
Lock: 5 1/2 inches x 1 1/4.
Furniture: Brass.
Weight: 7 pounds.

Another common type of musket used by the Volunteers was probably the Light Infantry Fusil. The dimensions of the fusil were —

Length: 60 inches.
Barrel: 43 7/8 x 1 5/8.
Caliber: 69 (bore .73).

Furniture: Brass (with Catalan style stock).
The type of weapon varied among the Catalonians." As each company changed commanders or merged, their style of weapons often changed. **SPANISH BLUECOATS**

CHAPTER 21: Recipe for Flan Caramelo, Champur-rado, and Empanaditas (see pages 196-199).

CHAPTER 21: Pious Fund. "[A collection of] money from which the missions paid for property and goods they needed. The Fund was established by the Society of Jesus (Jesuits) in 1697 after proposing that through the establishment of missions in *Nueva España,* the

Indians could be Christianized and practical working possession of the country perfected. The offer was accepted with the following restrictions: 1. Possession must be taken in the name of the Crown. 2. Occupation should be accomplished at no expense to the royal treasury.

"The Fund was created not only for present expenses but to create a capital fund, the income from which would support the California missions. The Jesuits acted as trustees of the Fund until 1767 when they were expelled from *Nueva España,* at which time it was taken over by the State. Distribution eventually began again to the missions. Some early colonization expeditions were financed by the Fund. The *Junta Directiva* managed the funds, including after the revolution against Spain. In 1842, *Santa Anna* by decree vested title and administration of the Fund back in the Republic and decreed the properties of the Fund were to be sold and paid into the public treasury. In 1846, the war between the United States and Mexico commenced and nothing more was heard of the Pious Fund."   **THE PIOUS FUND** - K. Johnson

CHAPTER 22. **Nootka.** See Chapter 2 Notes.

CHAPTER 22: List of men who served (or were supposed to serve) in Nootka with Pedro Alberni: Domingo Albarez, Antonio Baldez, Lorenzo Bentuna, Antonio Benilla, Bautista Bosch, Francisco Maria Bucareli, Saturino Buder, Gerónimo Burón, José Caballero, Estevan Cabre, José Campo, Antonio Cañizares, Simón Casasallas, Rafael Coca, Francisco Corbella, Antonio Domínguez, Sabastian Ducil, Baptista Escoda, Francisco Fabregatt, Mauricio Faules, José Antonio Ferre, Pablo Ferrar, Estevan

Figueredo, Francisco Flores, Diego Gálvez, Claudio Galindo, Antonio Gomez García, José Gómez, Sevastian Gonbara, Blas Gonzálas, Simon Gonzálas, José Guerrero, Tadeo Guias, Filipe Gutiérrez, Francisco Gutiérrez, Francisco Herrera, Andres López, Juan Maldonado, Manuel Mallen, Juan Manzanilla, Antonio Marín, Juan Marine, Francisco Martí, **Manuel Martínez,** José Mercader, Vicente Montenegro, Francisco Murguía, José Navarro, Domingo Nefrerias, Juan Ortel, Francisco Pacheco, Francisco Perez, Francisco Perez (another), Cayetano Ramos, José Ramos, Miguel Ramos, José Rey, Francisco Rodrígues, Rafael Romero, Francisco Rubiol, José Rubin, Juan Ruiz, José Sánchez, Juan Sánchez, Francisco Sarmiento, Damián Seguera, Miguel Seguera, Miguel Serera, Ygnacio Tejo (Ignacio Antonio Texo), Francisco Terricabres, **[José] Joaquín Tico,** José Tórres, Cayetano Valls, Augustin Vicens, Onofre Villalba, Francisco Villalba, José Vino, Francisco Ydalgo, Juan Yñiguez.   **SPANISH BLUECOATS**

CHAPTER 22: Burials at Sea. During this period, the Catholic Church did not permit burials at sea. Bodies were buried in the ballast of ships until they reached shore. Ballast consisted of gravel and sand.
          VENTURA, CALIFORNIA MARITIME MUSEUM

CHAPTER 22. Sergeant Tico. "Another Catalonian, Sergeant [José] Joaquín Tico who was with Alberni in the expedition to Nootka in 1789-1792 was later assigned to California. [José] Joaquín Tico's son, Fernando, was involved in California politics during the Mexican Period in the 1830's."
                              SPANISH BLUECOATS

◆

CHAPTER 23. Tides. See Glossary page 269

CHAPTER 24: "The list of Catalán Volunteers who came on that date (April 1, 1796) and landed first at San Francisco, a recently opened port of entry."

1796 mayo 30 S. Francisco
Pedro de Alberni Compañia
de Voluntarios de Catalán

Captain:	Lt. Col. Pedro de Alberni
Sargento:	**[José] Joaquín Tico**
Fambor: (Drummer)	**Juan Tico**
Cabo 1: (1st Corporal)	Francisco Rubiol
Obro:	Claudio Galindo
Cabo 2: (2nd Corporal)	José Miranda

Soldados: José Acosta, José Alari, Juan Alvarez, José Barrientos, Manuel de la Vega, José Espinosa, Diego Galves, José Gomez, Alejo Gonzáles, José Gonzáles, Juan Maldonado, Manuel Mallen, **José Martínez, Manuel Martínez,** Miguel Medoza, José Muruato, Faustino Oceguera, José Palafox, Benancio Ruielas, José María Serrano.

Ausentes en diferentes destino

Sargento:	Francisco Gutiérrez
Fambor:	**José Martinez**
Cabo:	Antonio Marin
Yd.2:	Mateo Bello

Soldados: José Caballero, José Campo, Simón Casasallas, Sabastian Ducil, Francisco Jiménez, José María Osio, Manuel Quesadas, Francisco Salas, José Servín, Narciso Tórres.

Teniente:	José Font
Sargento:	Juan Yñiguez
Cabo:	Onofre Villalba

Yd.2:   Francisco Sarmiento
Obro: Filipe de Haro

Soldados: Antonio Bacilío, Antonio Cañizares, José Carcamo, Alonzo Delgado, Sevastián Escribano, Victor Fernández, Rafael Fragosa, Sevastián Guevera, Antonio Llamas, José Lugo, Juan Ortel, Miguel Ortega, Francisco Pacheco, Jacinto Padillo, Bautista Pérez, Manuel Pérez, Cristóbal Rey, Rafael Romero, José Trujillo, Francisco Váldes, José Velis.

Subteniente: Simón Suarez
Soldados: Nicolas García, Tadeo Lisant, Manuel Mendoza, Teodoro Péna, José Rey, José Rocha, Juan Sobato, Pedro Sosano.

Total 72 hombres
BANCROFT LIBRARY, BERKELEY, CALIFORNIA
(Microfilm C-A-16)

On March 23rd and April 1st, the Valdéz and the San Carlos arrived at Monterey and San Francisco respectively with most of the Compañía Franca and the artillerymen, the rest coming up the following spring; the military force in California being thus increased by nearly 100 men.

HISTORY OF CALIFORNIA

CHAPTER 24: Fernando Tico's Baptismal Record.
#1942. April 8, 1798. "El octavo día de abril, 1798, en la capilla del presidio San Francisco bautiste un niño nacido el día antes, hijo legitimo ob José Joaquín Tico, Sargento Volunterio y de Señora Juana Carrera puede su nombre Fernando José Maria Ignacio [Martin]. Manuel (Blas?) de la padrinos."

SANTA BARBARA MISSION

<u>Translation of the original</u>: "On April 10th 1798, in the Chapel of the Fort of our Father Saint Francis, I baptized a baby boy born the day before at 8 o'clock in the morning. A legitimate son of Don José Joaquín Tico, first sergeant of the First Company "Franca de Voluntarios" Cataluña, and of Doña Juana Carrera and Pico, his lawful wife. I gave him the names:
FERNANDO JOSE MARIA IGNACIO MARTIN
His godparents were Manuel Martinez, a soldier from the same Company, and Ramona Noriega, the wife of the cavalry sergeant of the same Fort, whom I instructed of their spiritual relationship and of the other obligations that come with the Sacrament. And, so it may appear and be valid wherever it may be convenient, I sign it at the above mentioned Fort on the same day, month and year. Signed: Friar Martin de Landaeta."

The original and complete translation provided to Mrs. Juanita Callender by Msgr. Francis J. Weber.

CHAPTER 24: María Rafaela's Baptismal Record.
#2000-123, October 13, 1799. "El 13th dia de octubre 1799 en la del real presidio de San Francisco bautice somnemente a una hija nacio la niña antecedent, hija legitima de Joaquín Tico, sargento de la Compañía Franca de Voluntarios de Cataluña, del Pueblo de Sedo en Cataluña y señora Juana Carrera, natural de pueblo de Tepíc en la nueva España le puse por nombre María Rafaela Eduarda, fueron sus padrinos Juan Nepomucino Tico y Ana Maria Nunez agvienes adventi et Pazen tesco (?) y demas espiritual, obligaciones para conste forma. (signed) Padre Ramon Abella.
SANTA BARBARA MISSION

CHAPTER 24: Assigning Lands. The commander of the presidio is authorized to assign lands to communities and also to such individuals as disposed to work; but all must dwell at the *pueblo* or mission and all grants to be made with due regard to the formalities of the law. Missions may be converted to *pueblos* when sufficiently advanced, retaining the name of the patron saint. **HISTORY OF CALIFORNIA**

CHAPTER 24: **Captain & Trade.** The military captain is charged with recruiting soldiers to complete the full number. Married recruits must bring their families. Unmarried ones must have papers to prove they are single. No trade with foreigners.
HISTORY OF CALIFORNIA

CHAPTER 24: **Farallon Islands.** These are seven small islands thirty miles west of San Francisco. Seven miles divides them into two groups.

CHAPTER 24: **Fort Point.** This is probably the Fort that Sargento Tico was helping to rebuild at the San Francisco presidio.

CHAPTER 24: **Preparations if Invaded.** (Constant preparations for hostilities that never occurred.) "Among the many instructions the viceroy in New Spain gave to Governor Borica of Alta California in the event of foreign invasion were: Seize the vessels. Commandants to redouble precautions. Friars to give prayers and Indians if needed. Send notice of invasion to Monterey. Concentrate military on threatened site. Drive livestock inland. Drill men in use of arms. Messengers to be kept in constant motion. Tell Indians that the English would violate women and are hostile to religion. Post sentinels at possible anchorage sites. Able bodied men to gather at presidio. Disabled men to protect women and children. Strict economy to be practiced due to possible non-arrival of supply ship. If invaded, destroy cannon if presidio is abandoned. Target practice every Sunday. Place archives at San Fernando as well as reserve arms and church vessels. Manila Galleons must remain at Monterey until the way is cleared of privateers."

In the meantime, Indian problems persisted everywhere.   **HISTORY OF CALIFORNIA**

CHAPTER 24: Preparations for the March. *Capatz* means foreman. *Caporal* is the *mayordomo's* assistant. The assistant looked after the oxen and indicated to the *mayordomo* which animals he should take. Ox drivers yoked each ox and, when all were ready, went in groups to the localities assigned.

CHAPTER 24: San Francisco Bay. In mid 1800's, Fremont gave it its present name. The channel at the entrance to San Francisco Bay, now called the Golden Gate, is four miles long and one mile wide. The Golden Gate bridge spans the channel at the entrance to the bay. It connects northern California with the peninsula of San Francisco.

CHAPTER 25: Monterey. In 1797, there was a barbette battery consisting mostly of a few logs of wood irregularly placed behind which stood about eleven pieces of artillery.   **HISTORY OF CALIFORNIA**

CHAPTER 25: Misión San Carlos Borromeo de Carmelo. Padre Serra had planned for a stone church and had ordered the quarrying of stone for it in 1781. It is possible that he even sketched out the design. A few days before his death (August 28, 1784), he told Father Palou, "When the stone church is built, you may place me where you will." And when the church

was actually completed sixteen years later, it was built
around the earlier church in which Serra was buried
and it thus encompassed his remains.... The present
church is the seventh of a series of churches dating
back to 1771 when the first crude shelter of logs was
erected at Carmel.   **CALIFORNIA MISSIONS**

EPILOGUE: **Balsa Canoes.** (see page 244)

EPILOGUE: **Misión San Francisco de Asis.** This is
the true name for Mission Dolores. The mission is
called by its second name because of its location close
to a stream that ran into a lake by the name of
Dolores.   **CALIFORNIA MISSIONS**

A few families with the de Anza party settled by
the mission. Costanoan Indians lived in the area.

EPILOGUE: **[José] Joaquín Tico, Hoja de Servicios.**
"No propongo para subteniente al sargento de la
expresada, Joaquín Tico que sirve a S.M. de veinte
años, diez meses y quatro dias a esta parte con buenas
notas, porque es casado, y no me constan las circum-
stancias de su mujer." The reply that Berenguer gave
to Caballero (both military officers) in a letter headed
Mexico, July 27, 1802, (AGI Mexico 1464). Roughly
translated: "I am not proposing Joaquín Tico for
second lieutenant although he has a good military
record because he is married and there is nothing on
record about his wife." Joaquín Tico, Hoja de Servicios,
December 1800, AGA, Guerra Moderna 7277, c:8; and
Joaquín Tico, Hoja de Servicios, December 1798, AGS,
Guerra Moderna 7275,C:7.   **SPANISH BLUECOATS**

EPILOGUE: **José Joaquín Tico.** "The sergeant in

Alberni's Company was Joaquín Tico, a forty-four year old Catalonian who had served with the Company nineteen years, three months and twenty-seven days. Tico had been to Nootka with Alberni and it was noted that he almost died there. First Sergeant Tico was the executor of Alberni's will. In 1796, the Company was reassigned to Alta California. In 1800, the First Free Company's officers were: Lieutenant Colonel and Captain Pedro Alberni. Captain José Font y Bermúdes, a nobleman from Coruña who was second in command. Sublieutenant Simón Suaréz, a nobleman, was from Navarre." **SPANISH BLUECOATS**

EPILOGUE: Widows Pension: Although José Joaquín Tico was not an officer, the application for Juana's pension may have looked something like this:

"Solicitation of Monte Pio. Partido del Casamiento, Testimonio del expedients formado en virtud de instancia hecha por (wife's name) viuda del (soldier's or officer's name) de la compañía franca de Voluntarios de Cataluña solicitando la pension de Monte Pio, que le corresponde por razon de viudad; hereinafter cited as Testimonio del expediente Superior Govierno, Ano de (year)." **SPANISH BLUECOATS**

EPILOGUE: Yerba Buena. The settlement was founded during Governor Borica's time, just before the Ticos arrived in 1796. "It was still a horse village as late as 1846 when the Stars and Stripes were raised. Alcalde Washington Bartlett in a burst of unofficial inspiration — not having consulted the town council — changed the name from Yerba Buena to San Francisco in 1847." There were almost 500 inhabitants at the time. **CALIFORNIA, AN INTIMATE HISTORY**

San Francisco was incorporated in 1850, the same year California was admitted into the Union.

Seals and otters are plentiful along the Pacific coast of San Francisco.

Fogs often lie along the coast for weeks.

EPILOGUE: Fort at Yerba Buena. "Beyond the constant repairs by which Fort San Joaquin was kept as nearly in its original state as possible, and some changes in the disposition of the guns under Córdoba's instructions, I find no evidence of further progress at Fort Point during this decade. There was, however, still another battery established in 1797. This was to the east on Point Medanos, later called Point San Jose, and Black Point, renamed Mason, and long occupied by a battery. It was known as the Battery Yerba Buena, designed to command the shore stretching westward to Fort Point, and that stretching eastward to what was called later North Point, together with the body of water between that shore and Alcatraz Island, already so called, known as the anchorage of Yerba Buena, though it does not appear that any vessel except that of Vancouver (the explorer) ever had anchored there. Thus it will be seen that the name Yerba Buena, while it may have been given in a general way to the whole eastern part of the peninsula from Black Point to Rincon Point, was applied in these early times particularly to the North Beach region and not as is commonly supposed, and as was the case after 1830, to the cove south of Telegraph Hill. Of the battery (Bateria de la Yerba Buena), we know but little save that it was a less elaborate work than Fort San Joaquin, being hastily constructed of brushwood fascines for the most part, with eight embrasures and 5 eight-pound guns not needed at the fort. No permanent garrison was kept here, but at least until after 1800, the works were visited daily by a sentinel and to a certain extent kept in order."

HISTORY OF CALIFORNIA

EPILOGUE: Vancouver's Observations. The explorer, Vancouver, was the first foreigner to visit San Francisco Bay. "...his visit was one of the chief interruptions of the dull monotony of San Francisco life during the decade.... As Vancouver entered the port at nightfall November 14, 1792, he looked in vain for the lights of the town which he supposed to be planted here, and next morning the only sign of civilization was the herds seen in the distance. After a quail-shooting expedition on the hills where the city now stands, he came into contact with Commandant Sal and was entertained at the presidio where the wife of Don Hermenegildo received him 'decently dressed, seated cross-legged on a mat, placed on a small square wooden platform raised three or four inches from the ground, nearly in front of the door, with two daughters and a son, clean and decently dressed, sitting by her; this being the mode observed by these ladies when they receive visitors.'" He visited the mission and was taken everywhere. "...though greatly surprised at the weakness and poverty of the Spanish establishment and the lack of 'those articles which alone can render the essential of life capable of being relished,' yet for the kindness and hospitality of the people he had nothing but words of praise. ...[He] found Yerba Buena a better anchorage than the usual one nearer the presidio.

"Every facility was afforded him for obtaining wood, water, and supplies, though the carts placed at the disposition of the sailors were found to be a more clumsy and useless contrivance on land than the rude balsas of the natives as water craft."

HISTORY OF CALIFORNIA

EPILOGUE: Volunteers leave. In the autumn of 1803, the first contingents left *Alta California* with their families on the *Princesa* and the *Activa.* The rest left in 1804.

Definition of the Volunteers and their duties: *"Compañía Franca de Voluntarios de Cataluña* — An unattached unit with respect to regimental organization referred to as a *Compañía Suelta,* or Free Company, to be used in the employment of Royal interests as a troubleshooting reserve unit in *Provincias Internas* of New Spain."

REAL PEOPLE, MILITARY UNITS, AND SHIPS IN THE STORY

Sergeant [José] Joaquín Tico. First Sergeant of the first company of Catalan Volunteers. Born in old Spain, he came as a soldier to New Spain (Mexico) where he met and married Juana Carrera.

Tico children.

Juan Nepomucino	Born in New Spain, 1790
Rosalía Joaquina Josefa	Born at Presidio San Francisco, September 4, 1796
Fernando José María Ignacio Martin	Born at Presidio San Francisco, April 9, 1798
María Rafaela Eduarda	Born at Presidio San Francisco, October 12, 1799
Antonio Tomás	Born at Presidio Monterey, May 4, 1801

José Martínez. Drummer. His name is on the list of arrivals to Alta California in 1796.

Hernan (Hernando) Cortez (Cortes): Soldier and explorer for Spain; conquerer of the Aztec and Maya peoples. From Cuba, in 1519, he left his hacienda and slaves to sail with soldiers to "Veracruz, Mexico," conquering and killing for the gold and silver in the country.

Gaspar de Portolá. Governor of Baja California commissioned to accompany Father Serra and Pedro Fages to Alta California in 1769.

El Rey Carlos IV. Charles the Fourth, King of Spain, of the House of Bourbon. "El Rey Carlos III ruled 1759-

1788, el Politico; Carlos IV ruled 1788-1808, el
Cazador."   **HISTORIA DE ESPAÑA**

Cristóbal Colón. Navigator and explorer for Queen
Isabella of Spain. Discovered the New World in 1492.

Antonio Pol. A recruiter of Spanish Troops to go to
Havana, Cuba and New Spain in 1767.

Coronel Francisco Elizando of the Dragones de
España and officer in charge of operations during the
Sonoran War (1767-1773).

Captain Augustine Callis. He was born sometime in
1718 in Vich, a Principality of Catalonia. At seventeen
he enlisted in the Regimiento de Fusileros de
Barcelona, rising through the ranks to become a
lieutenant. Then in 1748, his company was
extinguished after thirteen years of military
campaigns, mainly in Naples and Italy.
    At age thirty-one, he returned to Vich, married, had
two children, and intended to settle down as a farmer.
But when the call went out to go to battle against
Portugal, he didn't hesitate and joined the Second
Regiment of Light Infantry of Catalonia as a lieutenant.
Obviously, Don Augustine preferred the life of a soldier
to that of a farmer.
    In April 1767, Callis, now 49 years old, committed
himself to the organization and leadership of the
Catalonia Volunteers. His family was not pleased with
his decision. He made monetary arrangements before
he left so that his wife and children would be taken
care of. He, like José Joaquín Tico and many others,
received an emotional farewell as he began the march
to Cádiz via Madrid and Sevilla.

Teniente-coronel Pedro de Alberni. Lieutenant-

Colonel and Captain of the first company of Catalonian Volunteers. At one time in his military career, he was cited for insubordination after he had asked eighteen times that his soldiers be given two-months back pay owed them. He joined the army at a very early age. One record says he entered an academy at age twelve.

Juana Vélez de Alberni. The above officer's wife. She was from Tepíc, Nayarit, Nueva España. Pedro Alberni probably met her while stationed there.

Teniente Pedro Fages. Lieutenant and Captain of the second company of Catalonian Volunteers. He accompanied Padre Junípero Serra to Alta California. Both men spoke Catalán as their first language. Serra and Fages were never good friends. The problem between them apparently arose when they vied for authority in Alta California.

Padre Junípero Serra. Miguel José Serra, born at Petra on the Island of Mallorca, Spain, entered the Order of St. Francis of Assisi and took the new first name, Junípero. He received his Doctor of Divinity degree, then became professor at the University of Mallorca where he taught and preached for nine years. In 1749, at the age of thirty-six, he sailed from Cádiz, Spain with Padre Francisco Palou.

He walked 275 miles from Vera Cruz to dedicate his mission vocation at the shrine of Mexico's Lady of Guadalupe. Serra helped build five missions in the Sierra Gorda Mountains of Central Mexico on his first assignment. Then he served out of Mexico City as a home missionary for nine years.

In 1767, when the Franciscans of Mexico were asked to take over the remote missions in Baja California, Serra was given the responsibility of doing so. In 1769, at the age of fifty-four, he accompanied the Portolá expedition overland to establish presidios and missions. He established nine missions of the twenty-one. Serra died at the age of seventy at Mission San Carlos Borromeo where he was buried. He was president of missions in Alta Californa 1769-1784.

Padre José Ramon Abella. Served at the presidio chapel when María Rafaela Tico was baptized in 1799 (possibly he traveled from Mission Dolores).

Padre Diego Garcia. Served at the presidio chapel when Rosalía was baptized.

Padre Ferman Francisco de Lasuén. President of the California Missions from 1785-1803.

Padre Martin Landaeta. Served at the chapel (possibly coming from Mission Dolores) when Fernando Tico was baptized in 1798.

Gobernador Diego Borica. Governor Borica was born in Spain. While serving in Monterey in 1799, he applied to the viceroy in Mexico City for a leave of absence to recuperate his health. He said he had served thirty-six years, twenty-five of which had been spent in active campaigns against Indian tribes, and tours of inspection of presidios, mining camps, and other settlements in the Provincias Internas.

He said he had been on horseback approximately 10,475 leagues which had given rise to a malady which demanded medical treatment. He was given an eight-months leave. He left for his period of recuperation accompanied by a packtrain from Pueblo San José that had been ordered for him by the replacement governor. He boarded the Concepción to San Blas at San Diego. He died in 1800.

He was a well-educated man who spent much time with his family. Borica introduced compulsory education in Alta California; years later it became reality throughout. Some priests taught colonists' sons. Generally they resisted teaching anything more than was necessary for use at the missions.

Borica insisted that fathers train their sons in mechanical occupations. Family pride in the best military families caused resistance to the idea.

The military post, Yerba Buena, was established during his term.

"As long as he was in office, he did not permit the natives to be hunted down like dogs, nor did he permit the lashing of natives until they bled."

José de la Guerra y Noriega. Born of a noble family in Spain. He was sent to New Spain at the age of thirteen to live with an uncle who had an import business; he worked well with figures; later became a military cadet and trained in New Spain.

Served at Presidio Monterey in 1802.

Married (with the king's permission) María Antonia Carrillo of Santa Barbara.

Became commander of Presidio Santa Barbara in 1815 where he remained in authority after the revolution against Spain in 1821, in spite of other Spanish-born having to leave. He died February 18, 1858 at the age of seventy-nine.

Virrey Marqués de Branciforte. Viceroy Branciforte's complete name was don Miguel de la Grua Talamanca y Branciforte. Marqués of Branciforte was a native of Sicily and belonged to the family of the Princes of Carine. He was invested with the Order of the Golden Fleece by Carlos IV. In spite of the fact he was an unpopular viceroy to those in New Spain, the third civil pueblo was named for him. The two other civil

pueblos were San José and Los Angeles. Villa
Branciforte was where the Ticos expected to retire.
The pueblo lost its name and was absorbed into
Mission Santa Cruz.

Marqués de Croix. The viceroy in Mexico City, 1767.

Captain George Vancouver. British explorer. Entered
navy as an able seaman at age 13. Vancouver Island
was named after him.

Lieutenant Peter Puget. British naval officer and
explorer. Puget Sound and Puget Island named for
him.

**Native tribes north of Guymas and those encount-
ered in the Sonoran Wars:** Tepoca, Salinero Tiburon
Islanders, Seri, Piatos, Yaqui, Pimo, Suaqui, Sibubapa,
and Apache.

**Segundo Regimiento de Infanteria Ligera de
Cataluña.** Second Regiment of Light Infantry,
Catalonia, Spain. Tico joined up in Barcelona with
this company of foot soldiers headed for Havana,
Cuba. On the march to Cádiz, the regiment was
divided into two companies known as Compañia
Franca de Voluntarios.

**Raymundo Carrillo, Ramona Noriega, Ana Marie
Nuñez, Maria Antonia Carrillo.** Real people in the
story.

The San Carlos. A coastal frigate built in the shipyard
at San Blas in time to transport troops to Sonora in
1767. Later it was used as a troop transport to Nootka
and to Alta California. It was wrecked in San
Francisco Bay in 1797, a year after the Tico family
arrived in Alta California.

La Concepción. A coastal ship used as a troop transport to Nootka, as well as to explore the northern coasts.

The Juno. Spanish ship bringing troops to Santacruz, New Spain from Cádiz, Spain.

The San Juan. The storeship accompanying the Juno on its voyage from Cádiz to Santacruz.

La Laurentana. A coastal packet boat and troop transport to Guaymas.

La Princesa Real. A coastal packet boat and troop transport to Nootka.

The San Antonio. A coastal packet ship, and troop transport to Sonora.

The Valdéz. A coastal packet boat carrying Catalan Volunteers to Alta California in 1796.

Don Antonio de la Colina. Captain of the Juno.

Don Francisco Eliza. Captain of the Concepción. He had a good reputation because of his naval training. In 1805, he became head of the Spanish Navy.

Don Manuel Quimper. Captain of the Princesa Real.

Don Salvador Fidalgo. Captain of the San Carlos when troops went to Nootka.

LOCATIONS MENTIONED IN THE STORY

The United States of America

California (Alta California). "After 1769, the northern country was for a time known as the New Establishments, Los Establecimentos de San Diego y Monterey, or the Northern Missions. ...without any uniformity, the upper country began to be known as California Septentrional, California del Norte, Nueva California, or California Superior. But gradually Alta California became more common than the others, both in private and official communications, though from the date of the separation of the provinces in 1804, Nueva California became the legal name, as did Alta California after 1824. In these later times, Las Californias meant not as at first, Las Islas Californias, but the two provinces old and new, lower and upper. Down to 1846, however, the whole country was often called a peninsula by Mexicans and Californians, even in official documents."

HISTORY OF CALIFORNIA

Alaska (Unalaska). Many coastal towns were declared Spanish possessions. Maps today show that some places still retain their Spanish names.

Carmel, California. The location of Mission San Carlos Borromeo. You may visit it today.

Monterey, California. The capital of Alta California at the time it became a state. Some early spellings are Mont y Rey and Monterrey. Among the many historic sites to be seen is the Monterey Presidio on Pacific Street, which is now the U.S. Army Language School. The Royal Presidio Chapel where Antonio Tomás Tico was baptized is called San Carlos Cathedral and is on Church St. Founded in 1770, it was to be the mission church of the port. It became the church for the Spanish colonists and soldiers instead when the mission moved to Carmel in 1771.

San Diego, California. The first mission and presidio in Alta California were founded here. The mission may be visited; the Serra Museum marks the site of first presidio. Here Father Serra waited for the San Carlos carrying Lt. Fages and Catalan soldiers to join his land force. When the ship arrived, most of the sailors and soldiers were sick or had died from scurvy. Fages returned to New Spain for replacements.

San Francisco, California (Yerba Buena). The earliest *pueblo* was under present-day Oakland Bay Bridge. Mission Dolores is at 16th and Dolores Streets; presidio site near Golden Gate Bridge.

Los Angeles, CA; San Jose, CA; Santa Cruz, CA (Villa Branciforte). Real places existing today, except Branciforte.

The United States of Mexico

Baja California. The division of the two Californias is just below San Diego. The name California may have come from a popular Spanish novel written in the middle 1500's.

Guadalajara (Capital of Jalisco). 290 miles (467 kilometers) northwest of Mexico City, in a rich farming and mining region. Tree-shaded public square and parks date to old Spanish days.

Gulf of California (El Mar de Cortez, Vermillion Sea). On Mexico's western coast; **Gulf of Mexico** on its eastern coast.

Guaymas. A Mexican port on the Gulf of California at Sonora. Early spelling was *Guajmas.*

Mazatlán. Today it is Mexico's largest Pacific Ocean port. It is located at the foot of the Sierra Madre Mountains, near the mouth of the Gulf of California.

Mexico City (la Ciudad de Méjico). The capital of Mexico. It is 7,575 feet above sea level. Founded about 1325 as Tenoctitlán, the Aztec capital.

Puebla (Capital of the state of Puebla). It lies 65 miles (105 kilometers) east from Mexico City. The city still has many beautiful Spanish style churches and other buildings. The chief products are cotton textiles (begun during mission times), glass and fine pottery.

San Blas (A coastal mainland city on the Gulf of California). It is located almost midway between Guadalajara and Mazatlán. A very important port at the time of the Ticos.

Sonora (A state in northwestern Mexico). Its mountains contain rich deposits of copper, lead, graphite, and some silver. Farmers in the river valleys grow rice, wheat, chickpeas,

tomatoes, vegetables, and cotton. At the time of the Ticos, it was
a large desert and mountain area that stretched into Arizona,
New Mexico, and Texas. Hermosillo is the capital and largest city
and was the starting point for several groups of Spanish/
Mexicans that came to Alta California as colonists.

Tepic. Located on the west coast in the Nayarit Mountains of the
Sierra Madre chain.

Veracruz. Founded by Hernando Cortez in 1519, it is Mexico's
first Spanish settlement. It is 200 miles (320 kilometers) east of
Mexico City. Today it is the chief port on the Gulf of Mexico.

Canada

Nootka. Nootka, the city is on an island also named Nootka in
the Pacific Ocean. It is connected by waterways to Vancouver
Island. The name, Nootka, comes from a tribe of Indians
inhabiting the island. Early writing designated the place as Nuca.
Nutka, Puerto de Nuca, Puerto de San Lorenzo de Nuca, and
Friendly Cove. The strait of Juan de Fuca is at the southern tip
of Vancouver Island.
      Many locations still retain their Spanish names. The San
Juan Islands are a group of over 170 islands that lie between the
state of Washington and Vancouver Island. They are bounded by
the Haro and Rosario straits and belong to the U.S.

Cuba

Habana (La Habana). The Capital of the island country, Cuba,
where Cortez had his hacienda and from which he sailed to
conquer the Indians in New Spain. Cuba lies off the Florida Keys
between the Gulf of Mexico and the Atlantic Ocean.

Spain

Spain (España). Until Ferdinand united the country, the Iberian
Peninsula was inhabited by separate groups of very diverse
people. Modern-day provinces still retain much of their original
individuality.

Barcelona (Capital of Catalonia). It has always been an
important seaport.

Cádiz: Believed to be the oldest seaport in continuous use in Europe. It is on the Atlantic coast.

Castile. Once a powerful kingdom. It was united to another powerful kingdom called Aragon in 1479. From there, Ferdinand and Isabella ruled at the time of Christopher Columbus. Today the map shows Old Castile and New Castile. Each Castile has been divided into modern-day provinces. The Castilian language is taught in most Spanish language classes.

Catalonia (Cataluña). A northeastern Spanish province on the shore of the Mediterranean Sea near the Pyrenees Mountains.

Madrid (The capital of Spain). It is located about 300 miles inland from Barcelona.

Pueblo de Sedo. No one seems to know where it was located in Catalonia. Many small villages disappear over periods of time.

Pyrenees Mountains (los Pirineos). A natural boundary between Spain and France.

Seville (Sevilla). An important inland port near the Atlantic Ocean. It lies 60 miles (87 kilometers) northeast of Cádiz on the Guadaquiver River. It is the capital of the province of Seville.

Belgium

Belgium (Bélgica). A small country bordering Germany and the North Sea. In earliest times, it was known as a Low Country. Spain, Austria and France governed the area at different times. The Low Countries lie between France and Germany and the North Sea. All the area was once known as the Kingdom of the Netherlands. In 1830, the Low Countries were divided into Belgium, Luxembourg, and The Netherlands.

Cyprus

Cyprus (Chipre). An important island country in the Mediterranean Sea.

England

Gibraltar. A 2.3 square mile (6 square kilometers) Peninsula that belonged to Spain until the treaty of Utrect in 1713. A neutral strip of land separates the British possession from Spain. The "rock of Gibraltar" is 1,398 feet high (426 meters). All food is imported; collected rain water in reservoirs supplies the people living there. It has been of strategic military value to the British.

France

France (Francia). shares the Pyrenees Mountains with Spain.

Italy

Italy (Italia). Resembles a big boot, located between the Adriatic Sea and the Tyrrhenian Sea, at the Mediterranean Sea.

Venice (Venicia). Was a separate city-state early in its history. It is now a city of canals within Italy.

Russia

Russia (Rusia). Russians sailed across the Bering Sea to Alaska because of the fur trade. By 1812, they had come as far south as Alta California where they established a trading post approximately 100 miles from San Francisco called Fort Ross. Mr. Sutter, of Sutter's Mills, purchased the fort in 1841.

Philippine Islands

Philippine Islands (Los Filipinos). Manila, the capital, was established very early as an important trade center with Nueva España because of its location and favorable sea currents.

Other Countries

Africa; Portugal; China

South America: Chile, Perú, Argentina

Regarding coffee: Ethiopia, Arabia, Turkey, Brazil, America

Regarding cacao: Central America, Amazon-Orinoco River Basin, South America, Mexico, Italy, Austria, Spain, France

INDIVIDUALS CREATED FOR THE STORY

Amparo (refuge, shelter)	— maid at señora Carrera's house during the party.
Antonio	— sargento Tico's older brother
Consuelo (consolation)	— spoken of by compañero aboard the Juno
Compañeros	— soldiers aboard the Juno
Couriers, soldiers officers, colonists	— at Veracruz
Graciela	— Juana's good friend
Jaime	— Juana Tico's cousin
María	— sargento Tico' sister
María	— maid at señora Carrera's when José revisits Tepíc
Mother	— José Joaquín's mother
Musicians	— at señora Carrera's
Padres	— except the Jesuits and those listed in "Real People"
Pablo (Paul)	— José's fisherman cousin
Pedro (Peter)	— José's younger brother
Pepe	— cook for señora Carrera
Relatives	— at señora Tico's house
Sailors and guards	
Señora Carrera	— mother and grandmother
Señora Fernandez	— at the plaza
Señora Flora	— herb lady
Señora Mendoza	— neighbor who sells milk
Señora Rojas	— neighbor who sells eggs
Señores Gómez, López, and Rodríguez	— friends, neighbors
Señor Galindo	— old soldier
Señor Sobato	— coffee house owner
Calle de Soldado	— where señora Carrera and Juana lived

GLOSSARY OF ENGLISH WORDS AND
EXPRESSIONS AS USED IN THE STORY

A

abandoned	-	deserted; forsaken; rejected; vacant
abruptly	-	quickly; unexpectedly
absolutely true	-	positively; without question it is right
accept	-	receive; take from someone
accompaniment	-	a drum beat to keep in step; an orchestra to dance to; a piano for a singer to keep the melody and time
accomplish	-	achieve; realize; finish; do
accustom	-	habit; to get used to
A.D.	-	(anno Domini) signifies time since Christ Jesus was born - a marker for determining when historic events took place
additional	-	more
adjust	-	getting used to
adjustment	-	getting used to something new
administrator	-	director; manager; supervisor
admonition	-	warning; advice; caution
adventure	-	quest; look for interesting experiences
advised	-	told what to think or do
afterthought	-	a thought added later
agreement	-	after two people say something is ok
ailment	-	sickness; problem
alert	-	mindful of; watchful of; signal
allotted	-	only a certain amount; what is allowed
allowance	-	money paid to people in need
aloof	-	not friendly
altar	-	an important table on a platform in the front of a church
altitude	-	elevation; height
amazed	-	surprised; awed
amber	-	a shade of yellow
amble along in a rolling gait	-	type of walking; feet wide apart, swaying somewhat from side to side
anchors	-	very large heavy metal hooks on the end of heavy ropes or chains

		dropped into the water to keep a ship or boat from floating away when stopped
ancient	-	very, very old
announcement	-	someone tells something important to others
anticipating	-	awaiting; expecting
anvils	-	a heavy iron block with a smooth face where white hot metals are hammered into the desired shapes
anxious	-	worried
apologies	-	what one says on being sorry
applauding	-	clapping hands together
appoint	-	name; nominate; select
appointed	-	selected; chose
appreciative audience	-	those present like what they see and hear
apprehensive	-	worried and perhaps frightened
approach	-	comes toward
approval	-	consent; permission
approximately	-	about; almost; nearly; roughly
Arabian dhows	-	a type of sailboat from Arabia
argues	-	debates; quarrels
armor	-	heavy metal suits to protect the soldiers
aroma	-	smell; fragrance
arrangements	-	preparations; plans; provisions
ascend	-	go up
assigned	-	appointed; names the job and place
assignment	-	chore; duty; job; task
assortment	-	many different kinds of a thing, or different things
assurance	-	guarantee; promise; certainty; security
assure	-	promise; says everything is fine; confirm
astonishment	-	amazement; awe; surprise; wonder
at ease	-	to stand in a relaxed manner - not stiffly
at the mercy of	-	no one had control over the actions of the ocean - it had full control over them
authorized	-	enabled; told to be in charge; appointed

available	-	at hand; obtainable
avoid	-	evade; escape; dodge; avert; bypass
awkward	-	clumsy; not what one is used to
awnings	-	heavy material suspended over objects to protect them from sun or rain; canvas

B

bales	-	large bundles closely compressed
ballast of sand & gravel	-	placed in the bottom of a ship to keep it balanced and upright
balsa canoe	-	canoe constructed of multiple bundles of wands, canes, reeds, sedges or bark rolls lashed together and arranged in such a fashion as to create a cavity or hold
bamboo	-	a sturdy tall grass with hollow stems
bandana	-	kerchief or scarf tied around the head
banns	-	notice of marriage given three times in the church of each of the ones to be married
baptize	-	the priest sprinkles the head of the baby with water, gives it the name the parents want, and blesses it; now the baby has become a member of the Catholic Church
barbecued	-	cooked over, or next to, wood or coals
barely enough	-	just enough - nothing left over
barracks	-	building or several buildings to house soldiers
bartering	-	bargaining; trading
basin	-	bowl
bawling	-	the sound a calf makes when it cries out
bay	-	cove; harbor; protected body of water
bazaar	-	type of market where all sorts of things are sold
B.C.	-	before Christ Jesus was born; a marker for determining when historic events took place
bearable	-	able to tolerate; able to endure
bearing	-	going toward a particular direction

befallen	-	occured; took place
beggars guild	-	there were so many beggars that they formed a group and decided where they would stand and beg for food and money; formed for aid and protection
bill of lading	-	paper sent with goods telling what is being sent and where it is to go
blast	-	the great sound the musket made when fired
blazing	-	burning; flaring up
blazing torch	-	bundle of twigs and branches set afire, then used to set fire to the hut
blinders	-	flaps at the sides of an animal's eyes, limiting the animal to seeing only straight ahead.
blistered feet	-	the place where shoes keep rubbing often forms a pocket that is filled with liquid and called a blister
bluffs	-	cliffs; bank of hills
blurt out	-	exclaim; speak out
board	-	to get on a ship
boisterous	-	rowdy; noisy
bonus	-	reward; something extra in the way of money or privileges given by the military
boring	-	something that does not create interest
bothersome	-	pestering; annoying
bouts of sickness	-	being sick many times
bow	-	the front of the ship; the stern is the back
branding time	-	in the spring, the missionaries, ranchers, and presidios with cattle burned their "brand" or mark into the hides of the new calves to distinguish ownership of them
brave	-	courageous; without fear
brawl	-	fight
brawny	-	muscular; tough
breeze	-	soft wind
brief	-	short
brief farewell	-	not much time to say good-bye
brig	-	used in the story as the holding cell for prisoners; also means a brigantine - a type of ship

broad smile	-	big smile that almost covers the face
broad sweep	-	the soldiers fanned out, then went forward
browse	-	just looking around
bulging picnic basket	-	a basket completely filled with food, making the sides stick out more than usual
buried	-	put into the ground
bustling	-	busy; many people moving about
butchered	-	slaughtered and cut up for cooking

C

cadence	-	rhythm; beat
calloused	-	hard, rough skin
calm	-	quiet; composed; serene
camel caravan	-	a group of camels traveling together carrying men and goods
campsite	-	a place to put up tents & make a bonfire
cane	-	a wooden stick to help one walk
canopies	-	type of roof made of material or wood
canvases	-	large pieces of heavy material, often oiled to keep out the rain
canyons	-	a deep valley with steep sides
capital	-	the official seat of government
capsize	-	when a ship turns over in the water, it "capsizes"
captive audience	-	people had to stay, there was no place to go
casually mentions	-	something said as an afterthought — as though it were not important enough to emphasize
cathedral	-	a place of worship
caulked the hull	-	filled cracks where leaks occurred
cavalry units	-	soldiers on horseback
cemetery	-	a place to bury people after they die
centuries	-	hundreds of years - 100 years is one century
chamber pot	-	because there was no indoor plumbing, a pot was placed under the bed or in a small cabinet to be used when it was not convenient to go to the outhouse; Juana probably poured the contents over the railing into the sea

channel	-	strait; passage; course
chanteys	-	songs sung by sailors in rhythm with their work
chapel	-	a small church; smaller dedicated room within a large church
chariot	-	a two-wheeled vehicle or cart drawn by horses and used in races, processions and wars by ancient Romans
chieftains	-	leaders of the tribes
chimes in	-	rings in; someone adds his opinion in a discussion between other people
choice	-	to select from two or several
chores	-	work that needs to be done
civilized	-	those who behave themselves in a decent polite manner and keep themselves clean
clever	-	alert; illusive; knew where to hide
click to the donkey	-	sound made by putting tongue to roof of one's mouth and sucking in
clumsily	-	heavy-handed; rough; awkward
clustered	-	gathered together; swarmed; grouped
coarse	-	rough; thick and rough; not fine
coasts	-	land on the edge of an ocean
cobbler	-	shoemaker
cobblestone street	-	rough street made of medium-size stones
cockade	-	ornament worn on the hat such as feathers or plumes
cockfight	-	a fight between two male chickens (cocks)
cockroach	-	an insect that looks for food everywhere and isn't particular about what it eats; boxes of food and open dishes with food should be tightly covered to keep them out; brown in color, some with wings; move quickly
coffeehouse	-	a place to drink coffee and talk with friends, or listen to someone give a talk
collect my wits	-	compose my thoughts; gather my thoughts

colonies	-	conquered possessions, or settlements of people under the control of a foreign power
comical	-	funny; humorous
commotion	-	noise; disturbance
companies (military)	-	divisions of soldiers into groups
compared to	-	making a decision between two or more things; to weigh the similarities and differences
complaints	-	telling of things that do not please one
completely	-	totally; wholly
compose one's thoughts	-	taking time to think about what one will say before saying it
concentrate	-	to think long and seriously
concessions	-	land given by permission - borrowed land
(his) condition	-	how he felt and looked
confession	-	(to the priest) telling of bad things one has done and asking forgiveness (since he believes he may die in the storm)
confining	-	storm kept everyone below deck like prisoners
confirm	-	to say that something already said or done is true
confused	-	not sure what something means
confusion of	-	jumble of (odors, smells)
congratulations	-	best wishes
congregating	-	a group coming together
conjures up	-	calls to mind; imagines
conquest	-	captured the country and its people
considerate	-	thoughtful; thinking of others' well-being
console	-	comfort someone
constant	-	all the time
constructed	-	built
consultation	-	to ask another's opinion on something
consulted	-	asked
contract	-	a signed agreement between two or more persons
conversation	-	talking together
convinced	-	reassured; persuaded; satisfied
copying	-	doing what someone else does; mimics

corporal	-	one of the first ranks given a soldier in the army - not an officer rank
corridors	-	halls; passageways
couriers	-	mailmen; in the story, the couriers rode on horseback, probably changing horses at several places along the way
cowlick	-	where one's hair is naturally unruly
cravat	-	a type of men's tie
crescendo	-	a rise in the noise level
crevices	-	cracks; very narrow places
crew	-	sailors aboard ship
crewless	-	without a crew; no sailors aboard
crippled	-	disabled; injured legs or arms
crisis	-	turning point; plight
crucifix	-	religious item; a cross
crude	-	coarse; uncouth; undeveloped
crudely made	-	very roughly made
cultivate (-ation)	-	plant crops; keep the land planted
culture	-	customs; such as the American culture, Japanese culture, Spanish culture, Mexican culture, etc.
customs house	-	the place where ships and people had to stop before they could do business, or come into the country; taxes and duties were paid there after inspections by the customs officers
cutting down on expenses	-	not spending as much as before

D

dab	-	touch several times without rubbing
damask	-	a type of material
dangerous	-	something to fear
dash to his side	-	ran quickly to his side
dead serious	-	absolutely serious
decide, decision	-	the result of making up one's mind about something
decks	-	the name for "floors" of a ship
deep furrows etched on leathery, sunburned faces	-	deep lines permanently set on leather-like, red-brown faces — near eyes, mouth and forehead
defeated	-	lost; didn't win
defend	-	to keep out an invader by weapons

		or by words
delegated authority	-	assigned command
deliberate fury	-	purposeful fierceness; intense
deliberately	-	purposely; planned to do it or say it
dense woods	-	forest thick with trees
depend on seeing	-	one expects to see something
depending on	-	put faith in something
deport, deportation	-	banish; exile; expel
depressed	-	exceptionally sad; gives up
description	-	telling what something looks like
deserter	-	escaped; ran away from the army
deserve	-	to earn
desolate	-	nothing there
despair	-	giving up hope; saddened
despondently	-	discouraged; downcast
destination	-	goal; aim; end
determined	-	firm; decisive
detour	-	to have to go around a place or thing
devastating	-	cataclysmic; calamitous; catastrophic; disastrous; very bad
diarrhea	-	a sickness of the intestines
dicker	-	argue over something; bargain
dignified	-	distinguished; honorable; stately
dimly-lighted	-	not bright; almost dark
disagreement	-	to differ; quarrel
disappears	-	goes out of sight
disappointment	-	feelings of sadness that something did not turn out as expected
discourage	-	saddened; frustrated
discussions	-	talks between people
disembark	-	to get off a ship
disgusted	-	repulsed; sickened; offended
disheartened	-	depressed; dismayed; discouraged
disheveled and haggard	-	unshaven, with straggly hair and clothes; gaunt, care-worn, exhausted
dismissed	-	told to leave
dismount	-	to get off a horse
dispatch	-	a message
displays	-	shows; arranges things to be seen by others
dispositions	-	behavior: happy, sad, touchy, etc.
distance	-	space; area: a short distance, long distance

distributing	-	giving; dispensing; disbursing; doling
disturbed	-	bothered; awakened
disturbing news	-	troublesome; bad news
doldrums	-	when there is no wind to fill the sails to push the ship along
dolphins	-	large thin-bodied ocean fish
doom the attack	-	destroy the attack; end the attack
doubting	-	questioning; wondering; wavering; distrusting
dozing	-	lightly sleeping
drafty	-	wind blows in through cracks, making it cold inside
drape	-	to place body over the saddle with arms and legs hanging down
drawing near	-	coming close
dreadful time	-	terrible experience
dregs	-	an extremely small amount
drift off to sleep	-	to gently go to sleep
drill practice	-	marching; practice marching with guns; obeying directions
dropsy	-	a sickness; it might have a different name today
drought	-	a period of no rain; very dry
drudgery	-	dull, irksome duties
dufflebag	-	a fabric or leather bag
duties and taxes	-	money the government collects
dysentery	-	caused by bad food, water or unsanitary toilet practices; to keep from having this illness, cook meat thoroughly, boil water suspected to be contaminated, wash hands after using toilet facilities and before handling food

E

earnest	-	devoted; diligent; serious
edict	-	proclamation; law
elation	-	joy; happiness
elite	-	special; one of a kind
embark	-	to get on a ship; to begin
emerge	-	to come out from
emergency	-	a great need for help
emigrants	-	those who leave one country and make their home in another
encircle	-	to go all around

encountered	-	met up with; experienced
enemy	-	foe; adversary; opponent; rival
energetically	-	spritely; speedily
engulfs	-	surrounds; envelops
enlistee	-	soldier who signs up to serve in the army
entertainment in Cádiz and Monterey	-	probably similar in many ways: dancing, watching dancers, visiting taverns, cock fights, bull fights, bull and bear fights, tricks with horses and horse races, etc.
entice	-	lure; tempt; induce; beguile
entrance	-	an opening through which to go inside
envelope	-	to cover entirely
envisions	-	imagines what something would be like
epidemic	-	general outbreak of disease
errands	-	going from one place to another to find things
especially	-	more than just special; purposefully
establish	-	organize; to build a foundation for an idea to get started
events	-	happenings
evident	-	an idea made clear; something that can be seen
excellent	-	superior; very good; perfect
exceptions	-	things that are different from the usual
excessive spending	-	spends more than is necessary
exchange of vows	-	swap promises
excited	-	delighted; thrilled
exclusively	-	only; no other
executor	-	administrator; one who acts for someone who has died to make sure that the money or items go to people mentioned in the dead person's will.
exhausted	-	very, very tired
expedition	-	exploration; voyage; mission
expensive	-	costs a lot
explore	-	search; investigate; examine; scout

F

fading coastline	-	as the ship sails farther and farther out to sea, the coast becomes just a line and finally disappears
faience	. -	earthenware dishes, vases, etc. decorated with opaque (not clear) colored glazes
flanks	-	the donkey's backsides over the rear legs
flash floods	-	rivers of water suddenly gush from the mountains and cover the land
flintlock	-	type of gun; musket
fond memories	-	thinking happy thoughts about long ago
ford	-	to wade across rivers or streams
foreigners	-	those who come from another country
foreign names	-	ships in port had names different from Spanish ships because they came from other countries
fort	-	fortification; a protected area with weapons and soldiers for the purpose of defending the land from invasion
frequent, frequently	-	often
frontier	-	outpost; farthest place; remote
frown	-	wrinkle one's forehead into a scowl
frustration	-	disappointed; not able to do what you want
full compliment	-	the expected number of soldiers in a company
fumigate	-	to expose to smoke or fumes; to disinfect
(big) fuss over	-	to pay more attention than is necessary

G

galley	-	kitchen on board ship
gallooned	-	decorated hat, with lace, embroidery, or braid of metallic thread, (see Notes Ch.9)
gambling	-	betting; taking a chance
gasps	-	to catch one's breath in surprise
gaunt and exhausted	-	thin, pale, drawn, and tired
gear	-	a soldier's equipment; outfit

generations	-	three generations would be grandfather, father and son
gestures	-	motions with hands and arms
giggles	-	small laughs
gilded	-	painted with gold
glinting	-	sparkling
gloomy quarters	-	dismal and dreary place to stay
gold pieces	-	money; gold coins
good fortune	-	good luck; prosperity
goods	-	items to sell; merchandise
goods-dealers	-	those who sell things
gossip	-	idle talk; small talk; rumor
gradual	-	little by little
granary	-	a type of barn to store grain - wheat, barley, etc.
grant	-	a measured amount of land given by the government with a title of ownership
grasped	-	to take hold strongly
grave, grave site	-	the place where someone is buried
grieving	-	being sad because of a death
guards	-	protectors
gunsmith	-	one who makes and repairs guns

H

haggling	-	arguing about the price
halyards	-	ropes that raise and lower the sails on a ship
handkerchief	-	a square of fine cotton to dab at one's eyes or nose; also used folded in a suit coat pocket
handout	-	something free
harass	-	bother; attack
hastily	-	in a hurry
hatch	-	hatchway; an opening, as well as the covering for the opening on a ship's deck
haul in	-	bring in or bring down (sails)
haul water	-	carry jugs of water from the stream
hawkers	-	vendors who shout out what they have to sell
headquarters	-	home base; head office
helter-skelter	-	going in all directions
hemmed towels	-	pieces of material that have had

		rough edges turned up and stitched with needle and thread to keep them neat
herbalist	-	a specialist who knows which plants are useable herbs
hesitate	-	doesn't do something right away; delays; waits
hideaway	-	a secret place
hides	-	skins
hired hand	-	a paid helper
hoisted	-	raised
horizon	-	where the sky and land, or the sky and sea, appear to meet in the distance
horsefly	-	very large fly with a big bite
huddled together	-	very close together
hull	-	the body of a ship
humid	-	damp
hunched over	-	shoulders rounded and body bent over
hurricanes	-	type of storm with much wind

I

imagination	-	something created in the mind
immediately	-	right away
impatient	-	in a hurry; does not like to wait
important	-	of great value
import license	-	a permit to bring goods into the country
impressive	-	a grand sight - one to remember
indentation	-	worn away; lower than the top
indignant	-	angry; offended; irate
information	-	news
(in) formation	-	in a particular manner such as in a line
inheritance	-	property received from a deceased individual
initials	-	the first letters of someone's name
insect-ridden	-	full of insects - mosquitoes, fleas, flies
insignia	-	distinguished by a mark or stamp
inspection	-	examination; looking it over
in spite of	-	a decision or action that goes on even when something else is happening

insubordination - rude to a superior officer
interrupted - temporarily stopped, then continues
invade - to come in without permission
invitation - asking someone to visit or do something with you
irate - very angry
issued new - giving out new military clothes, shoes, etc.
issues orders - officer tells soldiers what to do
it strikes me - an idea suddenly comes to me

J
jaunty angle - not straight; playful angle
jerky - dried meat
jester - a comic; clown; one who makes jokes
Jesuits - a religious group of the Catholic church; the Company of Jesus
jiggling - bouncing
jogs - a slow, steady type of running
journey - a trip; a voyage

K
kayak - an Eskimo canoe made of a frame covered with skins, except for a small opening in the center, and propelled by a double-bladed paddle
keg - type of barrel
kidnap - to steal a person
kilometer - 1000 meters; 3,280.08 feet; 0.621 of a mile (94 kilometers = 58.28 miles)
kindling - small pieces of wood only good for starting a fire

L
labor over a short note - those who had very little education, found it very hard work to write a letter; most soldiers could neither read nor write
laden - carrying a lot of things
lance - a type of long spear
land legs - after being on a ship for a long time and walking in a certain manner to keep one's balance (sea legs), it is often necessary to learn how to walk

		on land (land legs) after disembarking
lash	-	fasten; secure; tie
leak	-	place where water comes in
ledge	-	shelf
leisurely	-	slowly; in a relaxed manner
lieutenant	-	an officer rank
litter	-	device used to carry usually a single person
(to) liven dull meals	-	to make the same old meals more interesting
longboat	-	a very large rowboat
loyal	-	be a good friend to the king; one would respect and fight for him and his country
lulls	-	soothes
lurches	-	moves unexpectedly; jerks

M

machete	-	a large heavy knife used as a tool
makeshift	-	temporary
manages to find room	-	moves things around until there is enough space
maneuvering	-	dodging; going forward through obstacles
manservants	-	men assigned to take care of officers' food and clothing
marching briskly	-	marching in a lively way; energetically
marvel	-	to be awed or surprised by something
masts	-	high poles where sails are fastened
melancholy	-	depressed; sad; dejected; gloomy
merchandise	-	things for sale
merchants	-	those who buy goods to sell later
merge	-	to join together; become a single unit
midwife	-	a woman who understands childbirth and helps women having babies
miffed	-	insulted; wounded; angered
military	-	soldiers and their work
mimic	-	copy; imitate
miracle	-	completely unexpected and good
miserable	-	feels terrible; is seasick

misery	-	sorrow; woe; distress
misgivings	-	doubts; qualms; worries
misty air	-	fine rain in the air; fog
momentum	-	balance and speed
monopoly	-	no competition; the only one
monotonous	-	dull; same thing over and over
moodiness	-	irritable; sulky; sullen
motion	-	moving
mule train	-	a long line of mules carrying packs over their backs and sides
mumbled	-	did not speak clearly
musket	-	a type of gun
muster	-	a gathering of soldiers
mysterious	-	can't tell what it is; could be "spooky"

N

narrow gateway	-	ancient towns had walled cities and narrow entrances in order to keep enemies out
native	-	indigenous; national; natural; primitive; citizen inhabitant; resident
nauseating days	-	days (and nights) when most of the time is spent being seasick
nautical mile	-	a unit of speed of one nautical mile an hour
nautical mile. knot	-	see a dictionary for detailed discription
needlework	-	fancy sewing
neglected (condition)	-	did not keep something in good order
nestles	-	lies in a cozy, protected place
newcomers	-	people who have recently moved into the area
New World	-	The Americas - North, Central and South, as well as nearby islands
nimble	-	fast and accurate
nonchalant	-	casual; easy-going; relaxed
normal	-	typical; ordinary
notification	-	communicate; inform; announce
notorious warriors	-	well-known fighters
nursing her husband back to health	-	taking care of her sick husband

O

oars	-	type of paddles used to make the boat move (to row the boat through the water using oars)
object	-	does not agree
obligations	-	duties
obligingly	-	accommodates willingly; serves kindly
oblivious	-	doesn't know what's going on; doesn't see
obvious	-	noticeable; apparent; evident; clear
occasionally	-	once in a while
occupied	-	inhabited
official papers	-	sargento Tico's formal military papers that tell where he is going
omen	-	a sign; superstition
on edge	-	quick to take offense; nervous
opportunity	-	the right time to say or do something
optimistic	-	cheerful; confident; hopeful
orders	-	directive to go and do something
ornately	-	decorated with much design and paint
outgrown	-	too tall or too big to wear some item of clothing any longer
outhouses	-	outside toilets; usually there was a small, wooden, enclosed shed for men and a separate one for women
outskirts	-	the edge of a city
oxen	-	altered adult male cattle used as work animals and food

P

pace	-	stride; tempo; footsteps
parasols	-	umbrellas used against the sun's rays
passersby	-	people who walk by
patience	-	having time to wait; go slowly
patiently	-	gently waiting; slowly teaching
peacetime	-	a time when Spain was not fighting another country, or involved in a civil war
peers	-	looks at something
pension	-	money paid to a widow all at once, or at regular times during the year;

		money which had been saved from a military man's pay while he was alive and working; often the military would add to the money saved
persists	-	keeps coming back
personal requests	-	asking for themselves
pessimistically	-	a negative attitude; seeing only the problem
petitioned	-	asked; requested
petticoats	-	a skirt or skirts worn by a woman underneath her outer skirt or dress
pidgin	-	a language made up of other languages
pierces	-	punctures; stabs
pious expression	-	religious; showing devotion; serious
pitching	-	when putting up a tent, one is "pitching" it
placid	-	calm; peaceful
plague	-	epidemic of disease; outbreak of disease
plateau	-	smooth land rising above the land around it; "table" land
plod	-	walk heavily and slowly
poisonous snakes	-	rattlers, coral snakes, and other potentially lethal varieties
polishing	-	rubbing to make something shine
politely	-	with good manners
poorly equipped	-	does not have adequate supplies, cannons or guns
porcelain	-	a type of chinaware
port	-	a protected place for ships to anchor
position	-	place
post	-	a military assignment
pouches	-	bags; these were leather, had locks, and were sealed with the king's seal, or the viceroy's seal
poultices	-	a soft, usually heated, sometimes medicated, mass spread on cloth and applied to sores or other lesions for relief
practically	-	almost
precariously	-	dangerously; too close to the edge
prevails	-	that which is present; "calm prevails"
primitive	-	natural; not changed; rough; uncivilized

prisoners	-	captives; men put in jail
privileged men	-	men who have advantages others do not have, such as money, education or friendship with the king
(whole) process	-	entire procedure
procession	-	like a parade
prods (the oxen)	-	pokes the sides of animals with a long pole
progressed	-	made headway; advanced; growth; improvement
proper clearance	-	after inspection, and paying any duties or taxes on what one is carrying, being "cleared" to go on
prophecy	-	foretold; forecasting; known before it happens
protect	-	to take care of
protruding	-	sticking out
proud	-	happy about doing something well
provides	-	takes care of; gives
province	-	similar to a state
pull ourselves together	-	they stopped crying and grieving in order to do the necessary next thing
purposely	-	knowingly; intentionally; deliberately

Q

(crowded) quarters	-	a lot of people in a small space, home or room
quay	-	a dock made of stones
quilted	-	layers of skins or material sewn together with many rows of stitching
quota	-	the number of people needed to make up a "company" of soldiers

R

ragamuffin	-	poorly clothed, dirty, mischievous child
rages	-	rampages; raves; tempestuous
raiders	-	those who make sudden attacks
railing	-	trim that goes around the top of the hull
raise in rank	-	from sergeant to lieutenant
rancid	-	spoiled oil
rapid succession	-	quickly; one after another

rare occurrence	-	unusual; seldom happens
(to) ration	-	to use something in measured amounts; to use sparingly
realize	-	understanding; finally seeing the truth
reassure	-	cheer; encourage; assure; comfort
rebellious citizens	-	unhappy people who take up arms or in some way express their dislike of the government
reception	-	greeting
recognition	-	acceptance; aknowledgment; renown; remembers
recognizes	-	comes upon something or someone and knows what or who it is
recruiting officer	-	one who signs men up to become soldiers
refortify	-	to replace cannons; repair the old fort
regain composure	-	to get one's thoughts together once more after being sad, angry, or laughing; becoming calm
regardless	-	nevertheless; in spite of
rein in	-	pulling on reins for animal to stop
reins	-	lines of leather, sometimes rope, that are attached to a "bit" in the horse's mouth; the rider steers the horse by pulling on the reins
relax	-	not stiff or tense
release	-	remove from some imprisonment
reliable	-	trustworthy; dependable
relieved	-	happy that something turned out well
religious and territorial wars	-	wars to conquer people and force them to believe in the Catholic religion, and wars that are fought to get more land
religious relics	-	church artifacts; pictures; objects
reluctantly	-	does not really want to say or do it
remedies	-	medicines; herbs; to have answers to a problem
reminded	-	bringing a past happening to mind
rendezvous	-	a prescribed place of meeting
reorganizes	-	puts into better or different order
repaired	-	made right again
replacements	-	soldiers who are to take the place of those leaving a post

reputation	-	what you think of yourself or what others think about you - good or bad
respond	-	react; he did not react or respond to the remedies
responsibility	-	duty; in charge of something
restless	-	moves around a lot; fidgety
(unable to) resume his duties	-	not able to go back to work yet
retching	-	vomiting - often after food has already come up
retire	-	to leave one's job or work after many years
(cost of the) return passage	-	the money (cost) of tickets to go back (return passage) to New Spain on the ship
revelers	-	merrymakers; party people
reverberate	-	echo; resound; rumble; vibrate
rich goods	-	expensive things to sell
rigging	-	lines and chains used aboard a ship for working sails and supporting masts and spars
risky	-	dangerous
roll call	-	taking attendance out loud
root vegetables	-	grown underground - potatoes, carrots, etc.
rough water	-	the behavior of the sea; high waves or choppy waves
rounds a bend	-	goes around a curve in the road or path
routines	-	for the drummer to call to arms, call to eat, call to march, etc.; each activity would be represented by a different combination of beats; ruffle: a low continuous beating, less loud than a roll
rudderless	-	no steering mechanism; the tiller and rudder have separated; the rudder is located on the stern, underwater, and moves from side to side at the direction of the tiller, which is operated by a sailor
rude	-	someone with bad manners
ruffling hair	-	to run hands through hair; messing it up

rumors	-	gossip; hearsay
rungs	-	rounded sticks fitted into something on the sides and used as stairs
rutted path	-	in wet weather, carreta wheels sink into the mud; when mud dries, a rough dent is left where the wheels went through

s

sad	-	not happy
sailors	-	men who work on ships
sails	-	large sheets of canvas tied to masts to catch the wind in order to make the boat move; to sail
salute	-	recognition; placing the finger of the right hand to the forehead with palm open and thumb tucked in
sanctuary	-	a safe place; auditorium of a church
sashes	-	long pieces of cloth wrapped around waist
satisfied	-	completely happy at how things turned out
saunter	-	amble; stroll
scarcity	-	not enough; scant; sparse
scared	-	frightened; fearful
scarlet fever	-	a contagious disease
scarred-nose	-	the donkey had been into brambles or something else that scratched his nose, leaving marks
scoots across	-	slides across
scouts	-	special soldiers that spy out the land before regular soldiers go forward
scraggly	-	rough; irregular; ragged; shaggy
scramble	-	move fast, in any way possible
screeching	-	high pitched, unpleasant sound
scrubbing	-	washing with a brush; washing very well
scurried	-	ran away quickly
scurvy	-	an often fatal disease caused by not eating fresh fruit and vegetables for long periods of time
sea legs	-	a particular way one has to stand and walk while aboard ship to keep one's balance

seasick	-	some people are affected by the motion of the ship and become sick to their stomachs
seasoned sailors	-	sailors with many years of experience
secure havens	-	safe ports; safe anchorages
(to) secure ropes	-	to tie the ropes very well
separates	-	divides; goes in different directions
serenading	-	playing and singing to someone; a form of courtship
sergeant	-	the highest rank before becoming an officer
set aside the money	-	saved the money; put it into the pension fund; didn't spend the money
set sails	-	raise sails to begin a voyage
settlement	-	an area with very few people living there
severe	-	harsh; intense
share	-	to give to someone some of what you have
shark	-	a large fish in the ocean known to severely bite people who have fallen in the water or are swimming
shawl	-	a large piece of material placed around the shoulders
sheet	-	single piece of paper
(rain) sheets across the deck	-	raindrops falling hard and fast, so close are the drops they form a "sheet"
sheltered	-	protected
shelters	-	places of refuge for rest, probably made of poles and matting
ship's store	-	each ship had a store on board where people from the shore could make purchases
shiver	-	repeated quick moves by the body when cold or excited
shocked	-	very, very surprised; astounded; stunned
shocked and disbelieving	-	surprised, saddened, finds it hard to believe
shore-leave	-	sailors can go ashore after being on board ship for a long time
shortages	-	lack; scarcity; dearth

shouting	-	very loud talking
shrouded	-	head covered up, possibly the body too
shrugs his shoulders	-	lifts his shoulders up and down
(requesting) sick leave	-	asking to leave his post and return to New Spain for medical treatment
sigh of relief	-	a deep breath after things settle down
sighted	-	spied; see something one is looking for
signal	-	send a message; the captain shot off the gun
silhouetted	-	outlined against the sky
single swoop of flame	-	the thatch was so dry it burned up immediately
sizzling	-	sound made when a liquid hits hot coals
skeptical	-	doubtful
skillfully	-	cleverly; deftly; nimbly
skirmish	-	hand to hand fighting
sling and pulley	-	the sling is a wide strap placed under mules' bellies and fastened to a strong rope pulley which is fastened at the top of the mast; can be used to lift the mules up off the raft
slog	-	to walk or plod heavily
snuggles	-	sits very close to his father
sobbing	-	weeping; crying; wailing
social	-	being with other people
solemnly	-	dignified; serious
solitary	-	alone; one; single
son-in-law	-	daughter's husband
sow	-	a female hog; female pig
sow	-	to scatter seed; to plant seed
(if I could) spare the time	-	if I could take time from other activites
spars	-	masts; poles that hold sails
spellbound	-	captivated; entranced; fascinated; couldn't take his eyes off the sight in front of him
spire	-	a rod at the top of the church; may have a cross or other emblem at the top

spirits	-	an alcoholic drink like brandy
spit and polish	-	soldiers actually did spit on their shoes to polish them
splendid	-	elegant; rich-looking; special
sprigs	-	short stems with flowers attached
squashed	-	smashed
squawking	-	a raucous sound, loud and irritating
squeeze	-	to hold very close; to pinch
stake	-	a piece of wood or metal pounded into the ground
staples	-	basics; essentials; fundamentals
stares	-	gawks; watches
startles	-	surprises; frightens
stationed nearby	-	assigned closeby
stench	-	stink; smells bad
stern	-	rear part of the ship; the front part is called the bow
storage bin	-	a box or drawer; enclosed place for storing grain
storage space	-	where things are kept
stow	-	to store something
strain	-	tension; pressure; struggle
strait	-	a narrow body of water connecting two large bodies of water; body of water that runs between islands
stroll	-	a way of walking slowly
strong current	-	strong tide; strong flow of water
struggling	-	having trouble doing or thinking about something
stumble	-	falter; stagger; slip; fall
stunned	-	shocked; surprised; speechless
subdued	-	quieted; captured
success	-	accomplishment; what happens when one begins a project, finishes it, and the results are satisfactory
succumbed	-	gave into; became ill
suddenly checked	-	suddenly stopped
sufficient	-	enough
suggested	-	proposed; gave a possible answer
superstition	-	belief in things not true; omens
supply ship	-	carries tents, food, etc. - items needed for the soldiers once the ships reach their destination
(a) support to his wife	-	to be with her in her time of need; to stay with her so she does

		not feel alone
surprisingly	-	something returned to thought when it was not expected
surrounding	-	encircling
swashbucklers	-	on the order of pirates; tough sailors
swat	-	slap
swayback	-	not straight; caved in
sways from side to side	-	a rocking motion
swells and troughs	-	after a ship rides high on the sea's swell, or wave, the ship is then carried far down into the sea's trough, or channel between waves
swerve	-	to go around something or someone quickly
swiftly	-	rapidly; quickly
switched from	-	went from one thing to another
switched him	-	hit him with a switch - a common practice of that time; padres and fathers disciplined boys by hitting them with paddles or switches
symbol	-	something that replaces, or represents something; token

T

taking pity	-	feeling sorry for
tallow	-	animal fat used for making candles, soap, and oil for lamps
tanned pelts	-	animal skins dried and treated; pelts from muskrats, beavers, and seals were sold to be made into fur coats, hats, or capes for people in cold climates
tantalizing	-	mouthwatering; teasing
teakwood	-	a very hard wood grown in southeast Asia
teary-eyed	-	with tears in one's eyes
tease	-	to irritate or provoke
tedious	-	dull; unimaginative; wearisome
temporary	-	not permanent; can be moved or changed
terrifying	-	scary; frightening
thorns	-	needle-like growths on the sides of stems
threadbare	-	worn out in places

threading our way	-	walking single file; squeezing through
thrifty	-	economical; frugal; doesn't spend much money
tide	-	about every 24 hours and 26 minutes, the ocean and its inlets rise and fall; when it's flowing towards land (rising), the sailing ship comes in faster to its anchorage; when flowing out to sea, it makes it easier for the ship to get under way
tiller	-	a type of stick connected to the rudder that steers the ship
timid	-	shy; bashful
tirade	-	loud, long, unkind talk
(to) toast	-	raising glasses in a greeting or in good wishes to someone or group
toll	-	chime; peal; ring
torpid	-	slow, sleepy, sluggish; donkey's name is taken from this word
torrents	-	great quantity
tossed off course	-	strong winds and currents plus high waves carried the ship off its planned route
touchy disposition	-	quick to take offense and start a fight
tour	-	going around or through a place; sightseeing
tour of duty	-	length of time at one place for a soldier
tragically	-	sadly; devastatingly
tranquility	-	peacefulness; calmness
transferred	-	sent to another military post
transport	-	to carry by ship, wagon, mules, horses, or carts
treason, treasonous ideas	-	saying or doing things against one's country, usually punishable by death
treasury	-	where the money is kept
trek	-	long, difficult walk
tremendous	-	extremely great; terrible; extraordinary; dreadful
tribe	-	group of people living together
trim sails	-	to adjust the sails with reference to

		the direction of the wind and the course of the ship
tropical	-	humid; muggy; steamy; hot
trot	-	a gait; type of running
trudging	-	plod; wade; march
tunic	-	long brown robe priests wore
turbaned merchant	-	goods-dealer wearing a hat of cloth wrapped around and around his head
two-masted	-	a ship that has two main large poles (masts) from which the largest sails are fastened

U

uncharted	-	sea routes that are not recorded on paper; no map
uneventful	-	quiet; routine; boring; nothing important happening
unexpected	-	a surprise
unforeseen	-	something unpredictable; unexpected
uniform	-	special clothing which sets one apart from other people; shows type of work one does
unpredictable	-	can't tell what he, or it, will do
unrelenting	-	keeps it up without stopping
unsuspecting	-	not knowing; naive; didn't even think about it
upset	-	unhappy

V

vanished	-	disappeared; out of sight quickly
various	-	assorted; differing; several
vases	-	containers in which to put cut flowers
vendors	-	salesmen or women; merchants
vessel	-	ship
viceroy	-	the king's representative in his colonies; vice king
vie	-	compete; make it a contest
vigilance	-	alertness; attentiveness
voyage	-	a trip one takes on board a ship
voyager	-	one who travels by ship

W

waft through	-	drift; float; glide
wager	-	to bet; gamble
waistcoat	-	vest; short, sleeveless jacket
walked to and fro	-	walked back and forth
warehouse	-	large building for storing goods
wealthy	-	rich; has a lot of money
weapon	-	object with which to fight - gun, sword
weary	-	tired
weathered cheeks	-	sunburned and wrinkled face
weeping	-	silently crying
whales	-	large sea mammal
whiffs	-	puffs of smells or aromas in the air
whistles	-	pucker the lips, put the tongue in a special place, and blow air through the lips, making a musical or piercing sound
whitecaps	-	foam on choppy waves
whizzes	-	goes by very fast
will	-	document made by a living person listing where and to whom possessions should go after he or she dies; two witnesses must sign a will
wince	-	to make a face or grimace when something hurts
(something) within	-	Juan's mind begins to let in good thoughts about his father, making him feel happier.
without incident	-	nothing happened - especially something bad
without mishap	-	did not have an accident or something bad happen
wrestle the pigskins	-	the awkward shape of the pigskin made it difficult to handle
wretched	-	extremely terrible
wrings her hands	-	presses, squeezes, twists her hands

Y

yoke	-	a device around the neck of two oxen so they will move together

Z

zigzagging	-	first to the right, then the left

BIBLIOGRAPHY

BETTY CROCKER'S INTERNATIONAL COOKBOOK,
Random House, New York, Copyright 1980 by
General Mills, Inc., Minneapolis, MN

CALIFORNIA, AN INTIMATE HISTORY, Gertrude
Atherton, Blue Ribbon Books, Inc., NY

CALIFORNIA INDIAN WATERCRAFT, Richard W.
Cunningham, Copyright 1980, EZ Nature Books,
P.O. Box 4206, San Luis Obispo, CA 90403

CALIFORNIA RANCH COOKING, Jacqueline Higuera
McMahan, Copyright 1983, The Olive Press,
P. O. Box 194, Lake Hughes, CA 93532

EARLY CALIFORNIA COSTUMES, Margaret Gilbert
Mackey and Louise Pinkney Sooy, Stanford
University Press, Stanford University, CA,
Copyright 1932 by The Board of Trustees,
Leland Stanford Junior University

EARLY CALIFORNIA HOSPITALITY, Ana Béqué de
Packman, Copyright 1953, Academy Library
Guild, Fresno, CA

FODOR'S SPAIN, Eugene Fodor, Copyright 1970,
Fodor's Modern Guides, Inc.

HISTORIA DE ESPAÑA de José Terrero, Catedratica de
Historia Moderna de la Universidad de Valencia
(C), Editorial Ramon Sopena, S.A. *provenza*, 95,
Barcelona

HISTORY OF CALIFORNIA, Hubert Howe Bancroft, The
History Company, 1890, San Francisco, CA
Military records; correspondence; Catalonian
Volunteers; Pioneer Registry - (José) Joaquin
Tico, as well as his son, Fernando, listed
Joaquin: Compañia Franca, Vol.I-540; Vol. II-5;
PRV-748

HISTORY OF THE CONQUEST OF MEXICO AND
HISTORY OF THE CONQUEST OF PERU, William H.
Prescott, the Modern Library, New York, Random
House, Inc.

IBERIA, James A. Michener, A Fawcett Crest Book,
Fawcett Publications, Inc., Greenwich, CT,
Copyright 1968 by Random House, Inc.

LOS ANGELES, AN EPIC OF A CITY, Lynn Bowman,
Copyright 1974 by Howell-North Books, 1050
Parker Street, Berkeley, CA 94710

MEN, SHIPS AND THE SEA, Capt. Alan Villiers,
National Geographic Society, Washington, DC,
1973

100 PITFALLS IN SPANISH, Marion P. Holt (Staten
Island Community College and City University of
NY) and Juliane Dueber (University of Missouri,
St. Louis, MO), Copyright 1973 by Barron's
Educational Services, Inc., 113 Crossways Park
Dr., Woodbury, NY 11797

SPANISH BLUECOATS, Joseph P. Sánchez, University of New Mexico Press, Albuquerque, 1990 Permission obtained from The University of New Mexico Press to use experiences of the First Company as the setting for the military life of Sergeant José Joaquín Tico. Sergeant Tico and his son, Fernando, are mentioned on pages 80, 115 and 128. Sergeant Tico is mentioned relevant to his military duty in Nootka in 1789: experiences in Alta California and the reason that he did not achieve officer rank.

THE CALIFORNIA MISSIONS, Sunset Publishing Corporation, Menlo Park, CA

THE PAN-AMERICAN COOKBOOK, American Women's Club of Buenos Aires, Argentina, 1954

THE PACIFIC HISTORIAN, Vol. 22, No. 4, Winter 1978, University of The Pacific, Stockton, CA 95211

THOSE VULGAR TUBES, Joe J. Simmons III, Studies in Nautical Archaeology, Texas A & M University, College Station, TX

TRACK OF THE MANILA GALLEONS (Article), National Geographic Magazine, September 1990

WORLD BOOK ENCYCLOPEDIA, Copyright 1983 by World Book, Inc., Merchandise Mart Plaza, Chicago, IL 60654

275

ACKNOWLEDGMENTS

MRS. JUANITA RODRIGUES CALLENDER.
Mrs. Callender is the great-great-granddaughter of
José Joaquín Tico and the great-granddaughter of his
son, Fernando Tico. Born in Ventura, California,
Mrs. Callender presently lives in Ojai, California.
Mrs. Callender provided records of births, baptisms
and deaths of the early family. Thomas Workman
Temple of Los Angeles, California, researched the
birthplace of José Joaquín Tico in Catalonia, Spain.

THE BANCROFT LIBRARY AND ARCHIVES,
        BERKELEY, CA
MARITIME MUSEUM, J. PORTER SHAW LIBRARY,
        SAN FRANCISCO MARITIME NATIONAL
        HISTORICAL PARK, SAN FRANCISCO,
        CA
OJAI HISTORY MUSEUM AND LIBRARY, OJAI,
        CA
PRESIDIO SANTA BARBARA ARCHIVES, SANTA
        BARBARA, CA
PUBLIC LIBRARIES: FOSTER LIBRARY, VENTURA,
        CA.; OJAI LIBRARY, OJAI, CA
SANTA BARBARA HISTORY MUSEUM,
        GLEDHILL LIBRARY, SANTA BARBARA, CA
SANTA BARBARA MISSION ARCHIVES, SANTA
        BARBARA, CA
VENTURA COLLEGE LIBRARY, VENTURA, CA
VENTURA COUNTY MUSEUM OF HISTORY AND ART
        LIBRARY ARCHIVES, AND THE DOCENT
        LIBRARY, VENTURA, CA

INDEX

Art Work: Dust Jacket and Illustrations: Chris Martinez,
             Ventura, California.

Dust Jacket: Reproduction of original art by Chris Martinez,
               (mixed media) commissioned for PROMISES!
               PROMISES!
    Stock: #100 Gloss Book/White
    Film laminated

Jacket Design: Carl Rohkar, Ojai, California
    150 line screen color reproduction of original art

Cover Design: Carl Rohkar

Edition Bound Cover: National Blue; Gold foil front and spine
    Font: University Roman

Typesetter: Diane Rohkar, Ojai, California
    ASCII disks of author's manuscript translated to Macintosh
        Performa 6205CD computer by typesetter
    Printed from Macintosh LaserWriter 4/600PS
    Font: Adobe Bookman 12pt, 10pt

Printer: David Schaefer, Day and Night Premium Quality
            Printing, Carpinteria, California, U.S.A.
    Paper: Acid-free, white vellum, 60#
    End Sheets: Parchtone Natural
    Process: Offset printing from lithographic plates
    Press: Meihle

PROMISES! PROMISES!
ADVENTURES OF SARGENTO TICO
CATALUÑA TO CALIFORÑA 1766-1802
by Betty Louise Middleton Britton

Price   _____ $28.50

Postage   _____   3.00 Book Rate plus packaging

                   _____   4.20 First Class or Priority

Sub Total   _____

Sales Tax   _____   7.25% California Residents Only
                                (Does not apply to CA resale orders)

                                (Please supply resale number below)

Total   _____   Check or money order payable to:
                                JUANEZ BOOKS, 323 E. MATILIJA
                                ST., NO. 110-251, OJAI, CA 93023

MAIL TO _____

ADDRESS _____

CITY _____ STATE _____ ZIP _____

TELEPHONE (___) _____ RESALE NUMBER _____

PROMISES! PROMISES!
ADVENTURES OF SARGENTO TICO
CATALUÑA TO CALIFORÑA 1766-1802
by Betty Louise Middleton Britton

Price   _____ $28.50

Postage   _____   3.00 Book Rate plus packaging

                 _____   4.20 First Class or Priority

Sub Total   _____

Sales Tax   _____ 7.25% California Residents Only
                                (Does not apply to CA resale orders)

                                (Please supply resale number below)

Total   _____ Check or money order payable to:
                                JUANEZ BOOKS, 323 E. MATILIJA
                                ST., NO. 110-251, OJAI, CA 93023

MAIL TO _____

ADDRESS _____

CITY _____ STATE _____ ZIP _____

TELEPHONE (____) _____ RESALE NUMBER _____